MODERN HOMEBREW RECIPES

Exploring Styles and Contemporary Techniques

Gordon Strong

brewers publications

Brewers Publications
A Division of the Brewers Association
PO Box 1679, Boulder, Colorado 80306-1679
www.BrewersAssociation.org
www.BrewersPublications.com

Printed in the United States of America.

10 9 8 7 6 5 4 3 2 1

ISBN-13: 978-1-938469-14-5
ISBN-10: 1-938469-14-3

Library of Congress Cataloging-in-Publication Data

Strong, Gordon, 1962-
  Modern homebrew recipes : exploring styles and contemporary techniques / by Gordon Strong.
    pages cm
  Includes bibliographical references and index.
  ISBN 978-1-938469-14-5 (alk. paper) -- ISBN 1-938469-14-3 1. Brewing.
2. Beer. I. Title.

TP577.S796 2015
663'.42--dc23
                          2015008232

Publisher: Kristi Switzer
Technical Editor: Kristen England
Copyediting: Oliver Gray
Indexing: Doug Easton
Production and Design Management: Stephanie Johnson Martin
Cover and Interior Design: Kerry Fannon
Production: Justin Petersen
Cover Photo: Luke Trautwein

Carapils®/Carafoam®, Carahell®, Carafa®, Caramünch®/Caramunich®, Carared®, Caraamber®, Caraaroma®, Carawheat®, and SINAMAR® are registered trademarks of Weyermann® Malting Company.

To the Beavercreek (Ohio) Fire Department,
who saved my house and all who lived in it.

TABLE OF CONTENTS

ACKNOWLEDGMENTS

The original dedication of this book was to every homebrewer who ever shared a full, complete, and accurate recipe when asked. But as I started to write *Modern Homebrew Recipes*, life reared its ugly head. An electrical fire started in my attic on Memorial Day, 2014. Fortunately, I was home, our smoke detectors worked, and our local fire department responded in five minutes. They saved the house, but smoke and water damage took out much of my home office and other nearby rooms.

I was able to grab my computers and some notes, and much of my work was backed up on Dropbox. Fast-forward five or so months; we were able to move back into our newly rebuilt and remodeled home, and I got my restored possessions back. Two things I am grateful to have had during this situation are full replacement value insurance, and good off-site backups. Given that a barrel attacked me while I was researching my first book, and a fire tried to destroy my research during my second, I'm kind of avoiding barrel-aged and smoked beers now. Why does writing a book always seem to involve something trying to kill me?

Back to the matter at hand, I have a long list of people to thank. First, I would like to thank anyone who bought *Brewing Better Beer*, and gave me encouraging feedback. So many passionate, enthusiastic brewers took time at conferences, book signings, and beer events to tell me how much my book helped them. I remember an almost tearful brewer at a Brewing Network party telling me how my book had changed his life. I know that same person subsequently became a professional craft brewer. There is no better feedback for an author than letting them know that their time and effort was worthwhile and personally meaningful.

I'm indebted to those knowledgeable peers who enjoy talking about beer and brewing as much as I do, and who helped me understand recipe development and beer styles in greater depth. Thanks to Ray Daniels, Stan Hieronymus, Jamil Zainasheff, and Ron Pattinson. Writings from Roger Protz and Matt Brynildson also proved helpful.

I'd particularly like to thank those who shared recipes with me that I used or adapted in this book, including Frank Barickman, Kris England, Keith Kost, Jay Wince, Thomas Eibner, Darren Link, Jeffrey McElfresh, James Henjum, Dan George, William Shawn Scott, and Bob Kauffman. Thanks also to those who shared ideas or whose recipes inspired variations, including Curt Stock, Randy Scorby, Rodney Kibzey, Lee Jacobson, and Steve Fletty. I'd also like to thank Andy Tveekrem of Market Garden Brewery for inviting me to brew a professional craft collaboration beer with him.

I can't write a book involving beer styles without acknowledging all those within the Beer Judge Certification Program (BJCP) who have worked with me over the years, and those in my region who have continued to support me in elections. Involvement with the BJCP has fed my passion for beer and brewing, and has driven me to research and share what I've discovered. It's also allowed me to meet great new friends from all over the world.

Speaking of friends, I wanted to take a moment to remember my good friend Tom Fitzpatrick who passed away much too young. I probably would have had a recipe of his in this book anyway, but I wish it wasn't in here as a memorial.

My sincere thanks go to my long-time friend Randy Mosher for writing the foreword, and in helping me understand my place in brewing history. I've known Randy for as long as I've been brewing, and we've traveled together to many exciting places around the world. He gave me great advice and encouragement as an author when we were both speakers at a conference in Australia. Nobody beats Randy when it comes to passion and enthusiasm for homebrewing, so his endorsement is personally very meaningful.

Kris England deserves special thanks for his role as technical editor. An accomplished homebrewer for years before he went pro, he was one of the people who constantly challenged me for awards. It should then come as no surprise that he also challenged me over nearly every point in the book. He caught several errors, and worked with me to improve the book significantly. Even though it might look to some that we're fighting like two cats in a pillowcase, he's one of my closest and most respected friends.

Thanks once again to my publisher, Kristi Switzer, for her encouraging words as I've fought through the challenges of putting this book together, and thanks to Jill Redding and Betsy Parks, who both continue to publish my work in magazines.

Finally, I want to thank my wife Karla and my daughter Katya for continuing to put up with me as I obsessed over yet another beer-related project.

FOREWORD

A RECIPE FOR HAPPINESS

Brewing beer is a thrilling pursuit, but can be intimidating. While it may seem simple on the surface, it is a densely complicated art form, using a wide range of ingredients that are dependent upon complex biochemical transformations at every stage. To get the best results you can't just dump things into a pot as you would with a batch of spaghetti sauce. It takes a carefully chosen combination of raw ingredients subjected to a precise sequence of mixing, heating, filtering, boiling, cooling, and finally fermenting, to yield drinkable beer.

That's where a recipe comes in. A good one should offer the brewer a roadmap to success, with lists of ingredients and step-by-step guidance that culminates in delicious beer.

As long as there has been beer, there have been beer recipes. Shortly after the invention of writing, came a beer recipe—the earliest written recipe of any kind. Found in present-day Iraq and dating around 1900 BCE, the clay tablet contains *The Hymn to Ninkasi,* a song that steps poetically through the brewing process. Although quite foreign to us, there are parts (like the mixing of a mash and the rushing of sweet wort into a container) that are instantly recognizable to any homebrewer. In recent years, experimenters have filled in some of the gaps and actually brewed drinkable beer from this ancient set of instructions.

The Kalevala, a great Finnish-Hungarian epic compiled in the nineteenth century from ancient oral traditions, includes some thoughts about brewing. One section follows the travails of a brewster named Osmotar, who gives the loose outline of a brew:

"Osmotar, the beer-preparer,
Brewer of the drink refreshing,
Takes the golden grains of barley,
Taking six of barley-kernels,
Taking seven tips of hop-fruit,
Filling seven cups with water
On the fire she sets the cauldron,
Boils the barley, hops and water,
Lets them steep, and seethe, and bubble,
Brewing thus the beer delicious."

The epic goes on to chronicle several failed attempts to start fermentation, including "the spit of bears in battle," which would be a frightening way to brew, even for Vikings. At long last, honey "from the tips of seven flowers," gets the job done. It may be a questionable fermentation starter, but honey does contain certain yeasts, and its presence in ancient beer has been chemically confirmed by vessel residue from Iron Age burials.

Despite these high-profile tales, brewing recipes from earlier times are few and very far between. In the medieval period before the use of hops, beer was flavored by a secret mixture called gruit. We have some clues to its composition, but no complete recipe has ever been found. Until the dawn of the Industrial Revolution, the amount of malt required to brew a barrel of beer at a specific price was public information—mandated by law in most places—but, of course, it takes a lot more than the quantity of ingredients to make a recipe. Uncertainties around barley, malting and kilning techniques, hop varieties, and fermentation mean there are many pieces to the puzzle that have been lost, leaving us modern beer archaeologists to speculate and make somewhat educated guesses.

By the eighteenth century the world was exploding with brewing texts. Real, usable recipes show up in books such as *The London and Country Brewer*, attributed to William Ellis. With a little work, beers from Shropshire, Dorchester, Devonshire, London, and elsewhere saw new life in modern kettles (the versions I've brewed have been pretty tasty). However, at any given place and time, brewers made a limited number of products; often just one beer brewed in two or more strengths. Recipes were hardly needed when everybody in the town made the same kind of beer from the local malt using similar hops and yeast, so there are still lots of blank spots in the record.

By the early nineteenth century, advances in instrumentation and better recording of processes allow us to peer deeply into the minds of the brewers and recreate their beers pretty closely, although modern malting techniques don't exactly reproduce the original flavors. Large-scale industrialization and the lager juggernaut it made possible displaced dozens of quaint local beers in Northern Europe. As variety diminished, beer recipes became more technical, aimed at efficiency and consistency in commercial situations. As a result, the actual formulations became less important.

After alcohol sales were banned in the US in 1919, it all went underground—literally into peoples' basements. A typical Prohibition-era recipe stretches one can of hopped malt extract with an equal amount of sugar, fermented by baker's yeast. The resultant beer may have been better than nothing, but it makes for an intolerably thin and cidery product. Nonetheless, these primitive recipes lingered on in the shadows of the postwar decades until homebrewing was finally legalized federally in 1976.

And then, almost on cue, we started our most recent beer Renaissance. At the beginning of the current homebrew era, ingredients and information were scant. Most recipes came from British sources like Dave Line's books, referencing utterly unavailable beers and calling for exotics like golden syrup and treacle. But in those days of yellow, fizzy monotony in the commercial marketplace, even the humblest homebrew was a revelation and an act of rebellion.

As the hobby grew, so did the availability of information and ingredients. Fred Eckhardt and Greg Noonan wrote groundbreaking books drawing us into the world of all-grain brewing. Inspired by the writings and personal persuasions of Michael Jackson, the notion of beer styles began to take shape. At the same time, beer competitions started popping up, along with an organization to sanction and provide structure for them: the Beer Judge Certification Program (BJCP).

At some point Gordon Strong got involved with the BJCP. Volunteer organizations ebb and flow, but they depend on steadfast advocates— people willing to knuckle down and do the hard work year after year. BJCP has many such heroes, but for three decades, Gordon has been an active contributor. He took special interest in the continued clarification and accuracy of the BJCP style guidelines, and has helped shepherd them through at least two thorough revisions over the years. As the rest of the beer world looks to the US for guidance and inspiration, these efforts have taken on even greater importance in the growing global movement.

As our understanding of traditional styles, techniques, and formulations gets better, so do the beers. The brewing world is riddled with spurious myths and misinformation, but we're slowly building a clearer picture. Over the last decade or more there has also been progress in streamlining the homebrewing process to allow brewers to make the best possible beer without wasting time on unnecessarily complex techniques. Another trend acknowledges that each of us has different interests and priorities, and as a result, a wide range of techniques have been developed to suit everyone from the most casual weekend brewer to the paddle-wielding decoction warrior. It truly is a great time to be a homebrewer.

A brief overview of the evolution of beer recipes up to the present day would pale compared to the picture painted by the book you have before you. Developed and brewed by a keen enthusiast, organization stalwart, and creative brewer, the recipes in this book reflect the growth and maturation of brewing and recipe formulation in the twenty-first century.

He's been a strong advocate for a rational brewing approach with minimum fussiness and a very human touch. That combination of intense focus and easy accessibility is something I've always admired about Gordon, and I'm proud to offer a few words to help put it all in context for you.

So turn the page, dive in, and start quenching your thirst for great beer.

—Randy Mosher

INTRODUCTION

"I hate the notion of a secret recipe.
Recipes are by nature derivative and meant to be shared."

—Molly Wizenberg, "Orangette"

Since the release of *Brewing Better Beer* in 2011, I've given dozens of talks around the world to homebrewers and beer geeks. I gave one of my favorite presentations, *Practical Applications of Brewing Better Beer*, at the National Homebrewers Conference in Seattle (2012) and Philadelphia (2013). In that presentation, I talk about how to apply the lessons and techniques of *Brewing Better Beer* to develop new recipes. This book is based on the feedback received from those talks, and the suggestions from homebrewers to provide more examples. I'm happy to oblige, and hope you enjoy the result.

Brewing Better Beer included recipes, but wasn't a recipe book. I wrote it as an advanced lesson for homebrewers looking to better develop their skills, and to create their own personal brewing style. As such, the recipes merely illustrated some ways to employ new techniques. But many homebrewers wanted more recipes they could brew immediately.

Just like *Brewing Better Beer* was a different kind of homebrewing book, *Modern Homebrew Recipes* takes a novel approach to recipes.

Rather than simply listing ingredients and steps for various styles, I supply the thought process behind the formulation of each recipe, pinpointing the key aspects that make each one a success. I provide tasting notes and impressions along with thoughts on variations you can try. This additional information is meant to help you expand your ability and capacity to craft your own new recipes, whether you brew these recipes directly or tweak them to your own preferences.

GENERAL CONCEPT

Modern Homebrew Recipes is more than a book *of* recipes; it's also a book *about* recipes. Yes, there are over 100 ready-to-use recipes that have been tested and taste great. But my original goals from *Brewing Better Beer* still stand; to teach fellow homebrewers better brewing skills, and help them master the craft of brewing (including developing and adapting recipes).

In developing this book, I wanted to provide recipes that use current research, ingredients, and techniques that were applied using a consistent brewing method. When choosing examples, I thought it would be most interesting to brewers to cover several of the newest styles introduced in the 2015 edition of the Beer Judge Certification Program (BJCP) Style Guidelines, since not all of those styles have many published homebrew recipes.

Although recipes closely fitting style guidelines are important for competitions, some are for beers inspired by the flavor profile or balance found in some of my favorite commercial beers. These may or may not be great examples of the styles, or be intended for competition, but they are all beers that I enjoy making and drinking. I dislike the term *clone beer* so I'm just going to refer to these beers as being *inspired by* commercial beers, not replacements for them.

I have included some older recipes to contrast how various homebrew techniques and practices have evolved over time, and how recipes can be brewed in different ways. Older techniques aren't necessarily wrong, but they can often have different results, or at least side-effects. By comparing the different recipes for the same style, I hope the brewer will learn more about developing new recipes, and tweaking recipes to meet personal preferences.

The recipes in this book are the *real deal*—the actual, as-brewed ones that I developed and tested on my own system. They aren't converted, changed, modified, altered, or otherwise reworked. One of the things that readers told me they liked about my first book was that I gave actual opinions, preferences, and recommendations. I described everything exactly how I did it while being as specific as possible. I will be continuing that practice in this book, identifying and expounding on exact techniques and processes as well as giving recommendations on what ingredients and procedures I view as critical and which can be freely substituted (within reason, of course).

Although I describe and classify recipes in terms of style, this book isn't intended to be a successor to or replacement for *Brewing Classic Styles*, or other style-oriented books. Some BJCP styles are represented by a single recipe, some by multiple recipes, while other styles won't be covered at all. Providing multiple recipes for individual styles helps to illustrate the wide range that many possess, how variations of a recipe can be produced, and that a single commercial example (or recipe) should never completely define a beer style.

Each recipe in this book provides a lesson in procedure, technique, or ingredients. *Brewing Better Beer* contains more in-depth technical discussion on each topic, but I've described the basic techniques needed to brew any recipe in this book. I also highlight what I've learned since, and how my collection of techniques continues to grow and evolve. The best brewers are on a continual journey of learning. But learning is the means to an end, not an end in itself. Always ask yourself, "How can I apply these to my brewery, to my recipes, or to new styles?"

GOALS AND ORGANIZATION

I have several goals for this book. First and foremost is that you are able to use the recipes immediately, and brew something that sounds interesting (perhaps even a new style of beer). Brewing a great beer by trying something different in the process is a quick win, and often encourages you to learn more. A longer-term goal is that you learn how to apply and use a broader range of techniques, and understand which aspects of a recipe drive the final product.

The ultimate goal of this book is for homebrewers to gain a better understanding of how and why recipes are put together, how to use and adapt them, and how to create new recipes. Developing skills by brewing lots of different beers is the most effective approach; you often don't realize you've been learning until you're able to recognize your growth (or notice your neck hurts from all the medals you're wearing). Don't force the learning aspect; it will come. Try new things, have fun, and brew some great beer.

I've organized the book into two major sections: background information and recipes. The background information includes this introduction, a review of the brewing techniques required to execute the recipes in the book, and a discussion on how to work with recipes.

In the primer on brewing techniques, we'll review the major steps needed to make beer, the specific techniques used in this book, and how my brewing system is organized. I figured that if I share with you how I brew, you'll have an idea of how to adapt the recipes to suit your equipment and processes.

The discussion section includes how to read and interpret recipes, recipe formulation fundamentals, considerations for adapting recipes to your system, and substituting ingredients. Additional supporting material can be found in appendices to this book, including basic beer math, using recipe software, and converting all-grain recipes to extract, and vice versa.

The recipes themselves form the bulk of the book, and are organized into eight major groups: IPAs, everyday beers, strong ales, dark beers, lagers, Belgian favorites, spiced beers, and experimental. Organizing by theme makes it easier to discuss similarities and differences. All recipes use a common template, which includes the BJCP beer style and all information needed to brew the beer.

This is a practical book, not an academic study; its emphasis is on doing, not just sitting and reading. I use a conversational tone, just like I'd use if we were brewing, enjoying a beer, and talking together. That's what I'm visualizing as I'm writing, so please treat this like a private lesson from a friend, not getting lectured by a professor. When I sign books, there is nothing I like to see as much as a well-used, dog-eared, heavily-annotated copy, so by all means, get this book dirty (and bring me some of your beer to sample).

SECTION I
FUNDAMENTALS

1 | BREWING TECHNIQUES

"Recipes tell you nothing; learning techniques is the key."

—*Tom Colicchio, "Top Chef"*

Brewing procedures are the tactical choices and techniques that a brewer uses during the brewing process to solve specific problems and accomplish certain goals. They represent *how* a recipe is turned into beer. Different brewers will make individual choices, and those decisions often become patterns as methods are mastered. These choices are shaped by their experiences, knowledge, equipment, ingredients, stylistic preferences, available time and resources, and personal commitment.

Brewers often find themselves making the same choices over and over again when brewing certain types of beer; these represent standard practices. A brewer may have multiple sets of standard practices as part of their overall skill set. This collection of choices represents their own personal brewing style. A brewer's style is derived from the types of techniques used, how they are interpreted and executed, and what unique twists the brewer puts on them.

Each recipe in this book identifies the techniques I used to brew it. You don't necessarily have to brew the recipe the same way that I did; I made my choices to suit my own personal brewing style. I included this level of detail so you could understand what decisions I made in case you wanted to adjust them to suit your own preferences.

DEVELOPING YOUR STYLE

The key to developing (and maintaining) your style is to find your own set of efficient techniques or standard practices that work on your system with the ingredients you routinely use.

Unless you are experimenting or learning a new process, it's not worthwhile to constantly change the techniques you use. Select a subset of effective techniques, combine them into a few standard practices, and then use them repeatedly on a wide range of recipes. If you select the right procedures, learn them correctly, and repeat them frequently, you will ultimately master them. You'll be able to anticipate problems more quickly as the outcomes are more certain, and fix any issues more readily since you've likely encountered the situation before.

How many techniques are too many for your repertoire? That's hard to answer. It really depends on how frequently you brew. You should probably keep the number relatively low unless you brew often, and get a chance to use all the methods regularly. Otherwise you're introducing unnecessary variables into your process.

The exception, of course, is when you're consciously trying to learn and master a new technique. If you want to experiment with a something new, it's best to do it with a tried-and-true recipe, so you can see how it will impact your regular brewing processes. Whenever you do add a new technique to your procedures, decide if it is an addition to your standards, or a replacement for an existing technique.

You may know many techniques for brewing, yet use only a few of them regularly. That's understandable; it's a sign of experience to select a minimal but efficient set of techniques to accomplish your brewing tasks. But try to be open to change, there may be techniques that are unknown or unfamiliar to you that perform the task better than what you're using, even if your process is time-honored or cutting edge. Don't be anxious about trying a new approach just because you don't have experience with it. Assessing and updating your bag tricks is the normal learning curve of a brewer.

While searching for and incorporating new processes, remember that the world is full of self-appointed experts with sketchy credentials or no proven brewing accomplishments who flood the beer community with their *advice*. Take these recommendations with a grain of salt, particularly if they are trying to sell you something at the same time. The Internet has given many of these people an outlet, so be extra careful when perusing brewing forums.

Many world class brewers brew in completely different ways and still create excellent beer. The main lesson from *Brewing Better Beer* is to help people decide how to adapt their own brewing procedures and equipment to best meet their own needs. Understanding the interplay between techniques and recipes helps you understand how to brew your own unique creations.

THE BREWING PROCESS

While this is primarily a recipe book, it's still important to review all the steps involved in brewing beer. This is more of a quick summary than a tutorial, and is included in case there are any questions about specific terms within the recipes. In my view, here are the steps involved in the brewing process:

- **Review/Adapt/Formulate recipe** – Whether it's your own recipe or not, you need to review and finalize what you are going to brew in detail. Perform any alterations required for your system (conversions, efficiencies, utilization, etc.). Verify necessary ingredients are on hand, making substitutions if desired. Identify any missing pieces in the recipe.
- **Create brewing log** – Arguably one of the most important steps in the brewing process. You should create a log that describes everything you intend to do in enough detail that you can easily rebrew the beer. Use this log to track your progress on brew day, noting your readings and observations. You can't learn from your experiences unless you remember what you've done.
- **Set up equipment** – Check that everything is clean and functioning properly. This can be done as the first thing on brew day, or the night before (unless your equipment is permanently in place, as in a professional brewery). Note that this step involves not just your brewing vessels and heat supply, but all the tools, measuring equipment, cleaning supplies, and other gear you use on brew day. You don't want to miss a time-critical step because you are hunting around for a missing piece of equipment.

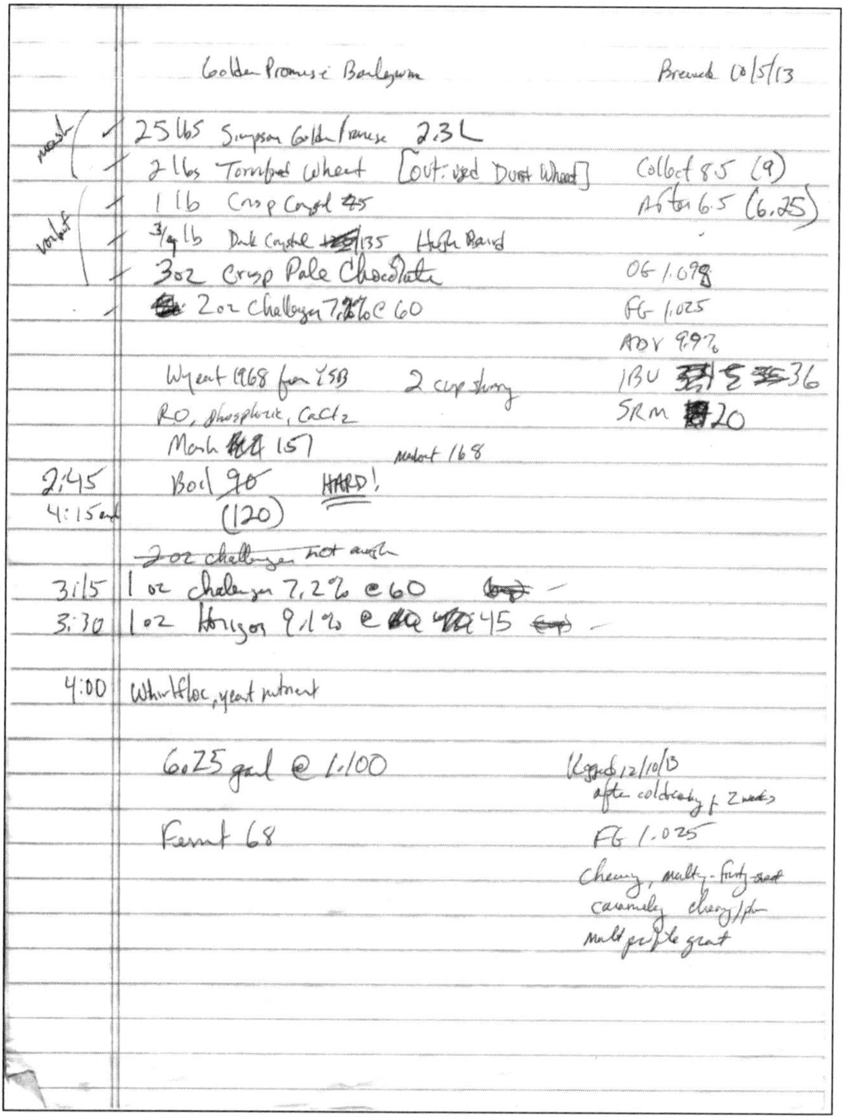
Golden Promise Barleywine
Brewed 10/5/13
mash
25 lbs Simpson Golden Promise 2.3L
2 lbs Torrified Wheat [out: used Durst Wheat]
Collect 8.5 (9)
vorlauf
1 lb Crisp Crystal 45
After 6.5 (6.25)
3/4 lb Dark Crystal 135 High Rand
3oz Crisp Pale Chocolate
OG 1.098
2oz Challenger 7.2% @ 60
FG 1.025
ADV 9.9%
Wyeast 1968 from ESB 2 cup slurry
IBU 36
RO, phosphoric, CaCl2
SRM 20
Mash 157 Mashout 168
2:45 Boil ~~90~~ HARD!
4:15 end (120)
~~2 oz challenger not enough~~
3:15 1 oz Challenger 7.2% @ 60
3:30 1 oz Horizon 9.1% @ 45
4:00 Whirlfloc, yeast nutrient
6.25 gal @ 1.100
Kegged 12/10/13
after coldcrashing for 2 weeks
Ferm 68
FG 1.025
Chewy, malty-fruity sweet
caramelly cherry/plum
malt profile great

Fig 1.1: The actual, handwritten (and edited) brewlog for Golden Promise Barleywine.

- **Prepare ingredients** – This is the *mise en place* of brewing. Most homebrewers prepare their ingredients on brew day or the day before (a yeast starter is the notable exception). Weigh out grains, separating them if they will be added individually. Mill the grain, checking that the grist is crushed consistently, and to the desired

Brew Number Gordian Strong Ale
Brew I.D. 20-3

Date 6/23/11

Malts		Lbs.		Salts	Oz.
Pilsner malt	✓ 7.5	412		CaCl2	10
Vienna	✓ 4	220		Kettle	
Acid	✓	28	24,4		
Caramunich II	✓	42	25,17		
Biscuit	✓	25	25		
Aromatic	✓	33	21,12		
Carafa Special III	✓	1.7	1.11		
Total Pounds:		761.7			

≈ 58.5%

Mash Profile	Time
131 for 15 min.	945/1000
146 145 for 30 min.	1007–1037
158 for 10 min.	1044–1054
170 for 5 min.	1101–1109

15°P

Water Gals.	°F
272	132
50	170

Water/Grist Ratio:
3 to 1

pH 5.33

Lauter	Time	Gallons	°P
Rest	1115–1130		
Vorlauf	1130–1150		17.8
Send to kettle	1150–		18.5
Sparge 170 gal	1200	155	
Kettle Full	2:10 – 3:25	372	

1.25 re-vorlauf

Hops	% Alpha		Time	2:10
Cz Saaz 6# 13oz	3.4	✓	2:25	60
				30
Cz Saaz 3#	3.4	✓	3:10	15
Cz Saaz 3#	3.4	✓	3:20	5
			3:25	WP

Whirlfloc
Yeast nutrient

Knockout Volume: 302gal @16.4 **°P** **°F FV**
Target Gravity: **17-18°P** **pH** 5.16 14

4 gal yeast from Blonde Tart FV13 17.2 302 gal to fermenter @ 58F

Fig 1.2: Professional brew log for Gordian Strong Ale with additional handwritten notes (note the smears from wort and water).

consistency. Make any adjustments to your water with brewing salts or acids to produce brewing liquor, or water prepared for brewing. Measure your hops, numbering them by addition or time. If you are adding any other ingredients (salts, finings, spices, etc.) during the process, have those measured out as well. All the

Batch	Date		Beer name - Style - Ver.				OG ~1.083						Vol
37	9/15/13		*Llamarada* Stout				BU 25 ABV ~8.4%						20 BBL

Sack	Wt.	%	Grist	Producer	Wt.	Sundries	Mash Schema:						
+.14	816	48.6	Pls	Patagonia	0	X Rice hulls		Time	BBL	Cm's 4.5/	Liq temp	Mash tem	Stood
+2	132	7.9	Oats, Flaked		7Kg	Coffee	Schedule						
"	132	"	Perla Negra	Pat.	1.1Kg	Milk Kun							
+1	99	5.9	Brown	"			Calcs		19.4	69cm	170	187	45
"	99	"	Chocolate, 550L	"		Steep 10min	All in	9:00	"	"	171	158	"
++	82	4.9	Quinoa, toasted	—		after K.O.	Steam On	9:45					
"	66	3.9	Especial 140L	Pat.									
							MO	10:05				166	10
					Wt.	Sugars	Vorlauf	10:15					20
					252	Honey, Acc.	Sparge	10:35					
						L&N w.p.	Ratio #/#:	2.5			Efficiency	85	
							pH	5.01			Actual	+.90	
							Boil time:	90			Kettle finings		
1426		Grist total			252	Sugar total	Start	12:00			Antifoam	1oz/7bbl	
Wt.	Hops (year)			AA%	Time	Bu	Amt	Liquor addition	BBL in	21.5		X	
9.0	Acc.	Cascade	(2012)	5.2	FWH	25	0	Lactic acid, 88%	P	19.75 P		Flock	1oz/10bbl
							300	CaCl2	Finish	1:30			
							—	MgSO4	BBL out	20		Zinc	25mg/bbl
							300	CaSO4	P	21.2		X	
									WP time	10		Stand time	10
								Remarks					
9		Lb hops				Lb extract	Great mash. High Gravity = Great extract from malt. pH a bit low						

Abbr: p-pellet, wl-whole leaf, calc-calculated

Fig 1.3: A different variation of a professional, printed brew log. This one is for my Llamarado Stout.

ingredients should be checked off in your brewing log and in place before you start the brew.

- **Heat water** – On homebrewing systems, heating water and keeping it hot during the brewing process takes considerable time and effort. The key is to plan your process steps so that you are doing other tasks while the water is heating. This way, the water will be ready when you need it, and you aren't stuck waiting around for it to reach the proper temperature. Multiple burners and vessels help considerably. When you heat your brewing liquor for your initial mash in, keep in mind that you normally have to heat the water hotter than your target mash temperature to account for heat loss during transfer, and that the mash tun and the ingredients in it are cooler than your strike water. Identifying this heat loss differential is an important step when calibrating your system.

- **Mash** – The goal of mashing is to produce wort, a sugar-laden liquid extracted from starches. Hot water and the milled grist (malt and grains) are mixed so that enzymes in the malt can convert starches into sugars. The infusion ratio (usually given in quarts per pound, or [qts/lb.]) listed in homebrew recipes is the amount of water to grist in the mash, which designates how 'thick' or 'thin' the mash will be.[1] The strike temperature of your mash water is the temperature of the brewing liquor added to the mash tun, which is always higher than the target mash rest temperature. A mash rest is a specific temperature where the mash is held for a specific period of time, which typically favors the activity of certain enzymes that produce the desired wort composition (types and quantities of fermentable and unfermentable sugars in the wort). The mash schedule is the set of rests used during the mash. Completion of the mash can be verified with a positive Iodine test.

- **Vorlauf** – *Vorlauf* is a German brewing term; *recirculation* is the equivalent English term. During *vorlauf*, wort is manually recirculated or pumped over the mash in the lauter tun to establish the grain bed as a filter, which removes large particles. This step is often done after a final higher-temperature mash out rest. Malts and grains that do not need to be mashed can be added during at this time so that they can contribute color and flavor.

- **Lauter/Sparge** – *Lautering* is the separation of wort from spent grains using a rinsing process called sparging. The goal of this step is to have clear, sweet wort with good flavor in sufficient volume to meet pre-boil objectives.

- **Boil** – Wort is boiled in the kettle for a specific amount of time, starting with a larger volume and lower specific gravity and ending with a smaller volume and a higher gravity. Hops, sugary adjuncts, kettle finings, and nutrients may be added during the boil. The addition of ingredients during the boil is normally specified in the recipe by stating the type and quantity of ingredient to be added, and the time they should be added to the boil. A hop addition at 5 minutes means they are added with 5 minutes remaining in the boil, not 5 minutes after boiling has started.

- **Rest** – A step used to help clarify the finished wort. On homebrew systems, this typically involves stirring it with a spoon then letting

---

[1] Note that professional breweries often use grist-to-liquor ratio instead, which is the ratio of the weight of grist to the weight of brewing liquor in the mash. It is a unitless measure that is easiest to calculate in metric units since one liter of water is defined as weighing one kilogram. You can calculate it as a ratio of kilograms of grist to liters of brewing liquor, and the result will be just a number without units. It can be a little confusing for homebrewers since the ratio is reversed (grist:liquor) from the typical homebrewer measure (liquor:grist).

it stand before chilling or running it off. On commercial systems, this is typically done using a whirlpool. Either way, the goal is to facilitate wort clarity by removing heavier particulates. Hops may be added during this phase.

- **Chill** – The process where finished wort is forcibly cooled to the desired temperature for pitching the yeast. The pitching temperature is not necessarily the same as the fermentation temperature (it is usually lower).

- **Fermentation** – Once yeast is introduced, the sugar in wort is converted into alcohol and carbon dioxide. The important things to note in your brewing log are the fermentation temperature and the yeast strain(s) used. Time estimates may be given for fermentation schedules, but fermentation should always be run until desired gravity is met and fermentation subsides.

- **Rack** – This step separates the fermented beer from yeast, hops, trub (sediment), and other unwanted particulates. The main goal is to transfer the finished beer away from the bulk of the yeast to reduce the chance of autolysis. A beer may be racked multiple times, and combined with finings or conditioners.

- **Condition** – This step involves aging and maturing finished beer, thus allowing the flavor to stabilize. It may involve other steps such as dry hopping, fruit additions, inoculation of 'wild' yeast and bacteria, and so on. Conditioning can also include lagering, a cold-conditioning step used to reduce undesirable flavor components in lager beer. To enhance clarity, beer may be fined or filtered at the beginning or conclusion of this phase.

- **Package** – The final step of transferring the conditioned beer into storage containers, such as bottles, kegs, or casks. The beer may be naturally carbonated in the container by adding additional sugar for the yeast to consume, or may be force carbonated using compressed CO_2.

- **Consume** – The fun part. I'll leave this step as an exercise for the reader.

SUMMARY OF TECHNIQUES

My goal is that you be able to understand and execute the techniques needed to brew the recipes in this book, not necessarily learn the detailed science behind them. Whenever a specific technique is used, you should also know what other information must be specified to properly brew the recipe. The brewing techniques I describe include water adjustment, recipe design, techniques used during mashing, lautering, boiling and hopping.

Many of my techniques are interrelated, so please read the "My Process" section before altering or substituting methods. Some of the choices made in one phase have implications for other phases; if you substitute methods, be aware that you may need to address the dependencies in other steps.

Water Adjustment

- **Using RO water** – My brewing water is awful—lots of calcium carbonate and high pH—so I've found that it's easier to use Reverse Osmosis (RO) water instead of trying to engineer my water every time I brew. If you're blessed with good brewing water, you might question why I do this. I fought through many different methods of adjusting water before I settled on this simple solution that drives my entire brewing process. I don't specify quantities needed since that depends on your system and batch size.

- **Adding acids** – I adjust my RO water with 10% phosphoric acid to produce brewing liquor with a pH of about 5.5 when measured at 68°F (20°C). I use the more dilute acid since it is easier to measure in the volumes needed for homebrew-size batches, and I prefer phosphoric acid since it's the most flavor-neutral of the commonly available acids. I perform this step so I can reach a good mash pH of about 5.1 to 5.3 (with a pale grist). Traditional methods for managing mash pH include using 88% phosphoric or lactic acid; using acidulated malt (or sauermalz the German way of weaseling around their own ingredient-limiting *Reinheitsgebot*); adding calcium sulfate (gypsum) to the mash to reduce pH through chemical interactions with the grain husks; adding calcium carbonate (chalk) to the mash to buffer acids in dark malts (or reducing added acid); and carefully replicating the ion content of water from classic brewing cities. I almost never use any of these techniques, but only because I'm managing pH in the mash differently, not because they can't be made to work. The type and quantity of each acid, and where and when they should be added will be specified in the recipe.

- **Adding salts to the mash** – Salts added to the mash can be used to adjust the flavor profile, provide desired ions that are enzyme cofactors, improve mash performance, and adjust mash pH. Since I use RO water, I add small amounts of brewing salts to almost every mash. The type and the quantity of salt is specified in the recipes. I typically add salts directly to the mash at the very start, but they can also be mixed in with the brewing liquor. The solubility of salts varies by type and pH (calcium carbonate has notoriously low solubility, which is why it can often be reduced by boiling), so I err on the side of caution by putting them directly in the mash. They are mixed into the mash after the grist and the water have been combined.
- **Adding salts to the boil** – The quantity of salts in the kettle is lower than the amount of salts in the mash, since they don't fully carry over. If you're using brewing salts to enhance the flavor profile of the beer (not just hit a target mash pH), then you may need to add salts to the boil. I don't use this technique very often, except where I want a more noticeable mineral profile in the final beer but don't want the salts in the mash. The type and quantity of salt should be specified in the recipe; I normally add them at the start of the boil so I don't forget them, but they can be added at any time.
- **Removing salts** – None of my recipes use this technique, but I used to adjust my brewing water by pre-boiling, adding pickling lime (calcium hydroxide), or adding acid (typically phosphoric or lactic) to reduce the calcium bicarbonate levels. None of these methods worked that well for me, and often required nearly as much time and effort as brewing. I just wanted to mention that there are alternative processes for removing unwanted salts if your water isn't good for brewing and RO water isn't readily available.

Mash Techniques

- **Infusion mash** – Sometimes called a single step infusion mash, this is the most basic mash program you can use. The way most brewers perform this step is by heating their strike water to the required temperature, then mixing the prepared water (brewing liquor) with the milled grain until it's well-mixed and has an even temperature throughout. This is called *mashing in* (sometimes called doughing in), and is where the mash starts. Single step rests are usually in the 144–160°F (62–71°C) range, but 149–151°F (65–66°C) is a reasonable average for most beer styles. This program is a compromise for enzymes, since it's typically in between the optimal ranges for alpha and beta amylase (See Table 1.1). Remember that you have to heat your water hotter than the rest temperature for it to settle in at the target. I recommend stirring the mash several times, not just around in circles, but scooping from the bottom towards the top; the goal is a well-mixed mash with an even temperature distribution. The rest temperature and time (duration) should be specified in the recipe.

COMMON BREWING ENZYMES

Enzyme	Active Range	Optimal Temp	pH	Denatured	Effect
β-glucanase	95-122°F (35-50°C)	113°F (45°C)	4.6-5.0	131-140°F (55-60°C)	Degrades cell walls, reduces gumminess
Peptidase	113-122°F (45-50°C)	113°F (45°C)	5.1-5.3	140°F (60°C)	Increases amino acids (nutrients)
Protease	122-140°F (50-60°C)	126°F (52°C)	4.6-5.0	158°F (70°C)	Reduces haze-forming proteins
β-amylase	136-149°F (58-65°C)	144°F (62°C)	5.4-5.5	158-162°F (70-72°C)	Produces maltose
α-amylase	149-165°F (65-74°C)	158°F (70°C)	5.6-5.8	172-176°F (78-80°C)	Increases dextrins

Table 1.1: Optimal temperatures for common brewing enzymes.

- **Step infusion mash** – This is similar to a single step infusion mash, but with multiple rest temperatures. Rests may be added for specific purposes, as each allows certain enzymes to work in optimal conditions to break down certain complex proteins and starches, degrade haze-causing particles, encourage the formation of certain acids, or adjust the fermentability and dextrin content of the wort. These rests can more squarely hit the active ranges of enzymes, depending on the type of beer being produced.
- **Infusion method** – There are different ways to change mash temperature, including infusing boiling water, applying direct

heat to the mash tun, or using some form of recirculation with heat. I prefer the latter, and usually direct-fire my mash tun while recirculating it with a pump. If you use the boiling water infusion method, you may wish to start with a thicker mash and use brewing software to calculate the volume of infusions needed. I start the burner and the pump, let them run, and then stop when I reach the desired temperature. Recipes may specify the method, but you can adjust it to your system.

- **Decoction (single)** – A decoction is a fraction of the mash that is removed and boiled separately, often passing through rest steps on the way to the boil. The method is also called decoction mashing, with the number of times the mash is boiled used in the name (single, double, or triple decoction). In the simplest version, the main mash is held at a rest temperature while a fraction (typically one-third the thickest part of the mash) is removed. This decoction is transferred to a separate boil kettle, and then raised to specific temperatures (think of this phase as performing a step infusion mash on just the decoction). However, the final *rest* is at boiling temperature. After the boiling is complete, the decoction is mixed back into the main mash, raising the temperature to the next rest step. A single decoction will always have at least two rest temperatures, with at least one rest being in the saccharification range. The recipe should state the rest temperatures and durations of the main mash, the time when decoctions should be pulled, and the rest temperatures and durations used in the decoction. If the recipe doesn't say how much of the main mash should be decocted, assume one-third of the thick part of the mash. Boiling of the mash aids in color and flavor development, improves extract, and degrades starches. Some brewers believe decoction mashes are unnecessary and don't accomplish anything, but I think color changes alone shows that is not true (not to mention flavor improvements, efficiency gains, body development, smoothness, and stability).
- **Decoction (double)** – Much like a step infusion is a repeated infusion mash at multiple rest temperatures, a double decoction mash is a repeated decoction. This means that there are two decoctions, (at least three different mash temperatures used). The recipe should

state the main mash rest temperatures and durations, as well as the rest temperature(s) and durations used in the decoctions. The recipe may specify how much of the mash to decoct, but it's generally around one-third the volume of the thick part of the mash.

- **Decoction (*hochkurz*)** – This is a German term meaning *high-short*, and is often used as shorthand for a form of single decoction (or step infusion) mash that starts with a rest at 144–145°F (62–63°C). It's an additional clarifying detail that explains intent, but doesn't really add any more information than is contained in the mash program itself. As with other multi-step mash programs, the important points are the rest temperatures, durations, and the methods of heating.

- **Hybrid** – My own term, it generally means mixing multiple methods. Most often in my recipes it means adding step infusion to a decoction mash regime. Traditional decoction mash schedules can be simplified by inserting step infusion rests for some of the decoction steps. I highlight this term so that the brewer sees that not all rest temperatures have to be achieved using a decoction. The mash program should specify the rest temperatures, durations, and how the changes in mash temperature are achieved (infusion or decoction).

- **Round-trip mash** – My own term again. I start the mash at a higher temperature, then recirculate as if performing a *vorlauf.* Allow the mash to naturally cool to a base temperature, then turn on the heat and start raising temperature until it hits the target (typically, the mashout temperature). This is performed slowly, so that the mash moves through the continuum of temperatures twice. I use this method when I want to maximize fermentability. The initial (high) temperature, base (low) temperature, and final (high) temperature should be specified in the recipe. The rate of change may be specified, but if not, plan for at least 30–40 minutes per phase (high to low, then low to high).

- **Cereal Mash** – A traditional method for breaking down starchy adjuncts (such as corn or rice) that don't have their own enzymes. I typically use flaked forms of adjuncts that can be mashed directly. Consider adding a short (5–15 minute) protein rest to the mash program when using flaked adjuncts.

Finishing the Mash and Lautering

- **Mashout** – After the mash is complete, many brewers raise the mash temperature to 166–172°F (75–78°C) and hold it for 5–15 minutes. This helps decrease the viscosity of the wort and improves lautering performance. Some believe it increases mash efficiency; I'm not totally sold on that idea, but it does get the mash closer to boiling temperature so it doesn't hurt. I often combine this with the *vorlauf* since it lets me meet both objectives simultaneously. On my system, I can direct fire the mash tun while I use a pump to recirculate the wort, so I can increase the temperature to mashout while recirculating. Treat this like another step infusion; the rest temperature and duration should be specified.

- **Mash capping** – One of my often-quoted techniques is to hold back the dark grains, dark malts, and crystal malts until after the mash has finished. Add the grains to the mash and let them steep for at least 15 minutes before lautering. I often perform this while heating to mashout temperature, and while I am doing a *vorlauf* (recirculation) to simulate sparging and encourage color and flavor extraction. Using the grains this way reduces the harshness in a beer since the husk materials are exposed to hot water for a much shorter time. There are other benefits as well that are explored in detail when I describe the method later in this chapter. A recipe may specify this method, or you may adjust an existing recipe to use this method by simply holding back any grain that doesn't need to be mashed until the mash is complete. These grains can be added during a fly sparge, but this approach also works when batch sparging.

- **Grain steeping** – An alternative to mash capping is steeping the roasted grains, dark malts, and crystal malts separately, using either a hot steep or overnight cold steep. Separate the liquid from the grain, then mix the liquid back into the boil, either late in the boil or after the boil has concluded. I like the flavors from this method, but it's more work and I find that I have to use more grains to get the same flavor effect. A recipe that specifies this method should state how long the steep should last, whether hot or cold water is used, and when the steeped liquid should be added to the wort.

- ***Vorlauf*** – This is a recirculation process that is used to clarify the mash runoff by establishing the grain bed as a filter. It is begun by starting to lauter, but catching the cast wort in a grant and returning it to the lauter tun by pouring it over the top of the mash. On some systems, this may be automated, with the cast wort being pumped directly back on top of the mash. This step is performed until the runoff is 'clear', and free from large particles. It can also be combined with mashout and mash capping, if desired. If combining all these steps, *vorlauf* for about 15 minutes. Some recipes might not mention the *vorlauf* because it is simply good brewing practice. I tend to include it in my recipes so that people don't inadvertently forget the step.

- **No Sparge** – This is pretty much like it sounds – lautering without sparging. *Vorlauf* as normal, then run off wort until the mash tun is empty or the target volume is reached. Some recipes or methods might refer to this as catching the *first runnings*. You can often identify a recipe that uses a no sparge technique if it has a low efficiency (more grain required to hit the target gravity), and that the water volume seems low. After the first runnings are collected in the brew kettle, hot brewing liquor is used to top off the kettle to the target volume. The idea of this process is that the first runnings have the best malt flavor, so only those are used. Often used with higher-gravity beers, this method also works well with smaller beers that have a malt-forward profile. The recipe should mention that a no sparge technique is used, since sparging is the typical (or assumed) process.

- **Sparge** – Some recipes may specify a fly (or continuous) sparge, or a batch sparge. Fly sparging involves spraying water gently on top of the mash while adjusting the runoff rate to match the sparge rate, so as to maintain a constant level of water on top of the mash. This method can extract unwanted tannins if the sparge water is too hot and at too high a pH above 170°F [77°C] and pH 6.0), so I normally adjust my brewing liquor to pH 5.5 with phosphoric acid to compensate. Batch sparging is like the no sparge technique, except once the lauter tun is drained, it is refilled with hot brewing liquor, remixed, recirculated until clear, and then lautered again. At homebrew volumes they are roughly equivalent methods, provided that sufficient water is used during batch sparging so that the proper starting volume is collected in the kettle.

Boil Techniques

- **The default** – The standard boil technique is well-known to every brewer. Heat the wort to a boil in the kettle, boil for the specified period, and then turn it off. Brewers should know the evaporation rate of their system so they can adjust the starting volume to reach the desired end volume. It's common to use a 60, 75, or 90 minute boil for most beers. The boil should be vigorous enough that bubbles are continually breaking the surface (a "rolling" boil), but not so violent as to cause boilovers. The recipe should state the boil duration, as well as the starting and ending volumes in the boil kettle.

- **Kettle caramelization** – A homebrew technique that boils down first runnings, either in the kettle or in an external pot, to create more caramel flavors through the browning of sugar. Typically, the amount of reduction is at least 75%. The process can create diacetyl flavors in the early stages, giving a butterscotch flavor. Care needs to be taken to avoid burning the sugar, which can create a charred flavor. This process is a substitute for brewing sugars or grist formulation, and is not a traditional brewing process. A recipe that uses this technique should specify the amount of first runnings to boil, and how much reduction to achieve. If not specified, assume the first gallon (4 L) is boiled down to a quart (1 L).

- **Spice additions** – I have quite a few recipes that use spice additions. I lightly crush the spices and put them in a tightly meshed hop bag. I put the bag in the boil near the end (typically in the last two to five minutes of the boil), and I may let it steep after the boil ends (for up to 10 minutes). I then remove the bag while continuing to process the beer. Limiting the contact time between the spices and the hot wort reduces unwanted tannin extraction. An alternate method is to make a tea out of the spices by pouring boiling water over them, letting them steep, and then straining the spices out. I cool the spiced water and add it in after the boil has ended. I also use this method to adjust the spicing level post-fermentation by making a tea with what spices need boosting, then blending it into the finished beer. The recipe will normally say when and how the spices are to be added, and how long they should stay in contact with the beer. I invariably avoid *dry spicing* or adding whole spices to the cold, finished beer.

This always seems to give a dusty, astringent flavor that ruins the beer. Having the spices exposed to some heat is important for quick extraction of flavors without the excessive tannins. Toasting whole spices gently in a dry pan over moderate heat is another way to intensify the flavors and aromas and bring out more of their essential oils.

- **Adding sugar adjuncts** – I normally add sugars, extracts, honey, molasses, or other sugary substances in the last 10 to 15 minutes of the boil. Honey has complex sugars that need some boil time to break down, but boiling the honey also removes desirable aromatics. To maximize its potential, I add honey in the last few minutes of the boil, like an aroma hop. Other sugars can be added at any time during the boil; the goal is to get the sugars dissolved and fully incorporated into the beer. Saving the extra sugars to the end of the boil improves hop utilization due to a lower boil gravity, but adding them at the start of the boil means you won't forget to use them. The recipe should identify the quantity and type of sugar adjunct, and when it should be added (similar to a hop addition).

Hopping Techniques

- **Boiling hops** – The traditional approach of adding hops (in any form) to the boiling wort. Recipes should specify the hop variety, form (pellet, whole, plug, etc.), alpha acid percentage (AA%), quantity (weight), and when they should be added. It is customary to express hop additions in terms of minutes remaining in the boil (e.g., "add bittering hops at 60 minutes" means to add hops with 60 minutes remaining in the boil). Collectively, the set of hop additions for a specific beer is known as the *hop schedule*.
- **First Wort Hopping (FWH)** – A special form of hop boiling, FWH consists of hops of any form added to the kettle before the boil begins. I typically add mine before I start lautering. FWH provides what many believe is a smoother, cleaner bitterness with significant hop flavor. Measured IBUs for FWH in a 60-minute boil is approximately equivalent to a 65 minute addition on the same system, but subjectively the bitterness level seems lower to the palate. If you want the same bitterness impact with FWH, you have to use more hops not fewer. However, I tend to use FWH more for their flavor than for their bitterness. A first wort hop

addition is expressed the same as a normal boiling hop addition, but the *when they should be added* component is normally expressed as FWH instead of the number of minutes remaining in the boil.

- **Hop bursting** – This technique involves a special hop schedule where most (sometimes all) the boiling hops are added in the last 15–20 minutes of the boil (and often within the last 10 minutes or after the boil is over). It may be used in conjunction with other techniques, such as FWH or whirlpool hops, but it implies that no traditional bittering hop additions (normally defined as hops added with 30–90 minutes remaining in the boil) are used. More hops must be used to reach the target bitterness level, but each hop addition contributes aroma and/or flavor to the beer. To my palate, the bitterness produced by this approach also tends to be cleaner and less harsh than traditionally bittered beers, much in the same way that adding dark grains at the end of the mash produces a less harsh beer. A recipe may or may not identify hop bursting or all late hop additions as a method.
- **Whirlpool hops** – A commercial brewing term for adding hops while the wort is spinning in the whirlpool (an external device used to separate hop matter prior to chilling). On a homebrew scale, this step commonly takes the form of adding hops after boiling has concluded but before the wort has been chilled. Simply stir the wort gently using a long-handled spoon in a circular motion. Even if not adding hops, this method can help improve clarity when used in conjunction with a stand. I tend to use one of two methods, either adding the hops immediately after the boil, or waiting 10 or 15 minutes to allow the wort to chill a bit before adding them (waiting a few minutes lowers how many IBUs are extracted from the hops). Contrary to popular belief, adding hops after the boil can add IBUs, as long as the wort is hot enough. How hot? I'm not sure that's been scientifically identified, but I'm speculating that IBUs are extracted down to the 180–185°F (82–85°C) range. If I'm using a large amount of a higher alpha hop variety, I wait a bit to add the hops unless the style can take more bitterness. In a recipe, this is just another form of a hop addition, and is typically shown as taking place at time 0 or time +10.
- **Hop steep or stand** – When I finish boiling or whirlpooling, I let the beer stand for around 20 minutes or so to help it clear before I start running it through a counterflow chiller. I sometimes use

this time to add more aroma hops, depending on the recipe. My system allows me to achieve good clarity when I use whole hops without performing a whirlpool, but this is not the case on many other systems. While I may use whirlpool hops and a hop stand interchangeably, these are technically two different processes.

- **Dry hopping** – Adding hops to finished beer to extract fresh hop aroma is called dry hopping. There are many different ways of doing it, but modern thought is that a relatively short contact time (3 to 5 days) at room temperature (about 60–68°F [16–20°C]) produces good hop intensity without excessively grassy characteristics. Multiple waves of dry hopping can be used to add more complexity and intensity, but be sure to remove one addition before adding the next. Cold-crashing can help separate hops that are not bagged. The goal of dry hopping is to extract hop oils but not excessive vegetal flavors. Keeping the hop contact time with the wort short and warmer is similar to my rationale for handling of dark grains and spices; avoiding tannins keeps harshness low. The final key to dry hopping is to avoid oxidizing your beer in the process. Oxidized hop compounds can be nasty, with big cheesy aromatics. Blow CO_2 on top of your beer, or add dry hops using an oxygen-free transfer process. Dry hopping in a recipe appears as a hop addition, normally with *dry hop* used instead of a time. The recipe may specify the time and temperature of dry hopping, but this is rare. Follow my time and temperature recommendations above if none are given.
- **Hopback** – Note that a hopback can also be used instead of, or in addition to, the hop stand or dry hopping. This involves filling a container with hops and running the beer through it on the way to be chilled. It's an inline step between the boil kettle and the counterflow chiller, and adds some fresh hop character while also serving as a filter. I tend not to use this technique, but some who are set up for it can use it as a substitute process.

Recipe Design Techniques

- **Single hop varietal beers** – Showcasing a single variety of hops in a beer allows the brewer to evaluate the characteristics of a hop. The techniques for brewing the beer are the same, but only one variety of hop is used.

- **SMaSH beers** – Single Malt and Single Hop (SMaSH) beers are popular with some brewers because they highlight the specific flavors of the ingredients and can be somewhat of a challenge to brew. Again, the brewing techniques are the same, but the ingredients are limited.

MY PROCESS

I avoided describing my end-to-end brewing process in *Brewing Better Beer* because I was trying to encourage you to improve your system and methods, not replicate what I do. However, this book is different, and it's necessary to describe my system and methods, as the way I brew informs most of my recipes.

My process is flexible, in that it allows me to have a similar setup for most styles, and doesn't rely on the local water profile, making it easily adaptable to brewing in different locations. It works well for me, but it's also designed around my equipment. I'm certainly not claiming that it's superior to other methods.

Equipment and Setup

I brew on a 15.5 gallon, three-vessel system that uses stainless steel kettles configured as a hot liquor tank, a mash/lauter tun, and a kettle. The mash tun and kettle each have a slotted copper false bottom; the unusual aspect of this configuration is that there is almost 3 gallons (11 L) of space underneath them. I use two pumps to move liquids between vessels and to recirculate. If I perform decoction mashes, I use a large, heavy-bottomed stockpot from my kitchen. I chill through a plate chiller.

The system is propane-fired, and I brew outdoors. Each vessel has an independent burner, although they are all fed from the same propane tank. It's a system I first put together in 1999, so it's not exactly what I'd build today if starting from scratch. It does however work well, and I don't want to invest the time in learning a new system as long as this one meets my needs.

Brewing Preparation Checklist

Tasks before brewing include:

- ❑ **Obtain sufficient water** – As I mentioned earlier, my local water is awful for brewing, so I buy RO water from a local supermarket in 5-gallon (19 L) plastic water bottles.

22

- ❏ **Determine water salts** – I prefer the taste of low mineral additions, so for most beers I simply add 1 tsp of calcium salts (calcium chloride or calcium sulfate) per 5 to 6.6 gallon (19 to 25 L) to get about 50 ppm of calcium.
- ❏ **Prepare brewing liquor** – On most batches, I add about ¼ tsp of 10% phosphoric acid per 5 gallons (19 L) of RO water to achieve a pH of 5.5 at room temperature.
- ❏ **Measure and crush grain** – If I'm adding grains at different times, I mill them separately. Otherwise, I just look for a good crush (husks torn but not shredded, starchy endosperm crushed into pieces). I store the grains in sealed containers.
- ❏ **Measure hops** – I weigh my hops and put them in separate bags or containers, numbered by sequence in the hop schedule. I store my hops in the freezer.
- ❏ **Prepare yeast** – Using a starter or a smack-pack, I have the yeast active and ready to pitch by brew day.
- ❏ **Check supplies** – I try to get most of the ingredient work done ahead of time as it allows me to check that I have necessary supplies on hand, and run to my local homebrew store if I don't. I always check to see that I have enough propane or a reserve tank handy.

Brew Day Procedure

I brew outdoors, so if the weather is good I can set up my equipment the day before. Otherwise, my standard process is as follows:

- ❏ **Set up equipment** – I set up my Hot Liquor Tank (HLT), mash tun, and burners first, adding my brewing liquor to both the HLT and mash tun. I heat both vessels at the same time for speed. On my system, my strike water is 15°F (8°C) above my initial mash temperature. Once burners are lit, I finish setting up the rest of my equipment.
- ❏ **Gather ingredients** – I bring the grain to the system, and complete any other ingredient prep (sometimes I prepare the hops on brew day).
- ❏ **Final equipment check** – I do one last inventory to confirm I have what I need, make sure my mash tun has enough foundation water to cover the false bottom, and that I have electricity for my pumps.

❑ **Mash in** – Once my water is at the proper temperature, I add my crushed grain and mash salts to the mash tun, typically while water is filling from the hot liquor tank. I stir with a mash paddle to break up any clumps, and to thoroughly mix the mash. I don't really measure water volumes; I'm looking for a mash of a certain consistency that can vary by recipe (if I had to estimate, I'd say most of my mashes are about 2 qts/lb., plus the water under the false bottom). I take an initial temperature reading at this point, and make any quick adjustments (typically by adding hot or cold brewing liquor).

❑ **Insulate mash tun** – I wrap duct insulation around my mash tun to help keep the temperature constant. On my system, it cuts heat loss dramatically.

❑ **Monitor mash** – I like to check after 15 minutes to make sure the mash temperature is stabilized, and make any adjustments if necessary (usually either direct firing the mash tun while recirculating, or adding cold brewing liquor) I typically stir the mash at this point to help get a more even temperature distribution. On my system, this also helps improve efficiency.

❑ **Perform mash steps** – Depending on the recipe, I might be doing a step mash, decoction mash, or other another process.

> ❑ **Step mashing** – I use a pump that recirculates wort from the false bottom to the top of the mash while I'm directly heating the mash tun. Boiling brewing liquor could also be used to raise the temperature.
>
> ❑ **Decoction mashing** – I pull decoctions using a large kitchen saucepan, and heat the decoction in a kitchen stockpot set up on one of my system's burners. I don't turn on the heat until I've finished transferring, and I stir constantly to avoid scorching. You don't want the decoction to stick to the bottom of the pot and burn; that will cause an ashtray-like flavor that will never go away.
>
> ❑ **Mashout** – When all mash steps are finished, I recirculate while heating to the mashout temperature. In most recipes, this is where I add dark grains and crystal malts. I normally mashout for about 15 minutes at 168–170°F (76–77°C).

- ❑ **Lautering** – Prior to lautering, I cut deep channels into the mash using a thin kitchen spatula. I make a checkerboard pattern in the malt, maybe 2 inch (5 cm) squares, taking care not to cut all the way down to the false bottom. This improves lauter performance and is similar to what mash rakes do in commercial breweries. If the recipe calls for FWH, I add them now. I run the wort off slowly into the bottom of the kettle, and stop collecting when I hit my target volume (I measure volume using a calibrated stick, measuring from the top of the kettle).

- ❑ **Sparging** – If I'm using a continuous sparge (my normal technique), I'll sparge while lautering, adjusting the rates to maintain a constant water level in the lauter tun. I normally sparge at a temperature of 170–172°F (77–78°C), but I heat my hot liquor tank higher since I lose some temperature during the transfer. It's important to keep the temperature in the lauter tun under 176°F (80°C) as this can increase haze.

- ❑ **Boiling** – After the kettle has been filled to the appropriate volume, I take a gravity reading so I can adjust the boil length and final volume if necessary to hit my target gravity in the finished wort. I manage the boil, adding hops and other ingredients per the recipe. Even if not specified in the recipe, I add a Whirlfloc tablet (or an Irish moss product) and some yeast nutrient (I prefer the Wyeast brand) in the last 15 minutes of the boil.

- ❑ **Whirlpool and stand** – After flameout, I stir the wort with a long-handled spoon to start a whirlpool, and then leave the kettle undisturbed for about 20 minutes to allow break material and hops to settle. I may add additional hops at this time. After the wort has clarified, I pump the wort out through an inline chiller. Note that I have a false bottom in my kettle which helps serve as a filter, especially when using whole hops.

- ❑ **Preparation for pitching** – I collect the chilled wort in a sanitized bucket, move it indoors, then take a gravity and temperature reading. As I prepare my fermenter and yeast, I give the wort another chance to settle in the bucket, where small hop particles can settle out. I rack the wort into a fermenter, oxygenate it (typically I run oxygen at full blast through a sintered stone for one minute), and pitch the yeast.

Fig 1.4: Measuring starting gravity.   Fig 1.5: Measuring final gravity (note clarity).

If I'm making multiple batches, I perform some of these steps in parallel for the next batch. For instance, I'll mash a second batch while boiling the first. I find that I can execute this process in 5 to 6 hours for one batch, adding 2 hours for each subsequent batch. Choice of techniques can affect those times considerably, as can batch size, since transfer times are doubled and a greater volume of liquid must be heated.

Remember to clean as you go, putting away unneeded equipment. I like to keep extra hot water around to aid in cleanup, and like to flush all lines that have touched wort with near-boiling water to dissolve and rinse away sugars. It's much easier to clean equipment while it is still warm.

I do think about the key control points, and the overall management of the process. I think ahead about the long lead time steps, and try to not lose time waiting on something else. One of the most important aspects of efficient brewing is to always keep your water hot. Reheating water is one of the biggest ways to lose time in the process. No one ever claimed brewing was easy, and it does take quite a bit of planning to brew 2 or 3 recipes on the same day.

KEY POINTS ABOUT MY PROCESS

While this process probably seems quite normal to experienced brewers, it has a few idiosyncrasies due to my equipment design and my water. The first is that I use what seem like oddly sized recipes. Most of my recipes are for 6.5 gallons (25 L), while you may see other recipes as 5 gallons (19 L). I size my recipes larger because I want to be sure I have 5 gallons finished beer in a keg at the end of the process. There is loss in wort transfer and racking when I move only the clearest, highest-quality wort or beer, so I scale my recipes larger to account for these losses. My recipes measure the volume of wort left in the kettle at the end of the boil, not the amount of beer in a keg when packaged.

The second idiosyncrasy is how my method is designed to work around my awful brewing water. In the course of seeking solutions, I settled on what I think has more general applicability due to its simplification and repeatability. When I was at Sierra Nevada's Beer Camp, they told me that they treated their brewing liquor so that it was at pH 5.5. If they can do it, why can't I? Starting with RO water is an obvious choice since my chalk-laden water takes too much effort to try to get into a usable state.

The goal of reducing harshness in my beer drove me to investigate various methods that could help. I determined that extended contact with grain husks and hop material was a bad thing, regardless of the pH. Sure, a higher pH will speed the extract of tannins, but they can still wind up in your beer if you leave them in contact long enough. That's what happens when I try to use dry spices in the secondary, and that's the same thing that happens with hops and grain.

I also try to reduce the contact time with compounds that contain tannins while maintaining an environment with less than a pH of 6. I do this by always just mashing what actually needs to be mashed: the base grains and specialty grains that have unconverted starches. This means that most of my mashes look identical regardless of the style of beer I'm making. This process is very repeatable and something I can optimize.

The dark grains and crystal malts steep at the end of the mash while I'm recirculating at mashout temperature and then again during the sparge to extract the desired color and flavor. This is similar to what extract brewers do when making their beer; the grains are steeped in hot water and then removed. The only difference is that extract brewers steep in plain water while I'm steeping in the recirculating mash water.

I find that I can further reduce harshness in my beers through the manipulation of the hop schedule. I use FWH, hop bursting, and hop stands frequently, as those tend to reduce the contact time of hops or the temperature where hops are exposed to the wort. The science behind FWH is not well understood, but the practical evaluation of the method shows that the quality of bitterness is smoother, and that more hop flavor survives than an equivalent amount of hops added to the boil.

Dry hopping can be a source of harshness and vegetal or grassy flavors. This can be minimized by keeping the overall contact time down, avoiding hop varieties with a grassy character, and sometimes by reducing the amount of pellet hops used. I don't dry hop too often, but I'm not as against it as I once was. I think the complexity of hop character is improved when hop bursting, hop stands, and dry hopping are all used together. I tend to use the dry hopping technique after having used other techniques, so I only use it when it seems like the beer needs an extra boost of hop aroma.

I use relatively light water treatments. Since I don't have to use salt additions to compensate for pH, I focus on what's needed for optimal mash performance and final beer flavor. As long as the mash settles into a range of 5.2–5.3 pH, the conversion should be complete and the beer should taste good. The actual acceptable mash pH range is a bit broader (5.1–5.5) but I try to aim for the center. Note that when referenced in brewing, pH is always reported at room temperature (25°C/77°F) since the measurement of pH is temperature-dependent. Using a standard reference temperature by convention makes it much easier to compare values.

I like the flavor from calcium chloride better than calcium sulfate, so I tend to use that in beers unless there is a need for the extra dryness that gypsum contributes. I did the calculations on how many grams are in volume measurements of salts; now I just measure my additions with teaspoons rather than gram scales since it's faster and has adequate precision for my needs.

I like this approach to water treatment since it's easy, and allows me to handle each beer in basically the same way. I'm also not sold on the various water calculators since they are simply models, and models aren't always accurate; they make necessary assumptions, but those assumptions may not be in line with how I brew. The models also don't really tell you anything about the flavor profile of the finished beer, either. I'd only be happy using models if I had taken the time to run extensive validation tests.

That's my full method. I find that it works well for me, and might be of interest to you, particularly if you are vexed by some of the same issues. At the very least, it should help you understand and interpret my recipes. Even if you have a well-developed process, you may still benefit from incorporating aspects of my methods. After all, that's what I do: continue to hone and refine my processes as I learn from other brewers.

2 | WORKING WITH RECIPES

"Don't let the secret recipe die with the inventor."

—Nathan Myhrvold, Intellectual Ventures, LLC

While many brewers may have spent years developing and honing their brewing processes, those skills are truly put to the test when trying to brew someone else's recipes. Another brewer may have formulated it on a completely different brewing system, or made a number of assumptions regarding the specifics of the ingredients, timings, and methods. This chapter explores how to tweak any recipe to make it work on your system.

INTERPRETING RECIPES

Recipes are like stories; some are better written than others. Missing information in a recipe can be as infuriating as an obvious, glaring plot hole in a novel. While mistakes in the writing of a story might annoy you, they don't really have important consequences on your life as a reader. Mistakes in the writing of homebrew recipes on the other hand, can have dire consequences on your life as a brewer (like a ruined batch of beer).

Have you ever looked at historical recipes? They can be frustratingly short on details. They usually only recorded the quantity of ingredients and most basic of parameters. The usual procedures were often not written down (the recipe assumed the brewers knew them), so other sources that describe or speculate on a brewery's legacy methods are used to make educated guesses. Similarly, the recipes of modern commercial breweries or homebrewers will probably lack details if the original author did not intentionally write them with other, external brewers in mind.

What at first glance may seem like missing information in a story may in fact just be a literary device. Maybe a detail was omitted because it wasn't relevant to the main story, or because the author felt it was obvious and didn't need to be explained. The reader sometimes needs to fill in the gaps to make the story complete. Recipes can have the same issue, because what is considered a *necessary* piece of information to one brewer might be obvious to another.

This section seeks to answer several important questions about the design and presentation of recipes:

- What are the main elements of a recipe?
- How are they structured, and what information do they convey?
- How should a brewer read, analyze, and understand a recipe?
- How can a brewer tell if a recipe is missing an important step or detail?
- Is it possible to determine or at least estimate any omitted details?

Recipe elements – Each recipe should have three basic sections: the parameters, the ingredients, and the process. The parameters describe the characteristics of the batch (batch size, the target style, the vital statistics, etc.) as well as system-related information (mash efficiency, boiloff rate, etc.). The ingredients section includes the types and quantities of malt and grains, hops, yeast, and sometimes water. The process section usually includes the mash schedule, the hop schedule, the fermentation schedule, and any unusual or special notes (it may also include water treatment).

To be fair, not all recipe writers have the same goals. In personal logs (including those used for commercial brewing records, see Chapter 1 brewing logs images), the author is the same as the reader (or at least trained the same way) and the recipes are more shorthand than anything. They are intended to remind the brewer of key details so they can replicate or troubleshoot a specific batch of beer. They aren't designed to teach someone how to brew.

Analyzing a recipe – Reading and understanding a recipe involves checking it for completeness. Your only goal is to identify whether or not you have enough information to brew the beer. If you have a standard template for your recipes, copying information from the recipe into your own format makes any gaps much more apparent.

What kind of information is typically missing from a recipe? Here are some of the more common problems I've seen, and how I typically handle the situations:

- **Mash efficiency missing** – Most recipes list a starting gravity, but not all provide the efficiency. This creates a problem, because you might not hit the target gravity if your system's efficiency is different. I use the grain bill, batch size, and starting gravity to derive the missing efficiency, typically using recipe software. I enter the batch size and the grain bill, setting the efficiency to my system default (70%). I then compare the estimated gravity with the target gravity for the recipe. If they are significantly off, I adjust the efficiency in the software until the gravities match (or are close).

- **Grain quantities missing** – Some recipes (particularly those from commercial breweries) are expressed in percentages. This is great for scaling a recipe and comparing it with other recipes, but many homebrewers don't know how to translate percentages to applicable quantities. I like to plug the recipe into brewing software, entering the percentages as if they were pounds. I then set the target gravity and let the software scale the grist accordingly.

  If you don't have recipe software, you can estimate the grist manually. First, calculate the total weight of malt needed to hit the recipe's starting gravity target using your system's mash efficiency (use equations in Appendix A if necessary), assuming the entire grist is base malt (use 36 points per pound). Second, apply the percentages of each grist component from the recipe to total estimated grist weight to estimate the weight of each ingredient in the mash. Third, calculate the gravity of this recipe. If the calculated gravity is different from the recipe target, scale each grist component by the percentage difference between the estimated gravity and the target gravity. Recheck the gravity of the updated recipe, repeating as necessary until the gravities match.

- **Grain details missing** – If the country of origin is missing, go with the native country if possible (for instance, if a recipe says Munich malt, go with a German maltster). If the maltster isn't specified, you can pick your favorite. You can sometimes use recipe software to help determine grain color if an overall color of the beer is given. However, many maltsters produce crystal-type malts within a certain range, and chocolate malt can be vastly different in color and flavor from one maltster to another. When in doubt, pick something reasonable for the style of beer.

- **Boil information missing** – Most recipes will give a batch size, but many will omit information on the starting volume or length of boil. The ending volume is the same as the batch size, and can be assumed if not explicitly stated. The starting volume is the most interesting piece of information since it determines how much wort I collect from the lauter, and suggests what kind of boil-off (or evaporation) rate is implied when compared to the final batch size. Even if the starting volume, ending volume, and length of boil are given, I'm looking for clues as to the vigor of the boil (i.e., how hard should the wort be boiling? Is it normal, or is it boiling hard?). If the implied evaporation rate is different than on your system, you will have to change sometime (starting volume, boil length, or boil vigor). If no boil time is given, assume 60 minutes (unless you see a hop addition that is earlier than that).

- **Hop information missing** – The typical hop schedule includes the variety, quantity, and timing of usage. If also often includes the alpha acid percentage of the hops, the format of the hops, and the IBU target for the beer. It rarely includes the IBU estimation method (unless the recipe is from a book or magazine where they list the method for all recipes). There are several cases of missing information to consider.

- **Recipe in AAUs** – Some homebrew recipes might give hop information in AAUs (alpha acid units, sometimes called HBUs, or homebrew bitterness units); other recipes may give hop additions in IBUs. Expressing hops in AAUs simply means multiplying the weight of a hop addition by the alpha acid percentage. For example, using 2 ounces of a 6% alpha acid hop gives 12 AAUs of bitterness. If you want to brew the recipe but can only find 4% alpha acid hops, you would use 3 ounces of them since 12 AAUs/4% AA = 3 oz. It's helpful for scaling hop additions based on what hops are available to you, but I would only use said hops for bittering additions. For flavor and aroma additions, you should be more interested in the amount of hop oils, so go by weight, not bittering contribution (since the bitterness of these hops is a secondary concern). Note that AAUs do not predict bitterness of the finished beer; they are simply a convenient measurement of the source ingredients.

Even if you don't use AAUs in your recipes, you might use them indirectly if you have to adjust the quantity based on the alpha acid content of your available hops. The alpha acid content of hops varies year to year too, so that's why you often see different alpha acids listed for the same variety of hops. When I fill out my recipe log, I write down what I actually used, because it might be different the next time I buy hops.

If designing a new recipe, I validate my recipe using software and the actual AA% of the hops I've chosen. The more modern approach is to list the IBU contribution of bittering hop additions rather than the weight and alpha acid percentage; it's understood you will use brewing software or a calculator to determine the actual amount needed (see Appendix A: Basic Beer Math for the specific calculation). Given the desired IBUs, the timing of the hop additions, the wort's gravity, the batch volume, and the AA% of the hops to be used, most software can determine for the weight of the hops required.

- **Alpha acid percentages missing** – If the alpha acid percentages are missing from the recipe, I can still figure out the value if I have the weight of the necessary hops and the total IBUs for the beer. I first check if I have those hop varieties on hand, and plug in the AA% from those. I then calculate the total IBUs using recipe software and check it against the target for the recipe. If that still doesn't work, I use the hops I have or can buy, add the indicated weight, and scale the bittering addition to hit the target IBU level.
- **Hop weights missing** – If I need to complete a hop schedule where weights are missing, I finalize the flavor and aroma hops first. I set the weight of those additions to give the expected perceptual impact for the style of beer. In a 5-gallon (19 L) batch, I

start with 0.25 oz (7 g) of hops for light impact, 0.5 oz (14 g) for moderate impact, 1 oz (28 g) for high impact, and 2 oz (57 g) for very high impact. Once those weights are set, I determine how many IBUs those additions contribute. The bittering addition is then scaled to provide the remaining IBUs needed to hit the overall bitterness target for the beer.

If I'm using recipe software to scale the bittering addition after I have set the flavor and aroma weights to desired levels, the software will often try to scale all the hops equally. When that happens, I need to manually reset (or lock, if that feature exists) the flavor and aroma additions quantities so I am varying only the bittering additions.

- **Beer style information lacking** – This issue takes one of two forms, either not clearly identifying the style, or providing a recipe that doesn't fit the stated style. Some beers are described with generic names, and others state they are following BJCP guidelines. Some recipes that are trying to match or clone commercial beers will state the brand name of the beer they seek to emulate.

  I handle this situation by trying to determine the author's intent. Were they trying to brew a classic example, or were they just trying to pick a name for their beer? If no style information is given, try to imagine the flavor profile and balance of the beer and see if it fits a defined style. Calculating the vital parameters using recipe software can also help. There may be several valid matches, and sometimes you must brew these recipes to evaluate them. Trained judges can help determine the closest style match.

  This is a problem only if you intend to enter the beer into a competition and are worried that your beer won't be judged properly, or if you don't like certain styles of beer and would rather avoid making them. Otherwise, just brew the recipe, enjoy your beer, and don't worry about the style.

- **Mash schedule deficient** – Some recipes don't provide a full mash schedule, or omit durations for different rests. If a recipe provides only one mash temperature, assume an infusion mash program and perform a one hour rest. Not all recipes specify a mashout; some brewers don't use it, and some simply don't include it as a mash step since it's a normal part of their process.

It's hard to write a recipe with a complicated mash program without describing the rests. Any brewer would be confused if a mash schedule said to do a decoction mash, for instance. If I ran into that case, my default mash schedule would be a *hochkurz* single decoction mash with a rest at 145°F (63°C) and another at 158°F (70°C), as described in the Brewing Techniques chapter. If it was a paler beer style, I'd boil for 5–10 minutes, and if it were a darker style, 15–20 minutes.

Regardless of mash technique, check through the mash schedule to be sure that there is at least one rest in the saccharification range of the diastatic enzymes (generally 144°F/62°C to 162°F/72°C). On the homebrew scale, a total mash rest time of at least an hour is typical.

- **Special ingredients or processes not described** – Sometimes in a recipe for an unusual or unconventional batch, a brewer will leave out abnormal steps. When I discuss my pumpkin ale recipe, I take extra time to explain how I prepare and use the pumpkin, since I know that most people mash it (while I put it in the boil). Some people like to keep their special methods secret, but many simply don't take the time to explain something they take for granted. All I can suggest is that you look through the recipe process carefully to see if it mentions how exactly special ingredients are used. Sometimes this information can be in several places, including part of the ingredient description.

- **Errata** – People are human and mistakes happen. Even in printed publications, errors can slip by editors and reviewers. You should review a recipe not only for completeness, but also for accuracy. Common errors that I see in recipes include transposing (swapping) digits, using the wrong units, incorrect metric conversions, dropped characters, off-by-one typing (hands shifted on a keyboard giving a different character or number), and cut-and-paste or reuse errors (using a template or previously written snippet, but not fully changing it). I can't describe every possible error, so use your judgment in questioning something odd.

Depending on your experience level (and sometimes your personality type), you might be able to accept a reasonable amount of uncertainty or ambiguity in a recipe. It helps if you already know how you are going to adjust it to your methods and system, unless you want to follow the recipe to the exact detail. Knowing the gaps that may exist gives you room to fix them, as discussed in the next section.

Fixing a recipe – If a recipe is missing a few pieces of necessary information, there are a few ways to go about fixing the problem. First, see if you can calculate the missing information given the information you have. I've discussed those methods in the previous chapter, but some additional formulas can be found in *Appendix A: Basic Beer Math*.

Next, see if you can resolve any unclear parts of the recipe. Maybe the original source of the recipe has more to say. If it comes from a book or magazine article, those sources may include information relevant to the recipe. If the recipe is from a person you know, see if you can contact them directly to ask your questions. I get a few emails a week from people asking me about my recipes; most authors are happy to help, as long as the requests are polite and to the point.

Finally, you may be able to make educated guesses about the recipe, or simply apply your own default processes. If you do add your own guesses or processes, be sure to re-read the entire recipe to see if there are any new inconsistencies. Regardless of the way you go about filling in the missing details, you should not brew until you have a final, executable recipe in hand. The recipe you actually brew may be a bit different than the original, but at least you're starting the brewing process with a plan.

RECIPE FORMULATION FUNDAMENTALS

You can develop solid skills working with other people's recipes. Adapting recipes to your system, scaling them, validating calculations, learning flavor profiles, and similar tasks all make you think about the structure and format of the recipe. However, when you reach the point when you want to create your own new recipes, or create a substantially different variation of an existing recipe, then you'll need to start applying some additional skills. This is true learning-by-doing, and cannot be forced or learned solely by reading. In this section, I explore how to approach this skill development and provide some recommendations based on what I do (and how I learned).

There is some additional background material in appendices that might be useful when working with recipe formulation. Appendix A includes basic beer math, the common equations you'll need to understand to work with recipes, and examples on how to use them. Appendix B describes how to work with recipe software, and how to select software to best support your needs. Appendix C discusses how recipes can be converted to use malt extract as a fermentable, and the special issues that extract brewers face when dealing with recipes.

Conceptualizing Recipes – When I start thinking about a new recipe, whether it is completely new or a major variation of an existing recipe, I don't rush to entering data into recipe software. I tend to start organizing my thoughts first before turning to any automated tools.

I use recipe software to support my recipe development, but mostly in the revising and refining phase. It's useful to know how to perform common calculations by hand, or to quickly validate the output of recipe software using rough approximations. It's equally helpful to know how to quickly use brewing calculators to automate otherwise tedious calculations you might need to make in the course of brewing.

My recipe formulation process starts with writing down ideas and adding notes, particularly if I'm doing online research or am considering multiple options. I start with a general idea of what I want to brew, such as the beer style, a similar commercial example, a set of general parameters, or a target flavor profile.

This is where experience comes into play. You are driven by intuition when you start building a recipe. Given enough experience, you will understand things that have or have not worked for you in the past, but also what has worked for other brewers. Understanding recipes created by other brewers pays off when you do start building your own.

When working with fermentables, it is helpful to develop the skill to think in percentages rather than weights. You may develop a feel for flavor contributions from different weights of grain if you have a standard batch size, but it's beneficial (to your overall brewing skill) to learn how different *percentages* of grain impact flavor since that knowledge is batch size-independent. The equivalent skill for hops involves learning how to think of bittering additions as bittering units, knowing that the specifics will be determined by the available hops.

The mental model I have for recipes is similar to the charts and tables in Ray Daniels' *Designing Great Beers*. For each style of beer you brew, you have a set of ingredients you might use. This isn't the full universe of ingredients; it's a constrained set of choices based on what you believe tastes good in that beer style. For each ingredient, you have a bounded range of percentages that you may use in your recipe (base malt may be 50–100% of the grist, while dark malts may be under 10%, for instance). This model isn't something someone tells you; it's what you build as you gain experience, updating as you learn.

When you create a recipe, you are making decisions using that model. You select individual ingredients from that constrained list, and you set their percentages of the recipe as a value within the range you've previously determined. You still have to learn to predict the flavor profile of the combination of ingredients you select, but at least you have substantially pruned the problem down to a manageable size.

Don't worry about precisely identifying a value for each ingredient in your recipe initially; you can start by including a range. This makes it easier to adjust later since you have some built-in flexibility. I start by specifying the ingredients that have the largest flavor impact on the beer, which isn't necessarily the ingredient with the highest weight or percentage. As you select specific ingredients, decide if you want to describe them generically (e.g., pale ale malt) or be more specific (e.g., Crisp Maris Otter). You have to make these detailed decisions immediately; you may wait until after the entire recipe is sketched out.

Once I have drafted an initial concept, I put it into a recipe program such as *Beer Alchemy* to validate the numbers and check the ingredient percentages. The review and revision process can be quite iterative, so it's useful to have recipe software make sure the ingredients add up and to see the target parameters of the beer. When a recipe built using percentages is expressed in weights, I often perform a final rounding step so that the weights are easier to work with on brew day.

Balancing flavors for a style – While recipe formulation involves quite a bit of math, there is also an artistic element to designing a beer that must not be ignored. Unfortunately, this side of brewing is hard to explain and teach – how does someone learn to be creative? Many people want how-to instructions, but that's not how humans learn creativity. To formulate unique, special recipes, you need to understand the ingredients, their flavor profiles, and how they change during the brewing process. You also need to understand what each contributes as part of a larger recipe. Finally, you need to understand how altering the balance of these components affects the overall impression of the finished product.

Learning ingredient profiles – I recommend tasting your ingredients at every stage in the brewing process to see how they change. Tastings steeped grains and hops can help you develop basic flavor and aroma familiarity, but there is no substitute for brewing, as the finished beer is much different than the basic ingredients. Brewing beers that feature single ingredients (such as single malt and single hop beers) allow you to vary and evaluate additional ingredients (such as specialty malts and yeast), which can be a very instructive exercise. Small batch brewing or homebrew club experiments can also help you gain an understanding of these flavors (with less work for yourself).

When thinking about the contributions from each ingredient, understand they can provide both flavor and aroma, but can also have other side effects such as changing the body, fermentability, appearance, and mouthfeel (like roasted grains adding tannins). Keep in mind that you must make tradeoffs when putting together a recipe; not every ingredient brings only positive contributions, and some may require additional work to compensate for their unwanted side effects.

Ingredient intensity – There is much to learn about how ingredients affect the final beer profile when used in different concentrations. There's a big difference between using 2% crystal malt and 10% crystal malt, or using crystal 40 versus crystal 120, or between 10% crystal malt and 10% Munich malt. When experimenting, try to brew beers with different concentrations so you can understand the difference between a background flavor and a primary flavor. If someone offers you their homebrewed beer, quiz them about the recipe so you can use their experience as a learning opportunity as well.

As with cooking, I think it's important to understand which ingredients have a strong flavor and will dominate the final profile if used too heavily. Biscuit malt, black malt, or the oft-abused peat-smoked malt for instance, can take over a beer as easily as pungent herbs like ginger, rosemary, or saffron can take over a food recipe.

Contributors to balance – I like to look beyond the numerical specifications for a beer, as I don't think IBUs or gravity readings tell a full story. Yes, the ration of bitterness to the beer's original gravity can tell you something about the balance, if the beers are generally of the same alcohol level and final gravity. But 50 IBUs will taste different in a 6% beer with a final gravity of 1.006 than in a 6% beer with a final gravity of 1.024. Even in a beer with similar numerical specifications, other flavors can affect the bitterness perception—think about 30 IBUs in a beer made with two-row versus a one made with Munich malt. The increased maltiness can *swallow* the bitterness, making it seem less bitter in comparison (even if the amount of malt is the same, numerically).

Just as some people confuse sweetness (the flavor of sugar) with maltiness (the flavor of malt), I also see people confusing sweetness with body. A beer can have body without being sweet (the dextrins mostly responsible for body in beer are not sweet). Sweet sugars can add body, but are not the primary source as they are normally fermented. You can have a beer that has a malty flavor and moderate body, but is not sweet (in that it has little residual sugar). However the presence of IBUs can affect the palate impression of sweetness; an absence of bitterness often makes you think a beer is sweet, even if it is relatively dry. It takes a trained palate or significant tasting experience to easily differentiate these characteristics in beer.

It isn't always easy to trace specific flavors in a beer back to a source ingredient. Fruity esters can come from yeast, but also from malts and hops. When looking at the overall flavor balance in beer, remember that you might be deriving similar flavors from different ingredients, and that those flavors may be supportive, may clash, or may become too intense.

Creating balance – Taking the various flavor components in beer and balancing them to suit a particular style or palate takes some work. At the most basic level, balancing the maltiness and sweetness in beer with bitterness (or roast, acidity, alcohol level, or harshness) is what makes beer taste good. Balance is always relative to the style of beer. A balanced IPA is quite different than a balanced *lambic,* for instance. Matching the flavor contributions from ingredients to the overall profile of a given style requires a deep understanding of what flavors come from what sources.

Even when you think you understand this process, there is still an experimental side to it, particularly if you have a complex recipe. You might not be able to accurately predict the flavors, and things you think might work together well might actually crash-and-burn when put into practice. Remember to test your creations and be willing to adjust them if they don't work as expected.

ADAPTING RECIPES

There are many situations where you need to adapt a recipe to work on your system. Sometimes you get a recipe from someone who brews on different equipment, with different efficiency, different processes, or different batch sizes. You might even need to adapt your own recipes if you have recently made significant changes to your brewing system or processes.

I'm assuming that you're working from a complete recipe at this point. If not, refer to the section on *Interpreting Recipes* for tips on how to fill in missing information. Some of the techniques described there are also used when adapting recipes. The main goal is to finalize the brewing decisions that control the outcome of your beer. Recipe software is useful for many of these techniques.

I'm also assuming that you understand your current system, and know how it responds to changing variables when you brew. If you are still learning your system, you can make educated guesses when you adapt the recipe, and gather data on how your system actually responds when you brew.

Batch scaling – This is probably the easiest adaptation. On the home-brew scale, batch scaling is linear. Simply change the quantity of ingredients by percentage difference. If you want to make a 10-gallon batch from a 5-gallon recipe, double all the ingredients. If you use the manual approach, you can double-check the result by entering the recipe in brewing software and checking the final parameters (original gravity, bitterness, and color, primarily). If scaling a recipe results in any unusual quantities, round the results to make them easier to measure while brewing.

Mash efficiency – Changing mash efficiency will change the amount of grain in the grist. While keeping the grist percentages constant, you can change the quantity of grain to determine the number of gravity points of the new mash efficiency. The number of gravity points extracted from grain is obtained by multiplying the weight of the grain, the potential extract of the grain, and the mash efficiency. Greater mash efficiency will use less grain, and vice versa. If I change the efficiency in a recipe using recipe software, I normally adjust the grain weights slightly to have round numbers.

Hop utilization – Changing the hop schedule or brewing on a differently sized system will affect hop utilization. Due to fluctuations in utilization, the hop schedule may need to be adjusted so that the recipe still hits the target bitterness level. Not all recipe software will model all hop additions correctly (such as first wort hops and whirlpool hops), so you may need to perform those calculations manually or enter them in the software in a way that will give you an equivalent value. For more detail in how the numbers are estimated, (see Appendix A: Basic Beer Math).

Boil rate and length – If a recipe specifies a starting kettle volume, ending kettle volume, and boil length, you should be able to check if those measurements work the on your system. Change the procedure to collect the necessary volume of wort required for the final volume given the boil length you are using. Double-check that the gravity in the kettle at the start of the boil will produce the desired target gravity at the end of the boil at the given boil length. If it is different, you will need to scale your recipe to hit that target gravity.

Waste and loss – Depending on your equipment, you may lose a fixed amount of wort during transfers, or may decide to select only the best fraction of the wort during transfers. Either way, the volume of beer you need at the end of the process reflects not only that loss, but all losses during the process (except boil losses, which are accounted for in the recipe). I like to make sure that I always have a full keg (or more), so I tend to brew larger batches (6.5 gallons, 25 L) even though I only need 5 gallons (19 L) at the end. If you find that you have less total yield when you are packaging, you may need to adjust your batch size. Use the batch scaling procedure to change your batch size so that it reflects your volume requirement (including loss). You may be constrained by equipment (like fermenter size), so check the volume you need at each step to make sure you can accommodate it.

Equipment availability and process substitution – Some recipes will specify methods that require equipment you don't have. For example, if you mash in a picnic cooler, it's unlikely you'll be able to directly heat your mash tun to step mash. Read through the recipe to ensure that you can actually execute all the steps on your system. If you can't step mash by direct heating, then you can either convert to a single-step mash, or perform the mash steps through infusing boiling water or by decocting. If the recipe specifies that you use a hopback, you can add the hops to the kettle after the boil, before you start to run off. You may also have to restructure the steps in the recipe if you don't have the necessary equipment.

INGREDIENT SUBSTITUTION

This is an advanced topic: those rare times where you need to change a recipe based on ingredient availability or substitute an ingredient you don't like out for one for one you do like. Everyone has their least favorite ingredients, whether it is peat-smoked malt, Summit hops, Ringwood yeast, or bourbon barrels. If you really don't like a specific flavor, ask yourself if it can be deleted without destroying the character of the recipe. If the ingredient *is* necessary, replace it with something you prefer. It may not taste exactly the same, but will at least be drinkable. In some cases, you'll be able to make a reasonable change without altering the character of the recipe; in other cases, you'll be hard pressed to brew the recipe without the missing ingredient. Keep in mind that not all ingredient substitutions are the same; some will work better than others. Process substitution (see *Adapting Recipes*) can also be used in conjunction with ingredient substitution or on its own as a way to compensate for missing ingredients.

Identifying key ingredients – The first step in substituting ingredients is to determine which ingredients are supplying the major flavor elements in the beer, and what role each ingredient is performing in the recipe. I provide this information in this book as a discussion point, but most other recipes will not have this level of detail.

Knowing about the basics of beer styles will help you brew as many styles are driven by well-known ingredients. The complexity of the recipe is also key, since the less complex the recipe, the more important an individual ingredients. However, some ingredients can have disproportionate impacts on the flavor profile. Examining the percentages of grist components can tell you relative quantities of grain, but you have to understand the intensity and distinctiveness of each element. This assessment needs to be done in the context of the overall flavor profile of the beer. For example, there may be only one malt in an IPA, but that flavor may be totally dominated by the hops even though it is 100% of the grist.

Dark malts have a large flavor contribution, but huskless equivalents are smoother and can be used in higher proportions. Don't go by color alone; the individual malt matters. Likewise, don't go solely by name; there can be a wide range in character for products of the same name (chocolate malt is notorious in this regard, but you can also see a large difference in Munich malts). Some toasted-type malts (amber malt, brown malt, Victory® malt, biscuit malt, and similar products) can have a disproportional impact on flavor, much more so than crystal-type malts of similar color.

With hops, the flavor contribution depends mostly on where in the hop schedule they are used. Hops that are used strictly for bitterness can generally be substituted at will, provided that they aren't known to have any other harsh qualities.

When in doubt, use more neutral bittering hops (like Magnum). Aroma and flavor hops are all about oil content; while you might be able to determine relative levels of oils, the overall impression of the hop character is what needs to be most closely assessed. Look for ones with similar descriptors (piney, citrusy, fruity, etc.) and try to use similar varieties. You don't necessarily have to match country of origin, although it sometimes helps.

Yeast is similar to hops; you have to understand its flavor and aroma contribution, in addition to its fermentation performance. Some yeast are relatively neutral fermenters, and can easily be substituted. Others have distinctive by-products; many Belgian strains produce a complex profile, and some strains are identified as phenol-positive (or phenolic off-flavor positive, POF+). Even some British and American strains are quite distinctive. As with hops, country of origin sometimes helps with substitutions, but shouldn't eliminate creative choices.

Specific substitutions – This isn't an exhaustive list because the possibilities are endless, but remember that using substitutions is an emergency measure; it should not be something you do because of laziness. The results from substitution won't be as good as using the specified ingredients. However, these may be able to get you closer to the desired flavor profiles if you absolutely must use other ingredients.

Note that in all the examples I give in quantities, the batch size is 5 gallons (19 L) with 10 lb. (4.5 kg) of base malt. Scale accordingly for different size batches. I also provide the quantities in percentages of the grist.

- **Two-row base malt** – This is fairly neutral stuff, so it's hard to substitute. It's also very easy to find. If I had to substitute for it, I might go with the most neutral pale ale malt I had and cut it 50-50 with Pilsner malt. The problem is that both of these malts have distinctive flavor, so your goal is to avoid a base flavor that tastes strongly of either pale ale malt or Pilsner malt. Assuming the two-row malt is North American, using other malts from the same region is better than getting English or German malts since European malts can have more flavor. Blending base malts often either enhances or reduces the dominant character of one malt.

- **Pale ale malt** – American pale ale malt is a little darker, maltier, and grainier than two-row, so I would substitute about 4 oz (113 g) of Munich malt (2.5% of grist) and 1 oz (28 g) of biscuit malt (1.25%).
- **English pale ale malt** – Belgian pale ale malt is probably the closest in flavor, but is also likely harder to find. Try adding 2 oz (57 g) of biscuit malt (1.25%) and 8 oz (227 g) of wheat malt (5%) to two-row.
- **Maris Otter** – This is a premium English pale ale malt with a strong bready and biscuity flavor. If you can get another English pale malt (or Scottish Golden Promise), you can start there and add a little extra biscuit malt (2 oz or 57 g) (1.25%). Otherwise start doctoring up two-row malt. Mix in small amounts of biscuit malt, maybe 4 oz (113 g) (2.5%). Half that amount of light crystal malt, perhaps 20°L, could give it some color and a touch more flavor. You can also lightly toast the base malt at 250°F (120°C) for 15 or 20 minutes to increase the bready-toasty flavors and darken it slightly.
- **Biscuit malt** – Amber malt is a bit more intense, so you can use it but in lower quantities (no more than 25%).
- **Amber malt** – Try toasting pale ale malt for 30 minutes at 300°F (150°C). Biscuit, Victory, or Melanoidin malts would be more distant substitutes.
- **Brown malt** – The flavors don't exist in other malts, in my experience.
- **Aromatic malt** – Try a 70-30 blend of light Munich and dark Munich malt.
- **Pilsner malt** – This one is difficult because it has a mostly neutral, clean flavor and a light, crackery-sweet quality without being highly grainy or bready. Add 4 oz (113 g) of flaked wheat (2.5%) and 8 oz (227 g) of flaked maize (5%) to two-row as a substitute.
- **Vienna malt** – Try toasting Pilsner malt for 15 minutes in a 300°F (150°C) oven, or use a blend of Pilsner and Munich malts in a ratio that gives the same color as the original Vienna malt.

- **Munich malt** – Add 8 oz (227 g) Aromatic or Dark Munich malt [5%] to Pilsner or Vienna malt.
- **Dark Munich malt** – Difficult to substitute. Try 80% light Munich malt and 20% Aromatic malt. Using a dark CaraMunich (120 or 150 L) can also work.
- **Chocolate malt** – There is such a wide range of chocolate malts, it's very hard to pin down the exact flavors to duplicate it. I'd use Weyermann Carafa II malt if I couldn't get chocolate malt, but it's harder to find. If you know the color (Lovibond or SRM) of the original malt, try to substitute one with a similar color (that will be a closer match in flavor).
- **Crystal malt** – German, English, and Belgian crystal-type malts can be substituted based on color but the flavors won't really be the same. Blending different colors of crystal malts can approximate the color, but not really the flavor. I'd rather go with a similar-colored crystal malt than blend crystal malts. Selecting an adjacent SRM-colored crystal malt from the same country might work in a pinch. If you want a shade darker crystal malt, you can try toasting your crystal malt for 20 minutes in a 350°F (180°C) oven.
- **Black malt** – Roasted barley or Carafa III could give similar colors, but not really the same flavor profile. You might try taking the darkest malt you have and dry-roasting it in a cast iron skillet over moderately high heat, shaking the pan frequently.
- **Peat-smoked malt** – It's much better to use a different smoked malt, like German *rauchmalz* instead. To me, this malt tastes like a handful of dirt, a pinch of ground cloves, and a dash of Chloro-septic® cough medicine. I think it has no place in brewing.
- **English Brewing sugars** – Make your own, or use combinations of treacle and invert sugar. See *UnholyMess.com*,[1] which not only explains invert sugar, but also includes a handy calculator for combining off-the-shelf ingredients to approximate invert sugar.
- **Bittering hops** – For hops that are not being used for aroma or flavor purposes, you can substitute hops with a similar cohumulone level, adjusting quantities so that they contribute the same IBUs as the original hops. When in doubt about variety, go with a clean bittering hop like Magnum. Otherwise, pick a higher-alpha hop variety from the country of origin of the beer style.

---

[1] http://www.unholymess.com/blog/beer-brewing-info/making-brewers-invert

- **Aroma and flavor hops** – Try to match the general character of the hop (hop pedigree and related information about hops and oil contents can be found in the Hopunion data book or on the web site: *www.hopunion.com*). If substituting hops, always choose fresh hops if you can. There are some very good US substitutes for German and Czech hops. I like Sterling for Saaz, Santiam for Tettnang, and Liberty or Vanguard for Hallertauer. I use these type of hops in English style beers as substitutes for Goldings, particularly when very fresh. Willamette is a great Fuggles substitute.

When looking at American and New World hops, match similar characters (citrusy, piney, stone fruit, tropical fruit, etc.). For instance, Galaxy and Amarillo both have ripe stone fruit characteristics even though the type of fruit is markedly different. We are seeing more hop varieties and blends that are meant to be general-purpose American-type hops, such as Mosaic and Falconer's Flight, that bring multiple characters in one package. If you can characterize the components of a hop you can't find (say, grapefruit and pine), then you can try to blend hops that have each individual component (say, Cascade and Chinook). For Summit hops, you could take a head of garlic, wrap it in cabbage leaves, steam it, and store it for two weeks in a bag holding used gym socks.

- **Lager yeast** – If you can't maintain lager fermentation temperatures but are able to lager, try using a neutral ale strain, fermented cool, then lager the resulting beer. *Kölsch* yeast is a good lager substitute. Or try the California lager yeast (Anchor Steam-derived) that can handle warmer temperatures. Still lager the beer, though; reducing and eliminating esters is an important part of the character.
- **Ale yeast** – Generally look to match character with character; look at the descriptors for the yeast and match keywords, such as malty, dry, minerally, or fruity. Don't feel that you have to stay within the same country to substitute yeast strains. For instance, two of my favorite ale strains are Wyeast 1272 American Ale II and Wyeast 1968 London ESB. I use the two of those interchangeably at times since they can both be moderately fruity, depending on fermentation conditions. I tend to keep the English yeast cooler and the American yeast warmer, but they can produce a similar profile.

- **Belgian yeast** – Belgian yeast strains bring so much character to beer that they are unique. However, strains can produce different by-products when fermented at different temperatures. I tend to think of Belgian yeasts by their overall character, and I choose my favorites in each family. I pick Wyeast 3787 if I want a spicy-phenolic, Wyeast 1762 or 3522 for a dark fruity-spicy, White Labs WLP510 or WLP515 for a more neutral Belgian character, Wyeast 1388 for a light fruity quality, and Wyeast 3711 or 3726 for *saison* character. So if you want to substitute, think about the flavor profile of the yeast.
- **Yeast substitution by vendor** – The go-to chart for comparing yeast strains from different yeast suppliers is at *MrMalty.com*.[2] The strains won't always be the same, as each yeast supplier many finalize a commercial strain differently. The yeast suppliers have done a good job mapping their yeast strains to the BJCP style guidelines, so that can often help you choose substitute yeast based on the style of beer you are brewing.

Hopefully, you'll be able to find the ingredients you need to brew these recipes (or choose a different recipe). Substitutions are an interesting way to learn about the character of specific ingredients, but if you're trying to match a specific recipe, it's not always a satisfactory experience. You might be able to use them in a pinch, but keep in mind that you're making a compromise. With that caveat in mind, let's move on to the actual recipes.

---

[2] http://www.mrmalty.com/yeast.htm

SECTION II

RECIPES

ABOUT THE RECIPES

"This is my invariable advice to people: Learn how to cook—try new recipes, learn from your mistakes, be fearless, and above all have fun!"

—*Julia Child,* My Life in France

Ah, finally some recipes. I expect many of you jumped directly to this section. That's expected, so don't feel guilty. I urge you to take a minute to understand the layout and format of the recipes, and how to look up additional information in this book. These are my actual, as-brewed recipes, and I haven't fiddled with them to put them into standard batch sizes, efficiencies, or methods. You'll probably need to adjust them a bit to work with your system and processes.

The recipes I've selected are grouped into broad general classes. These groupings aren't meant to directly represent BJCP styles or categories, only general similarities between beers:

- IPA: The modern craft beer favorite
- Everyday Beers: For when you're having more than one
- Strong Ales: For when you're not...
- Dark Beers: Come to the dark side
- Lagers: The big chill
- Belgian Favorites: Yes, all of them are my favorites

- Spiced Beers: Seasonal specialties
- Experimental: Styles, what styles?

For some categories, I've included multiple recipes to help illustrate the range of the style. I didn't want to imply that there is only one way to brew a given beer style, and I certainly don't want everyone entering the same beer into homebrew competitions (that would be incredibly tedious to judge!). I'm also including some older recipes to demonstrate some of my older techniques and styles, which make for interesting comparisons to current practices.

I sometimes mention names of commercial beers when discussing my recipes. I'm not really into clone brewing, or attempting to exactly replicate an existing beer. I'm instead using it as a form of shorthand. By using a popular example, I can describe the similarities between my recipe and a beer a brewer might have tried, and show how the recipe was perhaps inspired by it. I think every beer should be evaluated on its own merits, not on how well it matches a specific commercial product.

RECIPE FORMAT

I've used a standard template so that each recipe is in the same format. Most of the elements of the template should be fairly self-explanatory, but I will review each to ensure there are no misunderstandings:

When I include specific numbers for the style parameters (gravity, IBUs, color, etc.), I am using estimates from brewing software, not lab-analyzed values. I used Beer Alchemy on the iPhone configured with Tinseth bitterness estimates, Morey color estimates, and default hop format scaling factors. Batch size and mash efficiency settings are as described in each recipe. If you get different estimates than what are listed here, don't worry too much about it; your software might use a different ingredient database, or different calculation methods. I know this software doesn't take into account bitterness contributions from steeping or whirlpool hops, so the actual IBUs of beers using those methods are likely higher.

- **Title** – The name of the recipe. I name my beers after the style, and possibly include a batch number. Sometimes I name beers for competition, but it's typically an afterthought.
- **Comments** – Some background, personal notes, or a story about the recipe. Not technically important to brewing the beer, but these extra details provide some historical context.

- **BJCP Style** – The name of the associated beer style from the 2015 Beer Judge Certification Program (BJCP) Style Guidelines.
- **Style type** – This includes three types: *Classic BJCP Style* (existed as a named style in the 2008 BJCP Style Guidelines), *New BJCP Style* (new to the 2015 BJCP Style Guidelines), *Experimental* (something unusual that would be entered into one of the BJCP Specialty-type categories).
- **Description** – A general overview of the beer, with details as to how it might be differentiated from other examples within the style or compared and contrasted to other styles.
- **Batch Size** – The volume of the batch at the end of the boil (which isn't necessarily the finished volume of beer). Most batches are homebrew scale, ranging from 5 to 10 gallons (19 to 38 liters).
- **Efficiency** – The mash efficiency, or the percentage of potential sugars extracted from the source malts and grains. My efficiency is typically 70–75%, although some methods sacrifice efficiency for increased flavor or improved perceived quality in the end product.
- **Specifications** – The style's parameters: Original Gravity (OG), Final Gravity (FG), Alcohol by Volume (ABV), estimated bitterness using the Tinseth method and expressed in International Bittering Units (IBUs), and color expressed in Standard Reference Method (SRM) units.
- **Ingredients** – The quantity, type, and brand of each ingredient, as well as how they are used in the recipe. The format of each ingredient depends on the type of ingredient (fermentables, hops, yeast, other).
  - **Fermentables** (malt, grain, sugar, adjuncts) lists the quantity, type or name (sometimes the country of origin), brand, and where they are used in the process. Base grains are typically mashed, dark and crystal malts are often steeped during the mashout, and sugars are added during the boil (reference the mash technique and formulation notes in Chapter 2 for any additional details). Brands are the names of maltsters or producers; in many cases substitutions are no problem, but I like to be specific because flavors can change from one supplier

to another. If I reference a malt with a number (like *Crystal 65*), that represents the type of malt (Crystal) and the color in degrees Lovibond (65), note that maltsters often produce crystal malts over a broader range (like 55–65) or may call them something else (like "Medium Crystal"). When in doubt, check the specifications from the maltster. If I don't specify a maltster or country of origin, then the exact selection doesn't really matter; pick something close and readily available to you.

- **Hops** lists the quantity, type or name (sometimes the country of origin), alpha acid (AA%), format of the hops (usually pellets or whole), and the time they are used in the process. The format I use for hop timing is "@ *nn*" where *nn* is the number of minutes before the end of the boil. FWH means "First Wort Hops," and hops listed with a +*nn* means that they are added *nn* minutes after the end of the boil. Alpha acids vary by source and year of harvest, so be sure to adjust quantities based on the actual measured AA (AA% • weight in ounces = AAU [alpha acid units], which is what should always be used to calculate bitterness). For late hop additions (those in the last 15 minutes), use the actual quantity shown, but be sure to adjust the quantity of bittering hops accordingly to hit the target IBU level for the beer.

- **Yeast** is shown by brand and name, but other yeast suppliers often have equivalent yeasts. Yeast starters (1 L for 5–6.5 gallon batches) are assumed unless otherwise noted.

- **Other additives** will list any additional ingredients that are added to the beer. Normal brewing additives such as yeast nutrients and clarifying agents will not be shown as these are part of the standard brewing process.

- **Water treatment** – The type of water, water salts, acids, and other water treatments used in the recipes.

- **Mash technique** – The type of mash technique (or techniques) used in the recipe. Reference Chapter 2 for more information on the actual processes. The recipes won't include descriptions of how to execute the techniques unless they are unusual.

- **Mash rests** – The temperature and duration of each mash rest. Obviously the rests depend on the mash technique.

- **Kettle volume** – The volume of the beer in the kettle before the boil starts. I normally measure this using a marked stick.
- **Boil duration** – The amount of time the wort boils. The start of the boil is when bubbles start breaking the surface, and the end of the boil is when the heat is shut off (*knockout*).
- **Final volume** – The volume of the beer in the kettle at the end of the boil (typically measured with the same marked stick). The relationship between the starting kettle volume, boil length, and final volume is very system-dependent; you need to calculate your own boil-off rate and adjust accordingly.
- **Fermentation temp** – The temperature of the fermenting beer, not the ambient environment.
- **Sensory description** – My judging notes, describing the beer as I perceive it. These are my subjective observations; yours might (and probably will) be different.
- **Formulation notes** – My suggestions to the brewer, often identifying the key parts of the recipe where substitutions should not be made, or factors that are critical to the success of the recipe. The notes might also explain why certain choices were made.
- **Variations** – Ideas on how the recipe could be changed to make other beer styles, or adjusted to better balance or focus the beer.

3 | IPA RECIPES

"I have learned that a bitter experience can make you stronger."

—Mel Gibson, actor

Everyone knows that IPA means India Pale Ale, but the modern craft beer market has stretched that name well beyond its original roots. Most craft beers wearing the IPA label today bear little resemblance to historical English beers that were shipped to India, many aren't pale, and some aren't even ales. As the most popular craft beer category, the only thing 'IPA' has come to mean is a beer that has a very hop-forward aroma and flavor with moderately high to high bitterness levels.

It's best to not attempt to expand the IPA acronym; if we take it as a general name, all the modifiers (black IPA, session IPA, Belgian IPA, etc.) make much more sense. After all, why get so hung up on the name of beer styles when you could be just brewing and drinking them? If you tell a consumer that a beer is an IPA, they will have an expectation about the general balance and flavor profile of the beer, and will be able to understand how other adjectives change the implied target sensory description. The need for all the differentiation is simply because the category has grown so much, and features a lot of experimentation.

It's fascinating to see how the style description of IPA has changed over the years. The BJCP guidelines from the late 1990s describe a strong, highly hopped beer but not much else. One version said they were quite pale, while others said they could be almost brown. English hops or American hops were fair game, but the beers were also described as having caramel, toast, and fruit flavors. By 2004, the category had been split into English, American, and Imperial styles, and each focused on specific sensory expectations and overall character. The 2015 BJCP guidelines take it even further by acknowledging the various specialty IPAs that have been flooding the craft beer market. It's unknown whether these beers will have any staying power, but they are fun to brew and delicious to drink in the meantime.

As with the journey through the evolution of the IPA style category, this collection of recipes will showcase the differences in the classic and current formulations, as well as show off some of the more popular and creative variations on the style.

- **Four Seas IPA** – Once clearly an IPA, now more like an American Strong Ale. Reddish in color with a strong American hop character, inspired by Sierra Nevada Celebration.

- **Tomahawk Chop IPA** – An old school IPA heavy on the bittering, this beer needs significant aging to mature and come into balance. An American take on an English classic, but with my signature twist.

- **English IPA** – Often overlooked amidst the new specialty IPAs and bold American interpretations, this version uses classic English ingredients in a more modern interpretation.

- **East Coast IPA** – A more modern IPA in design with more late hop smoothness, but with a maltier and more balanced character. Features all Centennial hops, as a tribute to the classic Bell's Two Hearted Ale.

- **New World IPA** – My take on all that is new in IPAs using New World hops, in a dry and very pale interpretation. I was able to turn this one around in less than 3 weeks, which is a long way from a slow boat to India.

- **Sinamarian IPA** – A new kid on the block, the style is much different than a hoppy stout. For better or worse, this style appeared all over the place in much of the recent experimentation in specialty IPAs, but can be very enjoyable if done right.

- **Belgian IPA** – More than an IPA with Belgian yeast, there is a surprising amount of difficulty in properly pairing high hop levels with most Belgian yeast strains. Kind of like a smaller Belgian tripel crossed with an American IPA.
- **Spring IPA** – My own invention, *maibock* meets IPA in this springtime seasonal IPA. Encouraged by how well Belgian IPAs can work, I thought about other pale, stronger styles that might tolerate similar high hop treatment.
- **Session IPL** – All the hops, half the alcohol. What's not to like? In this version, I show how you can vary the hop varieties to create something completely non-traditional.
- **Halloween IPA** – Blood red for the season with enough warmth to chase away the chill. Pushes the boundaries of an American Strong Ale, but by tweaking the hop balance, it's clearly an IPA.
- **Mosaic Double IPA** – A stronger beer showcasing a distinctive single hop variety, this brew uses several of my signature techniques and ingredients.
- **West Coast Double IPA** – All that I love in today's IPA, plus a modern successive dry-hopping technique for extra aroma of hoppy freshness.

FOUR SEAS IPA

This was my first IPA (batch #15, brewed in 1997), and was inspired by Sierra Nevada Celebration. It won best of show at the Over the Mill competition in Michigan, where the grand prize was a custom kegerator. Somehow I stuffed it into the passenger seat of my Dodge Stealth and drove it back to Ohio, grinning all the way while hoping I didn't get pulled over.

Style: American Strong Ale (New BJCP Style)

Description: Darker and richer than today's IPAs, this was an American-style IPA at the time. Now it's probably more like an American Strong Ale or a big red ale. I was working on a new dark malt steeping technique to give it a reddish color. More of a drinking beer than a competition beer now, but useful to compare to more modern recipes.

Batch size: 5 gallons (19 L)   **OG:** 1.072   **FG:** 1.020
Efficiency: 70%   **ABV:** 6.9%   **IBU:** 90   **SRM:** 12

Ingredients:

12 lb (5.4 kg)	US two-row (Briess)	Mash
1 lb (454 g)	German Munich (Durst)	Mash
2 oz (57 g)	Wheat malt (Durst)	Mash
8 oz (340 g)	Belgian Caravienne	*Vorlauf*
4 oz (113 g)	UK Crystal 65 (Crisp)	*Vorlauf*
1 oz (28 g)	UK Roasted barley	Strike Water (*)
1 oz (28 g)	US Chinook 13.5% whole	@ 60
1 oz (28 g)	US Centennial 10.7% whole	@ 15
1 oz (28 g)	US Columbus 13.9% whole	@ 10
1 oz (28 g)	US Centennial 10.7% whole	@ 5
0.5 oz (14 g)	US Cascade 5.8% whole	@ 5
1 oz (28 g)	US Columbus 13.9% whole	@ 1
1 oz (28 g)	US Cascade 5.8% whole	@ 0
1 oz (28 g)	US Cascade 5.8% whole	@ +10
2 oz (57 g)	US Cascade 5.8% whole	dry hop
	Wyeast 1028 London Ale yeast	

Water treatment: RO water treated with ¼ tsp 10% phosphoric acid per 5 gallons
1 tsp CaSO$_4$ in mash
(*) Steep roasted barley in heated brewing liquor (entire volume of water to be used in the recipe) until it has a deep reddish hue, then remove.

Mash technique: Infusion, mashout, crystal malts added at *vorlauf*

Mash rests: 151°F (66°C) 60 minutes
168°F (76°C) 15 minutes

Kettle volume: 6.5 gallons (25 L)
Boil length: 60 minutes
Final volume: 5 gallons (19 L)
Fermentation temp: 68°F (20°C)

Sensory Description: Deep reddish copper color, but clear. Great, fresh hop aroma with citrusy and piney notes backed up with a light caramel malt richness. Quite bitter, but with a full finish and clean malty richness to balance. Not as dry and crisp as modern IPAs, but the combination of hops and malt work together very nicely. It won best of show when it was seven months old, so this IPA does take some time to age since the IBUs are quite high.

Formulation notes: The goal was to get a reddish color and feature classic old-school American hops (the 'C' hops, which leads to the play-on-words recipe name). A more modern combination of hops would certainly work, but I always like to return to some classics to keep perspective. Since this is inspired by Sierra Nevada, try to use fresh whole hops like they do. This does have some crystal malt, which is often frowned on today's IPAs, but think of it more of a winter IPA; the Munich malt adds a malty backbone without as much sweetness as crystal malt. This recipe is so old, I originally made it as a mini-mash beer (use 9.9 lb of pale liquid extract instead of the two-row), but like it enough that it's now in my regular rotation. In my older IPAs, I hop the beers heavily and age them for a considerable amount of time, which is more in the British tradition (and lets the bitterness mellow). Contrast this with some of the more modern turn-and-burn recipes, like the "Modern IPA" recipe.

Variations: Modern malts give more choices for reddish colors, so you can explore some. I discovered that most crystal malts really gave more amber-brown colors than true copper-red colors, so I decided to see if small amounts of a very dark grain or malt could give the red color (you can literally watch the red color come out of the roasted barley as it steeps). You are looking for color, not flavor, so don't overdo it. Carafa III Special might work as well.

TOMAHAWK CHOP IPA

The name of this recipe comes from the hop variety I used for bittering, and how they hit you when you take a sip. This is an aggressively bitter beer that takes a long aging time to come into balance. Loosely based on the "Sister Star of the Sun" IPA recipe,[1] this is one of the first hoppy beers where I used some honey as part of the recipe. I liked the outcome, so it has become one of my signature brewing moves. I was happy to see Bell's Hop Slam, an incredible Double IPA, use this technique as well.

Style: American IPA (Classic BJCP Style)

Description: An old school American IPA that has a huge bittering hop charge and takes considerable time to age. A throwback to the traditional English IPAs, but using American ingredients. Higher in alcohol than more modern IPAs.

Batch size: 5.75 gallons (22 L) **OG:** 1.072 **FG:** 1.014
Efficiency: 70% **ABV:** 7.6% **IBU:** all of them **SRM:** 10

Ingredients:

13 lb (5.9 kg)	UK Maris Otter (Crisp)	Mash
8 oz (227 g)	Wheat malt (Durst)	Mash
8 oz (227 g)	German Munich (Best)	Mash
4 oz (113 g)	Victory malt (Briess)	Mash
4 oz (113 g)	Crystal 120	Mash
4 oz (113 g)	Crystal 20	Mash
8 oz (227 g)	Belgian Caravienne malt	Mash
8 oz (227 g)	Orange blossom honey	Boil (@ 5)
3 oz (85 g)	US Tomahawk 16.8% whole	@ 60
1 oz (28 g)	US Tomahawk 16.8% whole	@ 15
1 oz (28 g)	US Tomahawk 16.8% whole	@ 5
2 oz (57 g)	US Cascade 4.5% whole	@ 0
2 oz (57 g)	US Centennial 10.5% whole	dry hop
	Wyeast 1272 American Ale II yeast	

[1] http://www.realbeer.com/hops/sister.html

Water treatment:	Untreated RO water for the mash, adding 1 Tbsp CaSO$_4$ to the mash
	Sparge water is RO water treated with ¼ tsp 10% phosphoric acid per 5 gallons
	1 tsp CaSO$_4$ in boil
Mash technique:	Infusion, mashout
Mash rests:	152°F (67°C) 60 minutes
	168°F (76°C) 15 minutes
Kettle volume:	7.5 gallons (28 L)
Boil length:	90 minutes
Final volume:	5.75 gallons (22 L)
Fermentation temp:	68°F (20°C)

Sensory Description: Absurdly bitter when young. I entered it in a competition when it was young, and national judge Steve McKenna wrote, "Your IPA is too bitter." I always admired his confidence in judging because of this comment. I can think of many people who would think that sentence makes no sense at all, but he was right. This beer only started winning awards after it was a year old, and then kept getting better and better as it aged. The base and character malts add rich bready flavor with a subtle malty and caramel complexity, but the hops carry this beer. The honey gives an extra fruity component that plays well with the citrusy and piney hops.

Formulation notes: My recipe software calculates this beer at 172 IBUs, which is physically impossible. Let's just say it's really bitter. Plan on cellaring it for at least a year. IBUs tend to fade over time, so you aim higher and let it come back into balance. Since it will be aging, having the extra character malts is important as they tend to fade over time.

Variations: Using all English hops would make this seem much more like a historical English IPA that needed a long maturation period to come into balance. Swap East Kent Goldings for the late hops, use something like Challenger or Target for the bittering hops, swap invert sugar for the honey, and choose Wyeast 1028 London Ale yeast.

ENGLISH IPA

An underappreciated style in many American homebrew competitions, this recipe is more of a modern take in that it has some crystal malt for color (sorry, colour) and a little flavor...er, flavour. The alcohol level is on the high side, but I was trying to make it a 1066 beer in honor of the Battle of Hastings.

Style: English IPA (Classic BJCP Style)

Description: Classic English flavors with a bready, biscuit malt base, a light supporting caramel component, and a big punch of floral, earthy, and fruity hops.

Batch size: 6 gallons (23 L)		**OG:** 1.066	**FG:** 1.014
Efficiency: 75%	**ABV:** 6.8%	**IBU:** 66	**SRM:** 10

Ingredients:

13 lb (5.9 kg)	UK Maris Otter (Crisp)	Mash
8 oz (227 g)	US Victory malt (Briess)	Mash
8 oz (227 g)	German Wheat malt (Durst)	Mash
8 oz (227 g)	UK Crystal 80 (Crisp)	*Vorlauf*
2 oz (57 g)	UK Goldings 5.5% whole	FWH
1 oz (28 g)	UK Target 10.5% whole	@ 60
1 oz (28 g)	UK Fuggle 4.5% whole	@ 0
2 oz (57 g)	Styrian Goldings 4.5%whole	dry hop
	Wyeast 1028 London Ale yeast	

Water treatment: RO water treated with ¼ tsp 10% phosphoric acid per 5 gallons
1 Tbsp $CaSO_4$ and 0.5 tsp $CaCl_2$ in mash

Mash technique: Step mash, mashout, crystal malt added at *vorlauf*

Mash rests: 151°F (66°C) 60 minutes
158°F (70°C) 15 minutes
168°F (76°C) 15 minutes

Kettle volume: 8.5 gallons (32 L)

Boil length: 120 minutes
Final volume: 6 gallons (23 L)
Fermentation temp: 68°F (20°C)

Sensory Description: On the strong side for an English IPA, but with substantial bitterness. Has a more rounded and characterful malt base than most American IPAs, with the hops providing a freshness that is assertive but not face-slapping. The fruity notes and sulfur character matches the Burton style.

Formulation notes: I stuck mostly with classic English ingredients that contribute meaningful elements to the flavor profile. The crystal malt should be restrained, so as not to intrude on the malt and hops.

Variations: I like the hop combination, but this could be brewed as a single hop varietal beer. I think there is a chance to play around with the base malt a bit, swapping in different maltsters and types of malt. I'd love to see what Golden Promise malt would do in this beer. A different yeast choice is certainly possible; I'd try the Wyeast 1335 British II yeast as an experiment, or Wyeast 1968 or White Labs WLP002 as a malty and fruity alternative.

EAST COAST IPA

East Coast of Lake Michigan, that is. Inspired by the deliciousness that is Bell's Two Hearted Ale, this is a very drinkable but not bone dry IPA. Compare to the Mosaic Double IPA, another single hop IPA.

Style: American IPA (Classic BJCP Style)

Description: A malty IPA that doesn't get too sweet, and showcases one of the most versatile hops available to brewers: Centennial. I just love the drinkability of this beer, and how it proves that you don't have to be over-the-top in IBUs or ABV to make a great IPA. I like to include a beer like this in an IPA discussion because it helps show the range of the style.

Batch size: 6.5 gallons (25 L)   **OG:** 1.063   **FG:** 1.011
Efficiency: 70%   **ABV:** 7.0%   **IBU:** 56   **SRM:** 6

Ingredients:

13 lb (5.9 kg)	US two-row (Briess)	Mash
2 lb (907 g)	German Vienna (Durst)	Mash
8 oz (227 g)	Belgian Caravienne	*Vorlauf*
4 oz (113 g)	German Carahell	*Vorlauf*
1 oz (28 g)	US Centennial 10.3%	whole FWH
1 oz (28 g)	US Centennial 10.3% whole	@ 20
1 oz (28 g)	US Centennial 10.3% whole	@ 10
1 oz (28 g)	US Centennial 10.3% whole	@ 1
2 oz (57g)	US Centennial 10.3% whole	@ +10
	Wyeast 1272 American Ale II yeast	

Water treatment:	RO water treated with ¼ tsp 10% phosphoric acid per 5 gallons
	0.5 tsp $CaCl_2$ and 0.5 tsp $CaSO_4$ in mash
Mash technique:	Infusion, mashout, dark grains added at *vorlauf*
Mash rests:	147°F (64°C) 60 minutes
	168°F (76°C) 15 minutes
Kettle volume:	8.5 gallons (32 L)
Boil length:	90 minutes
Final volume:	6.5 gallons (25 L)
Fermentation temp:	65°F (18°C)

Sensory Description: Clean malty base with some richness not always present in modern IPAs. The Centennial hops add complexity with citrus, pine, and grapefruit notes. The yeast adds another fruity element that helps tie the malt richness to the beer. The late hops gives a smooth bitterness that helps balance.

Formulation notes: The last hop addition is added 10 minutes after knockout for a 20 minute steep, which reduces the IBUs supplied by the hops while bringing out the fresh hop character. Transfer 5.5 gallons (21 L) to fermenter. Centennial really is a versatile hop, and the combination of first wort hopping, hop bursting, and hop steeping pulls all the character out without adding a grassy element.

Variations: Could dry hop instead of (or in addition to) the late steep. The base beer is malt neutral, so it should serve well as a platform for other single-hop IPA experiments. If the beer has too much malt or richness, cut back on the Vienna and crystal malts.

NEW WORLD IPA

I made this New World IPA as a retirement present for a co-worker. Using all of my favorite techniques, this typifies many of today's IPAs that are drinkable with a light malty backbone and tropical and fruity hop varieties. Best thing about this recipe is it was a 20-day turn-and-burn effort; from brewing to serving in less than three weeks! Two kegs were floating in less than an hour and a half, so I guess it was well received. Cases of Guinness, Corona, and Sam Adams sat next to the kegs, untouched; best compliment ever for a homebrewer!

Style: American IPA (Classic BJCP Style)

Description: Clean malt flavor with a rich base, but a dry finish that allows the huge fresh hop character to explode. I absolutely love this combination of hops; they are modern American craft beer classics. No crystal malt at all in this beer, which is why I like to say, "Munich is the new crystal" since it adds the desired extra malt flavor without the undesired crystal sweetness. A double-sized batch allows for a yeast experiments (everything can be halved for a normal-sized batch).

Batch size: 12 gallons (46 L)	**OG:** 1.066	**FG:** 1.012–1.018 (*)	
Efficiency: 65%	**ABV:** 7.2–6.5 %	**IBU:** 55	**SRM:** 6

Ingredients:

12 lb (5.4 kg)	Continental Pils malt	Mash
12 lb (5.4 kg)	US two-row (Briess)	Mash
2 lb (907 g)	Belgian Pale Ale malt (Dingeman)	Mash
3 lb (1.4 kg)	German Munich malt (Best)	Mash
3 lb (1.4 kg)	Orange blossom honey	Boil (@ 0)
1.5 oz (43 g)	US Amarillo 10.4% whole	FWH
1 oz (28 g)	US Simcoe 12.3% whole	@ 20
1 oz (28 g)	US Citra 15.6% whole	@ 20
1 oz (28 g)	US Amarillo 10.4% whole	@ 10
1 oz (28 g)	US Simcoe 12.3% whole	@ 10

2 oz (57 g)	US Simcoe 12.3% whole	@ 1
1 oz (28 g)	US Citra 15.6% whole	@ 0
1 oz (28 g)	US Centennial 10.8% whole	@ 0
1 oz (28 g)	US Simcoe 12.3% whole	@ 0
0.5 oz (14 g)	US Amarillo 10.4% whole	@ 0
	Wyeast 1968 London ESB Ale yeast	

Water treatment:	RO water treated with ¼ tsp 10% phosphoric acid per 5 gallons
	1 tsp $CaCl_2$ and 1 tsp $CaSO_4$ in mash
Mash technique:	Step Infusion, no sparge
Mash rests:	146°F (63°C) 45 minutes
	155°F (68°C) 30 minutes
Kettle volume:	13.5 gallons (51 L)
Boil length:	90 minutes
Final volume:	12 gallons (45 L)
Fermentation temp:	63°F (17°C)

Sensory Description: *One batch finished at 1.012 and was a perfect American IPA, so fresh and delicious, nicely dry and amazingly drinkable. The other batch finished at 1.018 and tasted a bit more like an American ESB, with a bigger malty backbone but still with a great hop profile. It wasn't quite as drinkable, but it reminded me of a great IPA that I had in Brazil from the *Cervejaria Colorado*. I find it fascinating to see how much the balance changes with a higher FG; it's like an entirely different beer. Still very good, but different in overall impression. The higher FG tends to get in the way of the hops a bit, but it depends on your preference.

Formulation notes: Honey can sometimes take longer to ferment, so watch how these beers finish. The yeast is also somewhat temperature sensitive, so raise the temperature at the end to help it finish strong. I used a heat-while-recirculate technique, so I didn't need to do a mash out. I also used a no-sparge technique, so the mash efficiency is kind of low, but the malt flavor is clean and strong. After boiling, I did a 20 minute steep of the hops, which aids in clarification and increases the hop character from the knockout hops. First wort hopping, hop bursting, and a hop stand help drive home the hop character. The IBU estimate is based on no IBU contributions from the steeping hops, which doesn't work out in reality; the actual IBU value will be higher, but the bitterness will be clean.

Variations: As I suggested, a split batch with different yeast would be a fun experiment. Wyeast 1272 American Ale II would be a natural choice for me, but you could do one batch with a well-known yeast and use the other batch as the experiment with a new or unknown yeast. Compare the two to see which worked better. While the hop character is intense, it could also be dry-hopped with any of the late hop varieties for an even more complex aroma. It might not be ready as quickly, though, so don't do this if you're in a hurry (I worry that dry hopping can reduce clarity in the short term).

SINAMARIAN ALE

I had avoided making a Black IPA for a long time because I wasn't sure if it was a passing fad or not, and because they style seemed overhyped. I should have ignored those feelings; this is a really nice beer, regardless of what you call it. The name comes from my first reaction when I heard of the style, "isn't that just an American IPA with Sinamar® added?"

Style: Black IPA (New BJCP Style)

Description: Smooth, dry, bitter, and fruity with a restrained roast flavor.

Batch size: 6.5 gallons (25 L)	**OG:** 1.064	**FG:** 1.014
Efficiency: 70% **ABV:** 6.7%	**IBU:** 60	**SRM:** 31

Ingredients:

10 lb (4.5 kg)	US two-row (Briess)	Mash
3 lb (1.4 kg)	UK Golden Promise (Simpsons)	Mash
8 oz (227 g)	German Munich (Best)	Mash
12 oz (340 g)	Carafa III Special (Weyermann)	*Vorlauf*
4 oz (113 g)	Carafa I Special (Weyermann)	*Vorlauf*
1 lb (454 g)	White table sugar or corn sugar	Boil
1 oz (28 g)	Australian Galaxy 13% pellets	FWH

1 oz (28 g)	US Citra 11.1% whole	@ 20
1 oz (28 g)	US Citra 11.1% whole	@ 1
1 oz (28 g)	Australian Galaxy 13% pellets	@ 0
0.5 oz (14 g)	US Simcoe 12.3% whole	@ 0
	Wyeast 1332 Northwest Ale yeast	

Water treatment:	RO water treated with ¼ tsp 10% phosphoric acid per 5 gallons
	1 tsp CaCl₂ in mash
Mash technique:	Infusion, mashout, dark grains added at *vorlauf*
Mash rests:	149°F (65°C) 60 minutes
	168°F (76°C) 5 minutes
Kettle volume:	8 gallons (30 L)
Boil length:	60 minutes
Final volume:	6.5 gallons (25 L)
Fermentation temp:	68°F (20°C)

Sensory Description: Very deep brown in color, light tan head. Big tropical fruit aroma, soft malt flavor with hints of cocoa. Dry but with a malty backbone. Bitter but not excessive. Malty flavor profile with bitterness taking over in the finish. Dry enough to encourage drinking but not bone dry. As it warms, more malt comes out. Clean and unobtrusive. The light roast notes enhance the dryness of the finish. As it was, it has light coffee and dark chocolate notes, which are enhanced by the fruitiness. Perfect IPA balance: no alcohol or hop bite, just very smooth. Not sweet, easy to drink.

Formulation notes: Avoiding harshness and clashing flavors is the key to this recipe. You must use the debittered dark malts, and avoid steeping them too long. Hops with a tropical fruit character are really nice in this beer, but I'd avoid using overly citrusy or piney hops. I'd also avoid using too much bready malt. The malt should take the background here so the hops can come through. Some sugar aids in attenuation, and a dry finish helps drinkability. FWH and late hopping keeps hop harshness down. I don't like my IPAs too alcoholic or bitter, and keep them no more than 7% and 70 IBUs. Steeping hops will add more IBUs than calculated, but they will impart a clean bitterness.

Variations: You can play with the roast and hop balance to suit your tastes. Dropping the roast entirely would make a very good American IPA; it could also serve as the base for making another specialty IPA with other character grains. Amarillo hops would fit nicely in this beer. Cascade or Centennial would be good substitutions for the Simcoe, as they add a counterpoint to the tropical character. Clean to fruity American or English yeast would work, as long as it attenuates. Obviously this could scale up or down as a session or double IPA as well.

BELGIAN IPA

My good friend Frank Barickman helped me develop this recipe. He does a collaboration brew with Eric Bean of the Columbus Brewing Company, and they call their beer "Big Frank." It's a Belgian Double IPA, but I have scaled it a bit and made some hop and yeast substitutions to fit my taste. When I make the standard-strength version, I like to call it "Little Frank" in his honor. Once I made it, I got very good efficiency and it finished unexpectedly low (not a bad thing for a Belgian IPA) winding up quite close to double IPA in strength (OG 1.070, FG 1.005, ABV 8.9%, IBU 42), but deceptively smooth (just like the best Belgian ales).

Style: Specialty IPA (New BJCP Style)

Description: Like a tripel combined with a modern American fruity and tropical IPA.

Batch size: 6.5 gallons (25 L)	**OG:** 1.064	**FG:** 1.009
Efficiency: 70% **ABV:** 7.3%	**IBU:** 56	**SRM:** 5

Ingredients:

8.5 lb (3.9 kg)	Belgian Pilsner malt (Dingeman)	Mash
3 lb (1.4 kg)	German Vienna malt (Weyermann)	Mash
12 oz (340 g)	Aromatic malt (Dingeman)	Mash
2 lb (907 g)	White beet sugar	Boil
2 oz (57 g)	German Tettnanger 4.5% pellets	FWH
1 oz (28 g)	Styrian Goldings 2.1% whole	@ 15

1 oz (28 g)	US Amarillo 9.2% pellets	@ 10
1 oz (28 g)	Styrian Goldings 2.1% whole	@ 5
1 oz (28 g)	US Amarillo 9.2% pellets	@ 0
1 oz (28 g)	US Citra 13.9% pellets	@ +10
1 oz (28 g)	Australian Galaxy 15% pellets	@ +10
2 oz (57 g)	US Amarillo 9.2% pellets	dry hop
	White Labs WLP510 Bastogne ale yeast	

Water treatment:	RO water treated with ¼ tsp 10% phosphoric acid per 5 gallons
	1 tsp $CaCl_2$ in mash
Mash technique:	Infusion, mashout, dark grains added at *vorlauf*
Mash rests:	149°F (65°C) 60 minutes
	168°F (76°C) 5 minutes
Kettle volume:	9 gallons (34 L)
Boil length:	120 minutes
Final volume:	6.5 gallons (25 L)
Fermentation temp:	62°F (17°C), allowing to rise to 75°F (24°C) to finish

Sensory Description: Huge apricot character with light pine background, dry finish, light phenols, and strong bitterness. The alcohol needs a little time to age, especially in the double IPA version. Medium body, fairly clean for a Belgian beer. The bitterness is strong but very clean; not harsh at all.

Formulation notes: I like the WLP510 Bastogne yeast (same as Orval), but Frank thinks that Wyeast 3787 Trappist Ale yeast does better in competitions since it gives it a more prominent Belgian yeast character. I think that bigger yeast character can clash with the hops, so be careful. I love the combination of Amarillo hops with the Bastogne yeast; it's something that I've seen done commercially in the *La Rulles Tripel*. Hops that are fruity (particularly tropical or stone fruit) work best. Highly citrus versions would tend to clash with yeast-derived phenols. Frank recommends not substituting out the Tettnanger hops, as they provide a nice floral spiciness. The hop techniques give a very clean bitterness without harshness. I think astringency could kill a beer like this. The yeast is a bit powdery, so I found it necessary to cold crash the yeast at near freezing after it had been warm conditioning for two weeks, which worked wonders, as the beer was incredibly bright afterwards. Additional cold conditioning can smooth out the beer quite well.

Variations: Obviously I've shown that it can work as a single IPA or a double IPA. When in the double IPA format, I found that it was like a very fresh Westmalle Tripel with a huge hop character. I don't know that I'd play around with this too much, except maybe to vary the fruity hops a bit or possibly increase the malt complexity and body. Add some flaked oats (maybe 5% of the grist) for something more inspired by Tripel Karmeliet. Possibly also play around with light spicing, adding a dash of coriander (perhaps a third of an ounce or about 10g).

SPRING IPA

The concept of this experimental beer is a Maibock-*style IPA. It doesn't match a commercial beer or style; this is just something that I thought would taste good. I'd enter it either as a Specialty IPA or as a Hybrid Beer, specifying helles bock and IPA, depending on how malty it finished (if more malty, enter as Hybrid Beer). In either case, I would briefly describe the concept, say that it uses ale yeast, and mention the style parameters and general hopping so judges could correctly evaluate it.*

Style: Specialty IPA (New BJCP Style, Experimental)

Description: The maltiness of a *maibock* combined with the bitter hoppiness of an IPA.

Batch size: 6.5 gallons (25 L) **OG:** 1.064 **FG:** 1.014–1.018
Efficiency: 70%   **ABV:** 6.1–6.6%   **IBU:** 60   **SRM:** 6

Ingredients:

9.5 lb (4.3 kg)	German Pils (Durst)	Mash
2 lb (907 g)	German Vienna (Durst)	Mash
2 lb (907 g)	German Munich (Best)	Mash
8 oz (227 g)	German Dark Munich (Weyermann)	Mash
8 oz (227 g)	Carahell (Weyermann)	Mash

12 oz (340 g)	White table sugar or corn sugar	Boil
1 oz (28 g)	US Liberty 3.7% pellets	FWH
1 oz (28 g)	Hallertauer Tradition 6.8% pellets	FWH
1 oz (28 g)	German Spalt 2.2% whole	@ 20
1 oz (28 g)	US Centennial 10.3% whole	@ 15
0.5 oz (14 g)	NZ Nelson Sauvin 12.5% pellets	@ 15
0.5 oz (14 g)	NZ Nelson Sauvin 12.5% pellets	@ 5
1 oz (28 g)	US Centennial 10.3% whole	@ 0
	Wyeast 1968 London ESB Ale yeast or Wyeast 1272 American II yeast	

Water treatment:	Mash water: RO water treated with ⅛ tsp 10% phosphoric acid per 5 gallons
	1 tsp $CaCl_2$ in mash
	Sparge water: RO water treated with ¼ tsp 10% phosphoric acid per 5 gallons
Mash technique:	Step infusion
Mash rests:	131°F (55°C) 15 minutes
	144°F (62°C) 30 minutes
	158°F (70°C) 15 minutes
Kettle volume:	8.5 gallons (32 L)
Boil length:	90 minutes
Final volume:	6.5 gallons (25 L)
Fermentation temp:	68°F (20°C)
Notes:	Use the settling tank technique to remove pellet hops and improve clarity.

Sensory Description: Great lemon-lime aroma with wonderful malt backbone. Beautiful gold color, crystal clear. The hop character is hard to identify; it has a fresh, almost dry-hopped presence that has floral, herbal, and spicy notes, but with hints of white grape and lime zest. The aroma carries over to the flavor. The hop aroma and flavor are big but not screaming like bold American hops. The German hops add a fresh note, but are a bit grassy. The malt flavor is wonderful and blends well with the hop varieties. Has that German richness of a *maibock* without the lingering malty intensity, and has a rich impression given the color. The alcohol is not noticeable as the malt stands up to it. The hop bitterness is clean. The late hop aroma and flavor persist.

Formulation notes: Getting the beer dry while retaining the maltiness is the first trick. The second involves blending in hops that allow the malt to shine through but also add a unique, distinct character. The lemon-lime character from German and Centennial hops with the white grape Nelson character adds a white wine impression. German or continental malts are key to the malty flavors, and the lower mash temperature helps get a dry finish. The late hop techniques keep the hop bitterness clean and increases the late hop presence; actual IBUs may be higher than estimated due to the steeping.

Variations: The balance of this beer can be changed significantly by playing with the FG. The 1968 yeast tends to finish a bit higher (1.018), while the 1272 can finish lower (1.014). Lengthen the primary mash rest to 60 minutes and eliminate the high temperature rest or double the white sugar from 5% to 10% to increase fermentability. If the beer is a little big or rich, try increasing the carbonation level or serving with a lime or lemon slice. The last Centennial hop addition can be doubled if a stronger hop aroma is desired; I probably wouldn't increase the Nelson since they can be overbearing at higher levels.

SESSION IPL

Who says IPAs have to be American or English? Or use ale yeast? Or be higher in gravity? IPAs are recognizable more by the overall balance than by any of those other aspects. This experiment uses German hops for a distinctively floral and spicy character, while the warm fermented lager yeast gives it a clean but fruity edge. The low gravity means you can enjoy this one all day. Some term IPAs made with lager yeast IPLs (India Pale Lager); since we're breaking rules anyway, why not? This idea comes from Frank Barickman, who calls it his "Hop ObSession."

Style: Specialty IPA (New BJCP Style, Experimental)

Description: This is like a session-strength German Pils with way more hops than you'd find in any German beer, but it comes across like an IPA in balance.

Batch size: 5.5 gallons (21 L)   **OG:** 1.036   **FG:** 1.009
Efficiency: 80%   **ABV:** 3.5%   **IBU:** 70   **SRM:** 3

Ingredients:

5 lb (2.3 kg)	German Pilsner malt (Weyermann)	Mash
1 lb (454 g)	German Wheat malt (Weyermann)	Mash
8 oz (227 g)	German Dark Munich (Weyermann)	Mash
2 oz (57 g)	German Hallertauer 5.0% whole	FWH
3 oz (85 g)	German Hallertauer 5.0% whole	@ 15
4 oz (113 g)	German Tettnanger 4.5% whole	@ 0
	Wyeast 2112 California Lager yeast	

Water treatment: RO water treated with ¼ tsp 10% phosphoric acid per 5 gallons
1 tsp $CaCl_2$ in mash
Mash technique: Infusion, mashout
Mash rests: 152°F (67°C) 60 minutes
165°F (74°C) 10 minutes
Kettle volume: 7 gallons (27 L)
Boil length: 75 minutes
Final volume: 5.5 gallons (25 L)
Fermentation temp: 60°F (16°C), letting it ramp up after two days to 65°F (18°C)

Sensory Description: Huge floral-spicy hop flavor and aroma, pronounced bitterness but with a smooth palate, and a clean and lightly fruity fermentation profile (without sulfur). German hops can be more subtle than their American cousins, but not if you use boatloads of them.

Formulation notes: The California Lager yeast gives you a clean fermentation profile without the sulfur of many German lager strains. At knockout, let hops steep for 30 minutes before chilling, to help drive the bigger hop aroma. After fermentation has finished, cold crash the yeast (chill to near 32°F/0°C), and then rack. No lagering is needed, so just force carbonate it and enjoy it fresh. Note that the blast of steeping hops can make the IBUs higher than estimated.

Variations: If you'd rather it have a more distinctly American character, swap in Cascade and Wyeast 1272. Want to make it British? Go with Goldings and Wyeast 1335. Playing around with other German or Saazer-type hops would be fun; I like Sterling as a hop choice since I can often get them fresher and better handled than imported hops at my local homebrew shop.

HALLOWEEN IPA

Another beer created for a work party, this time for Halloween. The smooth bitterness and rich malt is a good combination when the weather is cool, and the coppery-reddish color is kind of spooky. Boo.

Style: Specialty IPA (Red IPA) (New BJCP Style)

Description: A reddish fall seasonal IPA and a bit more body and supporting caramel fruit notes.

Batch size: 6.5 gallons (25 L)	**OG:** 1.065	**FG:** 1.014
Efficiency: 70% **ABV:** 6.9%	**IBU:** 67	**SRM:** 15

Ingredients:

12 lb (5.4 kg)	German Vienna malt (Durst)	Mash
10 oz (283 g)	CaraMunich III (Weyermann)	*Vorlauf*
2 oz (57 g)	UK Roasted barley, 675 L	Steep (*)
2 lb (907 g)	White beet sugar	Boil (@10)
1 oz (28 g)	Australian Galaxy 13% pellets	FWH
1 oz (28 g)	US Chinook 13.1% whole	@ 15
1 oz (28 g)	US Centennial 10.3% whole	@ 10
1 oz (28 g)	US Centennial 10.3% whole	@ 5
1 oz (28 g)	Australian Galaxy 13% pellets	@ 1
2 oz (57 g)	US Centennial 10.3% whole	@ 0
2 oz (57 g)	US Centennial 10.3% whole	dry hop
	Wyeast 1272 American Ale II yeast	

Water treatment:	RO water treated with ¼ tsp 10% phosphoric acid per 5 gallons
	1 tsp $CaSO_4$ in mash
Mash technique:	Infusion, mashout, crystal malt added at *vorlauf,* no sparge
Mash rests:	144°F (62°C) 60 minutes
	158°F (70°C) 10 minutes
	168°F (76°C) 15 minutes
Kettle volume:	8 gallons (30 L)
Boil length:	60 minutes
Final volume:	6 gallons (23 L)
Fermentation temp:	68°F (20°C)

Sensory Description: Fruity and caramel taste with the fruitiness of the Galaxy hops pairing well with the CaraMunich. Very elegant reddish color. The rich malty base supports the hop flavor and bitterness well. If it winds up too malty, or has a higher FG, then it's probably best to call it an American Strong Ale. It needs to finish on the drier side with some assertive bitterness to have the right balance as an IPA.

Formulation notes: *Steep roasted barley in hot strike water for a few seconds until a deep reddish color appears. No sparge technique. 20 minute hop stand at end. Settling tank used to separate hop residue prior to fermentation.

Variations: Could cut the Vienna malt with US two-row to reduce the malty punch, but that will significantly impact the resulting flavor profile. I was going for a quite malty IPA, but that increases the need to pay attention to the low mash temperature and not let the FG get too high. Dry hopping with different varieties, including Galaxy or Amarillo, would play up the fruitiness.

MOSAIC DOUBLE IPA

Introduced in the 2004 BJCP Style Guidelines as Imperial IPA, the style has been renamed to Double IPA in the 2015 BJCP Style Guidelines to better reflect current market usage. Mosaic is a relatively new hop, but well suited to single-hop beers.

Style: Double IPA (Classic BJCP Style)

Description: It's almost cheating to use Mosaic in a single-hop IPA because it has a more complex aroma and flavor than many hops, featuring several trendy hop characteristics like fruity, piney, citrusy, and floral. It's like instant IPA in a single hop variety. Uses modern hopping techniques to maximize hop aroma and flavor while giving a smooth bitterness and avoiding harshness.

Batch size: 6.5 gallons (25 L)   **OG:** 1.074   **FG:** 1.011
Efficiency: 70%   **ABV:** 8.4%   **IBU:** 72   **SRM:** 5

Ingredients:

12 lb (4.5 kg)	US two-row (Briess)	Mash
2 lb (907 g)	German Vienna malt (Weyermann)	Mash
1 lb (454 g)	Golden Promise (Simpsons)	Mash
1 lb (454 g)	German Munich malt (Weyermann)	Mash
10 oz (283 g)	White table sugar	Boil (@ 10)
1 lb (454 g)	Tupelo honey	Boil (@ 10)
1 oz (28 g)	US Mosaic 12.7% pellets	FWH
1 oz (28 g)	US Mosaic 12.7% pellets	@ 15
1 oz (28 g)	US Mosaic 12.7% pellets	@ 10
1 oz (28 g)	US Mosaic 12.7% pellets	@ 5
1 oz (28 g)	US Mosaic 12.7% pellets	@ 0
1 oz (28 g)	US Mosaic 12.7% pellets	@ +10
	Wyeast 1272 American Ale II yeast	

Water treatment: RO water treated with ¼ tsp 10% phosphoric acid per 5 gallons
0.5 tsp $CaCl_2$ and 0.5 tsp $CaSO_4$ in mash

Mash technique: Step Infusion

Mash rests:	144°F (62°C) 45 minutes
	158°F (70°C) 15 minutes
Kettle volume:	8.5 gallons (32 L)
Boil length:	90 minutes
Final volume:	6.5 gallons (25 L)
Fermentation temp:	68°F (20°C)

Sensory Description: Mosaic has a very complex profile that is fruity, citrusy, piney, and floral; it's like a blend of hops bred into one variety. The beer is pale amber with orange highlights, very clear. Big fruity, piney, and fresh hop aroma. Clean fermentation profile. High bitterness, but no harshness due to the late hopping technique. Fruity, piney flavor, dry finish, medium body. Very easy drinking, especially considering the deceptive strength.

Formulation notes: Mosaic is critical to this recipe, obviously. The base malt is supportive, but I use base malts to add complexity without crystal sweetness. Some sugar helps attenuation, and the Tupelo honey adds a little flavor as well. If you haven't used Tupelo before, it's a wonderful honey that can improve virtually any mead (or beer). I think the yeast selection adds some fruitiness as well. With the late steeping hops, the actual IBUs are likely higher than calculated.

Variations: I would love to see someone try to recreate this beer without using Mosaic hops. I'd be very intrigued to see how many different hops would need to be blended to get this level of complexity. Since the beer is fairly simple, it could serve as a base for other double IPA experiments by adding some other color or character malts. I'd be afraid of stepping on the hops too much, so tread lightly with those additional grains. The other obvious alternative is to dry hop this beer; I'd start with 2 oz (57 g) of Mosaic pellets and see where it goes from there.

WEST COAST DOUBLE IPA

I love the beers from Firestone Walker (especially Pale 31 and Union Jack), probably because many of brewmaster Matt Brynildson's ingredient preferences seem to match my own. While researching an article on dry hopping, I was intrigued by his short, successive hop technique and wanted to try it in a tribute to one of his beers, the Double Jack double IPA. He has talked about doing two successive dry hop additions, so I thought I'd give my version three. I'm using some of the hop choices he describes, but the recipe isn't meant to be a clone, just a beer I'd hope Matt would like.

Style: Double IPA (Classic BJCP Style)

Description: A double IPA with a fairly clean and malty grain bill and aggressive hopping. The dry hops are applied in successive additions to get the most oils from the hops without extracting too much vegetal matter.

Batch size: 6.5 gallons (25 L)		**OG:** 1.081	**FG:** 1.011
Efficiency: 70%	**ABV:** 9.4%	**IBU:** 99	**SRM:** 6

Ingredients:

10 lb (4.5 kg)	US two-row (Briess)	Mash
8 lb (3.6 kg)	German Pilsner malt (Best)	Mash
2 lb (907 g)	German Munich malt (Best)	Mash
4 oz (113 g)	German CaraRed malt (Weyermann)	*Vorlauf*
2 oz (57 g)	US Warrior 15.5% pellets	@ 60
1 oz (28 g)	US Centennial 10.3% whole	@ 15
1 oz (28 g)	US Cascade 4.5% whole	@ 15
2 oz (57 g)	US Centennial 10.3% whole	@ 0
2 oz (57 g)	US Cascade 4.5% whole	@ 0
2 oz (57 g)	US Cascade 4.5% whole	dry hop (*)
2 oz (57 g)	US Centennial 10.3% whole	dry hop (*)
2 oz (57 g)	US Amarillo 8.6% whole	dry hop (*)
1 oz (28 g)	US Simcoe 13.0% whole	dry hop (*)
	White Labs WLP002 English Ale yeast	

Water treatment:	RO water treated with ¼ tsp 10% phosphoric acid per 5 gallons
	0.5 tsp $CaCl_2$ and 0.5 tsp $CaSO_4$ in mash
Mash technique:	Infusion, mashout, crystal malt added at *vorlauf*
Mash rests:	131°F (55°C) 15 minutes
	145°F (63°C) 30 minutes
	158°F (70°C) 10 minutes
	170°F (77°C) 10 minutes
Kettle volume:	8.5 gallons (32 L)
Boil length:	90 minutes
Final volume:	6.5 gallons (25 L)
Fermentation temp:	64°F (18°C)

Sensory Description: Strongly hoppy, with a citrus, pine, and fruity aroma and a malty, sweet backing. Clean fermentation profile with supportive esters that work well with the hops. The malt is mostly neutral with enough richness to support the strong bitterness. The dry finish is clean with lingering bitterness and a boatload of hops. The alcohol is noticeable, especially when young, but the hops carry the beer.

Formulation notes: Combines a hop stand (20 minute post-boil steep) with a successive dry hop regimen. *Combine all the dry hops, then split into 3 equal portions; use each portion for a 3 day dry hopping period in succession at fermentation temperature, removing each addition of hops before adding the next. Be very careful to avoid oxygen pickup during this process. Crash cool when done. Does not include IBUs from the steeping, but we're pushing the limit of solubility for iso-alpha acids in this recipe anyway.

Variations: Any experimentation in this recipe is in the hop choices. Finding good combinations without producing a muddy result can be difficult. The base beer should provide a blank slate for creative hop use, whether a single hop beer or a combination.

4 | EVERYDAY BEER RECIPES

"The way I see it, you should live everyday like it's your birthday."

—*Paris Hilton, socialite*

Sometimes I'm in the mood for aggressive beers. But just as often, I find that I'd just like to enjoy a pint or two without making a big deal of it. As a result, I brew easy drinking beers that I can enjoy while watching sports, or (to fit the American stereotype) after mowing the lawn. I hesitate to call these beers *session beers*, because I think that's a narrow definition reserved for more classic English styles of lower gravity. I prefer to call these *everyday beers*, since they are the kind of beer you can drink basically any time you want, regardless of situation or weather.

I think the key characteristics of everyday beers are moderate alcohol level (around 5% ABV), with a good balance of malt and hops, flavors with more than one dimension, and (most importantly) an emphasis on drinkability. These styles aren't tied to any particular country, they're more a selection of worldwide beer styles that I like to drink regularly.

I've chosen multiple examples of some styles to demonstrate the range, how styles have changed, or to show how various techniques can be used to reach similar brewing goals.

- **Columbus Pale Ale** – A classic APA using mostly Columbus hops, this beer served as the prototype for most of my hoppy pale beers.
- **Galaxy Pale Ale** – A modern APA with New World hops. Uses Australian Galaxy hops exclusively, which gives the beer a big passion fruit character.
- **Classic Blonde Ale** – A versatile summer beer that has a malty finish and clean flavors.
- **West Coast Blonde** – A late-hopped session beer, more bitter than most blonde ales; a cousin to Session IPA.
- **New World Blonde** – A warm weather beer featuring tropical fruit flavors.
- **Ordinary Bitter** – There's nothing ordinary about this beer. My Michael Jackson tribute beer is modeled after Fuller's Chiswick Bitter.
- **Pride of Warwick Bitter** – Best bitter is one of my favorite English styles, and I made this one a bit more in the style of draught Bass ale.
- **English Pale Ale** – Don't call it an ESB; that's a specific brand name for a Fuller's beer. I prefer strong bitter if served on draft, and pale ale if in bottles.
- **Landlord Tribute** – A great best bitter, this can be made as a Single Malt and Single Hop (SMaSH) beer if you want.
- **Export Irish Red Ale** – After I learned that authentic Irish red ales have a different character locally than what they export to the US, I decided that I liked both of them. Here is my take on the export version with more caramel character, strength, and sweetness.
- **Scottish Heavy** – Very adaptable, this beer can be easily scaled to different strengths.
- **Killer Kölsch** – Balance is the key in this delicate style from Cologne, Germany.
- **American Wheat Beer** – Summer in a glass (at least in the US Midwest), but I'll drink this one year-round.
- **Nut Brown Ale** – A modern English brown ale to honor the very first beer style I ever brewed.
- **Honey Brown Ale** – Don't look at me like that; it was a request for a party. This is a split batch recipe for both a plain brown ale and a honey brown.

- **American Amber Ale** – A complex grain bill that uses Belgian, German, and English specialty malts with a modern fruity hop character.
- **Atypical Altbier** – Misinformation leads to deliciousness in this style from Düsseldorf.
- **Classic Altbier** – No misinformation here; this recipe closely matches the best commercial examples when fresh.

COLUMBUS PALE ALE

This is the all-grain version of the first American Pale Ale recipe that I put together after my local DRAFT homebrew club made a bulk purchase of Tomahawk hops (Tomahawk, Columbus, and Zeus hops are collective referred to as CTZ since they are the same hop). It represents the classic, old-school type of strong pale ale that was quite common in the early days of craft brewing. It uses a variety of character malts with a traditional hopping regime. This beer won a number of medals, along with a best of show at the Riverside Rumble competition in Ohio in 1999.

Style: American Pale Ale (Classic BJCP Style)

Description: My brewing notes of the time said that this was "excellent, almost an IPA." I was probably thinking along the lines of Anchor Liberty. Today I don't think many people would confuse this with an IPA. It's a strong pale ale.

Batch Size: 5 gallons (19 L)	**OG:** 1.056	**FG:** 1.012
Efficiency: 70% **ABV:** 5.9%	**IBU:** 43	**SRM:** 6

Ingredients:

8.5 lb (3.9 kg)	US two-row (Briess)	Mash
8 oz (227 g)	German Munich (Durst)	Mash
4 oz (113 g)	Wheat malt	Mash
8 oz (227 g)	Belgian Caravienne (Dingemans)	Mash
4 oz (113 g)	US Crystal 20	Mash
4 oz (113 g)	US Victory malt (Briess)	Mash

8 oz (227 g)	Orange blossom honey	Boil
0.5 oz (14 g)	US Columbus 13.9% whole	@ 60
0.5 oz (14 g)	US Columbus 13.9% whole	@ 15
0.5 oz (14 g)	US Columbus 13.9% whole	@ 5
1 oz (28 g)	US Columbus 13.9% pellets	@ 0
1.5 oz (43 g)	US Centennial 10.9% whole	dry hop
	Wyeast 1272 American Ale II yeast	

Water treatment: RO water treated with ¼ tsp 10% phosphoric acid per 5 gallons

0.5 tsp $CaCl_2$ and 0.5 tsp $CaSO_4$ in mash

Mash technique: Infusion, mashout

Mash rests: 152°F (67°C) 60 minutes

168°F (76°C) 10 minutes

Kettle Volume: 6.5 gallons (25 L)

Boil Length: 75 minutes

Final Volume: 5 gallons (19 L)

Fermentation temp: 68°F (20°C)

Sensory Description: Clean base malt with a little bit of toasty and lightly caramelly flavor as an accent. The orange blossom honey adds some aromatics that play well with the hops and yeast. Clean, lingering, bitter finish. Bright, fresh hop aroma.

Formulation notes: This was the prototype for many of my future hoppy beers, including those that include some orange blossom honey. It's not enough honey to turn this into a full-fledged honey beer, but it does add a little extra body, esters, and flavor. It also includes minor additions of character malts for a little extra background complexity, but none of them have a major impact on the overall taste.

Variations: The beer is a playground for classic American C-type hops. Use it to experiment with different combinations, or as a single hop varietal beer. Personally, I'd go with Cascade or Centennial (or both).

GALAXY PALE ALE

This is a recipe I put together when giving talks about Brewing Better Beer. *I wanted to feature the Galaxy hops I first discovered while in Australia in 2010, but also demonstrate how to use many of the new techniques from the book. While formulating, I thought it would be amusing to create a great American Pale Ale using no American ingredients.*

Style: American Pale Ale (Classic BJCP Style)

Description: Beautiful gold color with a huge fresh fruit aroma, and a clean, smooth bitterness on a relatively neutral malt base.

Batch Size: 6.5 gallons (25 L)	**OG:** 1.050	**FG:** 1.015
Efficiency: 70% **ABV:** 4.6%	**IBU:** 59	**SRM:** 4

Ingredients:

6 lb (2.7 kg)	Canadian two-row (CMC)	Mash
6 lb (2.7 kg)	Euro Pilsner malt (Dingemans)	Mash
1.25 lb (567 g)	German Munich malt (Best)	Mash
0.5 oz (14 g)	Australian Galaxy 13.7% pellets	FWH
1 oz (28 g)	Australian Galaxy 13.7% pellets	@ 10
1 oz (28 g)	Australian Galaxy 13.7% pellets	@ 5
1 oz (28 g)	Australian Galaxy 13.7% pellets	@ 0
1.5 oz (14 g)	Australian Galaxy 13.7% pellets	@ +10
	Wyeast 1968 London ESB Ale yeast	

Water treatment:	RO water treated with ¼ tsp 10% phosphoric acid per 5 gallons
	0.5 tsp $CaCl_2$ and 0.5 tsp $CaSO_4$ in mash
Mash technique:	Step mash
Mash rests:	144°F (62°C) 30 minutes
	153°F (67°C) 30 minutes
Kettle Volume:	8.5 gallons (32 L)
Boil Length:	90 minutes
Final Volume:	6.5 gallons (25 L)
Fermentation temp:	62°F (17°C)

Sensory Description: Huge punch of fruity notes with a tropical, passion fruit aroma and a little citrus. The bitterness is strong but clean and not at all harsh. The little bit of maltiness and body helps balance the hop bitterness. It doesn't seem nearly as bitter as the IBUs would indicate due to the first wort hopping, hop bursting, and a hop stand.

Formulation notes: The mix of Pilsner malt and two-row gives a fairly neutral base, but still has some flavor. It's not all one or the other; all two-row is a bit too neutral, and all Pilsner can make it taste too sweet. You can use any German or Belgian Pilsner malt, but I like the Belgian since it has a touch of fruitiness. I like using about 10% Munich malt instead of any crystal malt (remember, Munich is the new crystal) since it provides maltiness and body without sugary or caramel sweetness. The English yeast can give a fruity but clean note as long as it isn't fermented too warm. The Galaxy hops have great passion fruit character (or at least they did when I first tried them in Australia; more recent vintages seem to be more piney and tropical fruity). I used a 20 minute steep at the end, which can give this more bitterness than estimated.

Variations: Obviously you can use some US ingredients in this beer, particularly for the two-row base malt. Wyeast 1272 could also be used instead. I like to use some US Cascade hops late along with the Galaxy. Citra, Amarillo, or other fruity-type hops would work well, too. The base beer is so neutral that it could be used for almost any hop experiment. You could also tweak it by adding specialty grains to make it an amber or brown ale; just back off the hops somewhat if you go that route, as they can clash with character malts. If you want to go all out with hop aroma, you can dry hop it with 2 oz (57 g) of the same variety you brewed it with.

CLASSIC BLONDE ALE

American Blonde Ale is one of my go-to summer beers. I don't like to make them too strong or aggressive, but still want them to have significant flavor dimensions. This version closely matches the BJCP style description, and is what I'd use in competition. Judges are funny about this style; it's very broad, yet many of them are looking for specific interpretations. If I'm judging the style, this is what I'd look for. It's a double-size batch, so you can drink a keg and take another to a party.

Style: Blonde Ale (Classic BJCP Style)

Description: Flavorful base malt supporting a gentle bitterness from light American hops.

Batch Size: 11 gallons (42 L)	**OG:** 1.048	**FG:** 1.012
Efficiency: 70% **ABV:** 4.8%	**IBU:** 10	**SRM:** 5

Ingredients:

8 lb (3.6 kg)	US two-row (Briess)	Mash
6 lb (2.7 kg)	German Pilsner (Best)	Mash
4 lb (1.8 g)	German Munich (Best)	Mash
1 lb (454 g)	German Carahell (Weyermann)	Mash
0.25 oz (7 g)	US Citra 13.8% whole	FWH
0.75 oz (14 g)	US Citra 13.8% whole	@ 5
2 oz (57 g)	US Centennial 10.3% whole	@ 0
	Wyeast 1318 London III yeast	

Water treatment:	RO water treated with ¼ tsp 10% phosphoric acid per 5 gallons
	2 tsp $CaCl_2$ in mash
Mash technique:	Infusion, mashout
Mash rests:	151°F (66°C) 60 minutes
	168°F (76°C) 10 minutes
Kettle Volume:	13 gallons (49 L)
Boil Length:	75 minutes

Final Volume: 11 gallons (42 L)
Fermentation temp: 65°F (18°C)

Sensory Description: Clean but malty base with balanced bitterness (higher than estimated, but still a touch malty in the balance). The hops are light but expressive, adding a citrusy, tropical note. There is some residual malty sweetness to keep it from being too dry in the finish.

Formulation notes: I like to go with a clean malt base that has some malty flavors without going all caramel or crystal sweet. The German or Belgian base malts work well, as do low color German crystal malts for a little body and flavor. The US base malt cuts the flavor of the continental malts. The hops go in late, and can provide more IBUs than the calculation shows if they continue to steep before chilling. To keep the IBUs restrained, start chilling right away or use the Centennial hops in a hopback. Yeast that provides a malty profile is the best choice for this style, since you don't want it bone dry. You want some residual malt to help balance the hops, and give some malty flavors in the aftertaste without being sweet. The fruity-citrusy American hop character is clean and refreshing, and complements the malt nicely.

Variations: Compare this recipe to the Galaxy Pale Ale and other American Blonde recipes. In a style so subtle, it's easy to change the character by making some small adjustments. Fortunately, all those other versions are also very good beers, but this is the one that tends to do best in competitions.

WEST COAST BLONDE

I made this beer for my presentation at the 2013 NHC, and it helped demonstrate some educational facts about hop utilization. I was looking for a balanced blonde ale, but wound up with something that tasted a bit more like a pale ale. So I just called it a West Coast Blonde Ale, and everyone thought it was appropriate. Rebalanced with different hops, this beer is the predecessor to the Classic Blonde Ale recipe.

Style: Blonde Ale (Classic BJCP Style)

Description: Estimated to be 15 IBUs, but measured in a lab to be 27 or 38 (depending on the test method[1]), indicating a need for updates to recipe software formulas, and problems with how labs measure whirlpool-hopped beers. The beer is aggressively bitter for a blonde ale, which is more common on the US west coast. It features an identical grist to the Classic Blonde Ale but the different hops make it a completely different beer.

Batch Size: 11 gallons (42 L)	**OG:** 1.048	**FG:** 1.010
Efficiency: 75% **ABV:** 5.1%	**IBU:** 27–38	**SRM:** 5

Ingredients:

8 lb (3.6 kg)	US two-row (Briess)	Mash
6 lb (2.7 kg)	German Pilsner (Best)	Mash
4 lb (1.8 g)	German Munich (Best)	Mash
1 lb (454 g)	German Carahell (Weyermann)	Mash
1 oz (28 g)	US Meridian 6.7% pellets	FWH
2 oz (57 g)	US Centennial 10.3% whole	@ 1
2 oz (57 g)	US Meridian 6.7% pellets	@ 0
	Wyeast 1318 London Ale III yeast	

Water treatment:	RO water treated with ¼ tsp 10% phosphoric acid per 5 gallons
	2 tsp CaCl$_2$ in mash
Mash technique:	Infusion, mashout
Mash rests:	149°F (65°C) 60 minutes
	168°F (76°C) 10 minutes
Kettle Volume:	13 gallons (49 L)
Boil Length:	75 minutes
Final Volume:	11 gallons (42 L)
Fermentation temp:	68°F (20°C)

---

[1] For those lab geeks out there, ASBC manual isooctane extraction (bitterness unit method A) measured 38, and ABSC iso-alpha-acid by solvent extraction (method B) measured 27 according to Actual Brewing, Columbus, OH. Method A can pick up aroma hop additions as bitterness, so Method B is preferred for beers with a strong late-hop or dry-hop addition.

Sensory Description: Dry and bitter with an expressive hop notes that had a piney and citrusy character. The fruity qualities were somewhat subdued, or perhaps overshadowed by the hops. It reads more as a pale ale than a blonde ale, but it isn't a big pale ale.

Formulation notes: The hops were given a 20 minute steep prior to chilling, which clearly extracted more bitterness than recipe software estimated. Meridian is described as a hop that has lemon and blueberry flavors; it seems woody and citrusy to me. I was looking for some interplay between the lime character in Centennial and the fruit flavors in Meridian, but it came off a bit more 'Pacific Northwest' than I was expecting (in that it played up the more "evergreen" type flavors). I'd probably use different varieties if I was looking for a blonde ale. But in a west coast blonde? These hops are just fine.

Variations: I like the balance of this beer, but not really as a blonde ale. In the days of session IPAs, it follows a similar intent without making something difficult to drink. Meridian was an unusual hop, and it might not be to everyone's taste, so I'd play around mostly with the hop varieties. If you want this to be more like a blonde ale, don't use an extended steep of the hops; chill immediately after boil ends. Or wait 10 or 15 minutes after the boil ends to add the hops if you *do* intend to use an extended steep.

NEW WORLD BLONDE

Another take on an American blonde ale, this time playing up the tropical fruit combination of Galaxy and Citra hops. It is a bit lower in gravity than other blonde ales, and is a favorite of mine in the summer. These three blonde ales, taken together, are meant to show how you can vary recipes to come up with distinctly different beers. This type of information is also discussed in the "variations" section of most recipes, but here are some concrete examples. Concrete blonde examples (ha!).

Style: Blonde Ale (Classic BJCP Style)

Description: Beautiful gold color with a clean malt background and the flavor and aroma of tropical fruit.

Batch Size: 6 gallons (23 L)   **OG:** 1.042   **FG:** 1.011
Efficiency: 60%   **ABV:** 4.1%   **IBU:** 13   **SRM:** 5

Ingredients:

5 lb (2.3 kg)	US two-row (Briess)	Mash
5 lb (2.3 kg)	Belgian Pilsner (Dingemans)	Mash
12 oz (340 g)	German Munich (Best)	Mash
8 oz (227 g)	Belgian Caravienne (Dingemans)	*Vorlauf*
0.5 oz (14 g)	Australian Galaxy 13% pellets	@ 10
0.5 oz (14 g)	US Citra 13.4% pellets	@ 5
0.5 oz (14 g)	US Citra 13.4% pellets	@ +10
0.5 oz (14 g)	Australian Galaxy 13% pellets	@ +10
	Wyeast 1272 American Ale II yeast	

Water treatment: RO water treated with ¼ tsp 10% phosphoric acid per 5 gallons
1 tsp $CaCl_2$ in mash
Mash technique: Step Infusion, mashout, no sparge
Mash rests: 131°F (55°C) 15 minutes
152°F (67°C) 45 minutes
168°F (76°C) 15 minutes
Kettle Volume: 8 gallons (30 L)
Boil Length: 90 minutes
Final Volume: 6 gallons (23 L)
Fermentation temp: 68°F (20°C)

Sensory Description: The malt flavors are pure and clean, and the hops are noticeable but don't scream at you. The overall character is elegant, clean, and juicy, with a distinct tropical impression. A nice summer beer, especially if the gravity is kept low. The no sparge technique improves the quality of the malt flavor, and the late steep of hops keeps the bitterness restrained while adding a wonderful hop aroma.

Formulation notes: The efficiency of this recipe is lower because it is a no sparge recipe; sparging will make a stronger beer, closer to 5%. The hops need to be handled specially as to not extract too much bitterness. Put the boiling hops in mesh bags and remove them at the end of the boil so the bitterness doesn't continue to be extracted as the beer stands hot.

Let the beer chill to 185°F (85°C) before adding the post-boil hops (also in bags). Let steep for 10 minutes, then remove.

Variations: If you'd like to play up the hop aroma more, this beer can easily be dry-hopped with an equal mix of Citra and Galaxy. Start with 1 oz (28 g) for 3 days. Repeat if more hop aroma is desired. It's not meant to be a hoppy style, but you can take it that direction if that's your preference.

ORDINARY BITTER

I put this recipe together as a tribute to Michael Jackson after he passed away because he was known to enjoy an honest pint of ordinary bitter. This is a simple recipe that relies on ingredient quality above all else.

Style: Ordinary Bitter (Classic BJCP Style)

Description: Bready, caramel, and toffee malt flavor with a firm bitterness and a fruity yeast character. Wonderful on cask.

Batch Size: 6.5 gallons (25 L)		**OG:** 1.034	**FG:** 1.008
Efficiency: 70%	**ABV:** 3.4%	**IBU:** 27	**SRM:** 8

Ingredients:

6 lb (2.7 kg)	UK Maris Otter (Crisp)	Mash
2 lb (907 g)	UK Golden Promise (Simpsons)	Mash
6 oz (170 g)	UK Crystal 60 (Crisp)	*Vorlauf*
2 oz (57 g)	UK Crystal 80 (Baird)	*Vorlauf*
0.5 oz (14 g)	UK Challenger 7% pellets	FWH
0.5 oz (14 g)	UK Northdown 8% pellets	@ 20
1 oz (28 g)	UK Goldings 5.5% whole	@ 5
1 oz (28 g)	UK Goldings 5.5% whole	dry hop
	Wyeast 1968 London ESB Ale yeast	

Water treatment: RO water treated with ¼ tsp 10% phosphoric acid per 5 gallons
1 tsp $CaSO_4$ in mash

Mash technique:	Infusion, mashout, crystal malts added at *vorlauf*
Mash rests:	149°F (65°C) 60 minutes
	168°F (76°C) 15 minutes
Kettle Volume:	8 gallons (30 L)
Boil Length:	60 minutes
Final Volume:	6.5 gallons (25 L)
Fermentation temp:	Start at 63°F (17°C), allowing to rise to 68°F (20°C)

Sensory Description: Has the bready, biscuit malt, floral, woody hops, and fruity ale character so classic in English bitters. Enjoy fresh after it has dropped bright. Lovely on cask without a sparkler. I often serve it directly from the cask on gravity feed without a beer engine. Serving at cellar temperature (55–58°F /12–14°C) allows the malt and fruity qualities to open up and better support the hops.

Formulation notes: The British base malts have more of a bready, biscuit flavor; blending them adds complexity. The darker crystal malts give some extra color, as well as dark caramel and toffee flavors. The percentage of crystal malts isn't that high, so don't expect a lot of body and sweetness. Yeast adds a supportive fruitiness, but the hops come through with their floral, fruity, and woody qualities. This style is traditionally dry-hopped when served on cask. The Fuller's yeast strain (Wyeast 1968 or White Labs WLP002) is a superb cask strain; it flocculates very well.

Variations: I really like this recipe the way it is, but there is some variation in crystal malts between maltsters. The crystal isn't a dominant flavor, so you can really use just about any British maltster. Some of the very dark ones can be a touch burnt, so I prefer to add them at *vorlauf* rather than in the mash.

PRIDE OF WARWICK BITTER

I tend to name my English beers "Pride of Warwick" after my hometown in New York. Of course, we pronounce it "war-wick" instead of "warrick" like they do in England. The balance of the beer is similar to draught Bass ale, although the flavors are different.

Style: Best Bitter (Classic BJCP Style)

Description: A dry interpretation of the style with flaked maize to provide some roundness and depth, which is a traditional English approach.

Batch Size: 5.5 gallons (21 L) **OG:** 1.041 **FG:** 1.008
Efficiency: 70% **ABV:** 4.4% **IBU:** 31 **SRM:** 11

Ingredients:

7.5 lb (3.4 kg)	UK Maris Otter (Crisp)	Mash
8 oz (227 g)	Flaked Maize	Mash
4 oz (113 g)	US Victory malt (Briess)	Mash
8 oz (227 g)	UK Crystal 60 (Crisp)	*Vorlauf*
0.8 oz (23 g)	UK Black malt	*Vorlauf*
0.75 oz (21 g)	UK Goldings 5.5% whole	FWH
0.4 oz (11 g)	UK Challenger 7% whole	@ 60
0.5 oz (14 g)	UK Fuggles 4.5% whole	@ 15
0.75 oz (21 g)	UK Fuggles 4.5% whole	@ 1
0.5 oz (14 g)	Styrian Goldings 4.5% whole	dry hop
	Wyeast 1028 London Ale yeast	

Water treatment: RO water treated with ¼ tsp 10% phosphoric acid per 5 gallons
1 tsp $CaSO_4$ in mash, 0.5 tsp $CaSO_4$ in boil
Mash technique: Infusion, mashout, dark grains added at *vorlauf*
Mash rests: 151°F (66°C) 60 minutes
168°F (76°C) 15 minutes
Kettle Volume: 7 gallons (26 L)
Boil Length: 75 minutes
Final Volume: 5.5 gallons (21 L)

Fermentation temp: 68°F (20°C)

Sensory Description: Bready, dry, and lightly minerally with fruity, floral, and woody hop character. The malt has biscuit notes, but also a rounded flavor that implies sweetness while remaining dry. The bitterness level is prominent but not extreme. This beer is easy to drink and best enjoyed at cellar temperature.

Formulation notes: The back malt is only for color adjustment; using debittered black malt is fine. The rest of the ingredients are fairly traditional for English-style beers. The corn adds the rounded quality, with the Victory malt playing up the biscuit notes found in the base malt.

Variations: This beer can handle more dry hopping; the listed version is fairly gentle in that department. The mix of hops is one of my favorites for English beers, but the varieties can be played with to get a different character. Using something more daring than Fuggles and Goldings is fun, but the Styrians work very well. The yeast can be changed but it won't likely be quite as dry. Swapping calcium chloride for calcium sulfate in the water treatment will also reduce the dryness and sulfate content.

ENGLISH PALE ALE

This is a beer I brewed with my friend Ken Weems, who is one of the people who first taught me to brew. It was in the middle of winter, right before New Year's Eve, and we both wanted something warming and chewy we could enjoy during the rest of the winter. But the caveat was we didn't want a sipper; we wanted pints.

Style: Strong Bitter (Classic BJCP Style)

Description: Quite strong by modern English standards, this is in the range of export strong bitters. Probably borderline Strong Ale in England.

Batch Size: 11.5 gallons (44 L) **OG:** 1.055 **FG:** 1.014
Efficiency: 60% **ABV:** 5.6% **IBU:** 36 **SRM:** 14

Ingredients:

26 lb (11.8 kg)	UK Maris Otter (Crisp)	Mash
1 lb (454 g)	Flaked Maize	Mash
1.5 lb (680 g)	UK crystal 60 (Crisp)	*Vorlauf*
4 oz (113 g)	UK crystal 120 (Crisp)	*Vorlauf*
2 oz (57 g)	UK Black malt	*Vorlauf*
2 oz (57 g)	UK Goldings 6.6% whole	FWH
1 oz (28 g)	UK Challenger 7% pellets	@ 60
1 oz (28 g)	UK Northdown 8% whole	@ 5
2 oz (57 g)	German Tettnanger 4.5% whole	@ 2
2 oz (57 g)	Styrian Goldings 4.5% whole	@ 0
	Wyeast 1968 London ESB Ale yeast	

Water treatment:	RO water treated with ¼ tsp 10% phosphoric acid per 5 gallons
	1 tsp CaCl$_2$ and 2 tsp CaSO$_4$ in mash
Mash technique:	Infusion, mashout, dark grains and crystal malts added at *vorlauf*, no sparge
Mash rests:	152°F (67°C) 60 minutes
	168°F (76°C) 15 minutes
Kettle Volume:	13.5 gallons (51 L)
Boil Length:	90 minutes
Final Volume:	11.5 gallons (44 L)
Fermentation temp:	Start at 68°F (20°C), allowing to rise to no more than 72°F (22°C)

Sensory Description: Malty-rich with bread, biscuit, and toffee flavors and a fruity yeast quality. The bitterness is quite high, but that will reduce with age. The hops have a floral, fruity, and spicy quality.

Formulation notes: The no sparge technique reduces efficiency but improves the quality of the malt flavor. The Northdown and Tettnanger hops both add a spicy quality to the aroma. The increase in crystal malts add a more robust body and residual sweetness with dark toffee flavors. A warmer ferment adds additional fruitiness. The bready malt base easily supports the strong bitterness and fruity-spicy flavors.

Variations: The hops can be changed if spicy late hops are not to your liking. The late hop character can be increased with dry hopping or increasing the quantity of knockout hops. Scaling the beer up to the 7 to 8% ABV range changes the overall feeling of the beer since the fruity flavors are often more prominent as it ages. Since this is a no sparge beer, you can also just make a strong beer with the first runnings and not bother topping off the kettle to the target pre-boil volume.

LANDLORD TRIBUTE (SMASH)

I tried to think up a cutesy name for this, but why bother? Timothy Taylor's Landlord is truly a world-class beer. Enjoyed fresh from the cask, it is a sublime experience. This recipe is my tribute to this classic beer, which features the signature flavors of Golden Promise malt, Styrian Goldings hops, and Yorkshire yeast. You can't really substitute any of those ingredients and still make the same beer. If there is ever a reason to buy a cask beer setup, this beer is it. This beer is on the strong side for an everyday bitter in the UK, so it often competes as a strong pale ale.

Style: Best Bitter (Classic BJCP Style)

Description: Light amber color, moderate bitterness, dry and hoppy finish with bready, toasty malt flavors. The flavor dimension of this beer is astounding in its complexity given the simplicity of the recipe.

Batch Size: 6.5 gallons (25 L)	**OG:** 1.041	**FG:** 1.010
Efficiency: 70%	**ABV:** 4.1%	**IBU:** 36	**SRM:** 12

Ingredients:

10 lb (4.5 kg)	UK Golden Promise (Simpsons)	Mash
3 oz (85 g)	Debittered Black Malt (Dingeman)	*Vorlauf*
1.8 oz (51 g)	UK Goldings 5.9% whole	@ 60
1 oz (28 g)	Styrian Goldings 2.1% whole	@ 10
1 oz (28 g)	Styrian Goldings 2.1% whole	@ 0
	(40 minute steep)	
	Wyeast 1469 West Yorkshire Ale yeast	

Water treatment:	RO water treated with ¼ tsp (1.2 ml) 10% phosphoric acid per 5 gallons
	1 tsp $CaCl_2$ in mash, 0.5 tsp $CaCO_3$ in boil.
Mash technique:	Infusion, mashout, dark malt added at *vorlauf*
Mash rests:	152°F (67°C) 60 minutes
	168°F (76°C) 15 minutes
Kettle Volume:	8.5 gallons (32 L)
Boil Length:	70 minutes
Final Volume:	6.5 gallons (25 L)
Fermentation temp:	68°F (20°C)

Sensory Description: It is surprising how much character and complexity comes from the malt in this beer; if asked to guess, I would have suspected a more complex grist. The biscuit quality in Golden Promise is much less than Maris Otter, and is more balanced. The bitterness is average for an English bitter, noticeable but not extreme. The dryness and tannic hop character enhance the hop bitterness, and provide balance for the malt (along with the minerally yeast). I like to serve this beer at cellar temperature (55–58°F/12–14°C) to maintain the right balance. If served too cold, the malt won't be as tasty or impressive. Light amber color, a bit cloudy when young but eventually drops bright.

Formulation notes: I tried to use the classic ingredients in this recipe, and to develop the same flavor profile and appearance as the inspiration beer. Golden Promise malt is a must; you can vary the maltster to see which you like better. Styrian Golding hops are required as the aroma addition. The 1469 yeast is the same Timothy Taylor yeast from West Yorkshire, so you really do need that for the minerally character. The dark malt is for color adjustment; you can use other methods if desired. The long hot steep of hops is intentional to provide a drying quality. Note the boil time and volumes (this beer required a hard boil).

Variations: If you want to make this as a single malt and single hop (SMaSH) beer, use all Styrians for hops and decoct the grain to deepen the color. I think the brewery might use Fuggles as a flavor addition, so you might consider that as well if you are actually trying to clone the beer.

You could use this as a basis for a different bitter with perhaps Maris Otter as the base malt and any of the other well-regarded English yeasts (my preference would be the Wyeast 1335 British Ale II).

EXPORT IRISH RED ALE

After a trip to Ireland in February 2014, I learned a great deal about the differences between domestic Irish and export versions of Irish Red Ale. The local variety is like a grainy pale ale, while the export version is stronger and has a fuller body and more caramel character. Both are excellent beers, but I prefer drinking the export variety since it has a softer finish and more flavor. Many American craft brewers produce stronger versions of this style, but I prefer the more moderate strength version since the alcohol does not interfere with the malty flavors.

Style: Irish Red Ale (Classic BJCP Style)

Description: An export-style Irish Red Ale with a chewy body and slightly sweet balance. Caramel and toast flavors provide significant malt character. What most US judges think of as a classic example, so this tends to do well in competitions.

Batch Size: 6.5 gallons (25 L)		OG: 1.052	FG: 1.014
Efficiency: 70%	ABV: 5.0%	IBU: 15	SRM: 19

Ingredients:

7 lb (3.2 kg)	UK Mild ale malt (Pauls)	Mash
3 lb (1.4 kg)	German Vienna (Durst)	Mash
1 lb (454 g)	Carapils malt	Mash
1 lb (454 g)	Flaked maize	Mash
1 lb (454 g)	Crystal 40 (Scotmalt)	*Vorlauf*
4 oz (113 g)	UK Roasted barley	*Vorlauf*
0.5 oz (14 g)	UK Goldings 6.9% whole	@ 60
0.25 oz (7 g)	UK Goldings 6.9% whole	@ 30
0.25 oz (7 g)	UK Goldings 6.9% whole	@ 10
	Wyeast 1084 Irish Ale yeast	

Water treatment:	RO water treated with ¼ tsp 10% phosphoric acid per 5 gallons
	1 tsp CaCl₂ in mash
Mash technique:	Infusion, mashout, dark grains and crystal malt added at *vorlauf*
Mash rests:	151°F (66°C) 60 minutes
	168°F (76°C) 15 minutes
Kettle Volume:	8 gallons (30 L)
Boil Length:	75 minutes
Final Volume:	6.5 gallons (25 L)
Fermentation temp:	70°F (21°C)

Sensory Description: Rich, chewy malt with a caramel and toast flavor. Low bitterness increases the perception of sweetness. Reddish copper color. Light grainy dryness in the finish from the roasted barley without a noticeable roast quality.

Formulation notes: I picked unusual base malts so they could add more dextrins and mouthfeel to the beer. The corn gives it a rounded flavor, while the rest of the grains give it toast and caramel flavors with a drying finish. This isn't meant to be a classic commercial recipe from Ireland; I just matched ingredients to flavors.

Variations: If making this for competition, I would use a no-sparge technique to increase the intensity of the malt flavor. For a more authentic domestic Irish Red, lower the gravity to 1.044, cut the crystal malt in half, and drop the carapils entirely.

SCOTTISH HEAVY

I have played around with different versions of Scottish ales for a long time, but finally settled on the flavors I wanted when brewing with Golden Promise malt. The specialty malt suggestions in this recipe come from Jay Wince of Weasel Boy Brewing Company, who makes some outstanding Scottish ales.

Style: Scottish Heavy (Classic BJCP Style)

Description: Malty rich with low bitterness, yet easy to drink. Don't carbonate this too highly or the drinkability will suffer. Hops are definitely in the background, but the malt has some extra character that provides interest with every sip.

Batch Size: 6.5 gallons (25 L)	**OG:** 1.038	**FG:** 1.012
Efficiency: 75%	**ABV:** 3.5%	**IBU:** 11	**SRM:** 13

Ingredients:

8 lb (3.6 kg)	UK Golden Promise (Simpsons)	Mash
8 oz (227 g)	Flaked barley	Mash
4 oz (113 g)	CaraMunich II (Weyermann)	*Vorlauf*
2 oz (57 g)	UK Pale chocolate (Crisp)	*Vorlauf*
2 oz (57 g)	UK Roasted barley	*Vorlauf*
0.6 oz (17 g)	UK Goldings 5.9% whole	@ 60
	Wyeast 1728 Scottish Ale yeast	

Water treatment: RO water treated with ¼ tsp 10% phosphoric acid per 5 gallons
1 tsp CaCl$_2$ in mash

Mash technique: Infusion, mashout, dark grains and crystal malt added at *vorlauf*

Mash rests: 156°F (69°C) 60 minutes
168°F (76°C) 15 minutes

Kettle Volume: 8 gallons (30 L)

Boil Length: 60 minutes

Final Volume: 6.5 gallons (25 L)

Fermentation temp: Start at 58°F (14°C), allowing to rise as high as 68°F (20°C) to finish.

Sensory Description: Malty and toasty with a clean and lightly caramel finish. Low bitterness allows the malt to be the star. The roasted barley adds some dryness towards the finish that helps compensate for the low hopping. The flaked barley adds some dextrins and body.

Formulation notes: Boil the wort hard for 60 minutes to hit target volume. The Golden Promise malt runs the show here; it provides such a rich flavor that it can almost carry the beer alone. The rest of the malt components enhance the complexity.

Variations: This recipe can be scaled up or down to make any type of Scottish ale of any strength. Weasel Boy uses Wyeast 1318 as a house yeast, so that can be used successfully in this style as well. Maris Otter as the base malt would make a bready, more biscuit heavy version, which should also taste good.

KILLER KÖLSCH

I fell in love with this style after a visit to Cologne in 2006. I had enjoyed it before, but it didn't remember it being anything special. Trying it fresh made all the difference. I also saw how very few Cologne brewers used wheat in their recipes, and I now leave it out of mine (the graininess of the wheat doesn't help the style at all). I also noticed how the various beers made by traditional Cologne breweries were similar, but distinct. The style allows for subtle changes in balance from several components (malt, hop flavor, bitterness, fruitiness), but all hovered around moderate intensity. I won a number of NHC first round medals with this recipe, which is in the style of a Früh or Reissdorf.

Style: Kölsch (Classic BJCP Style)

Description: Delicate, pils malt-driven beer with moderate hop flavor, a hint of esters, and a soft, dry finish.

Batch Size: 6.5 gallons (25 L)		OG: 1.046	FG: 1.011
Efficiency: 70%	ABV: 4.6%	IBU: 16	SRM: 3

Ingredients:

11 lb (5 kg)	German Pilsner malt (Durst)	Mash
4 oz (113 g)	German Vienna malt (Best)	Mash
4 oz (113 g)	Belgian Caravienne (Dingemans)	Mash

0.33 oz (9 g)	US Liberty 4.5% whole	FWH
1 oz (28 g)	German Hallertauer 4.3% whole	@ 30
0.4 oz (11 g)	US Crystal 3.5% whole	@ 5
	White Labs WLP029 German Ale/Kölsch yeast	

Water treatment:	RO water treated with ¼ tsp 10% phosphoric acid per 5 gallons
	1 tsp $CaCl_2$ in mash
Mash technique:	Step mash, mashout
Mash rests:	131°F (55°C) 10 minutes
	145°F (63°C) 45 minutes
	158°F (70°C) 20 minutes
	168°F (76°C) 10 minutes
Kettle Volume:	8.5 gallons (32 L)
Boil Length:	90 minutes
Final Volume:	6.5 gallons (25 L)
Fermentation temp:	58°F (14°C), allowing to rise to 68°F (20°C) after 4 days to finish. Lager 2 months at 40°F (4°C).

Sensory Description: Delicate, rounded pils malt flavor with a slightly sweet impression. The hops have a floral and spicy quality, with just a hint of fruit in the background. The taste profile is clean and the finish is dry, with a rounded malt flavor and supportive bitterness. This version has lower bitterness than others, but there are variations within the style and I prefer the lower bitterness when paired with the dryness (especially when lagered).

Formulation notes: I use some American versions of German noble hops in this recipe since I can often get them fresher than the German varieties. Fresh malt is a must, since the malt character needs to be support the beer. Step mashing helps produce attenuative wort. I also use kettle finings since clarity is important for the style. The yeast is quite powdery, so it generally needs to be fined with gelatin or filtered clear (but the powdery yeast *does* help it mature while being lagered). Modern commercial versions are turned around quickly with a short, cold lagering time, but I like to lager mine longer to help reduce sulfur notes and let the flavors blend better.

Variations: Since the balance can be adjusted so much and still make credible versions of the style, the easiest ways to vary the beer is to increase the bitterness, increase the hop flavor and aroma, vary the fermentation temperature, and to play around with the mash schedule. You might make a double batch and try the two different yeast strains to see if you like one better than the other.

AMERICAN WHEAT BEER

If I'm going to brew an everyday wheat beer, I'll usually make a German hefe-weizen. My favorite recipe for that style is in Brewing Better Beer, *but I also make an American wheat beer for parties or to serve as the base for a fruit beer. This recipe is in the style of Bell's Oberon, but is lower in strength and dry-hopped.*

Style: American Wheat Beer (Classic BJCP Style)

Description: A golden wheat beer with a full-bodied malty flavor, a fruity yeast quality, spicy-floral hop flavor, and somewhat citrusy hop aroma.

Batch Size:	6.5 gallons (25 L)	**OG:** 1.054	**FG:** 1.016
Efficiency: 70%	**ABV:** 5.1%	**IBU:** 21	**SRM:** 6

Ingredients:

6.5 lb (2.9 kg)	German wheat malt (Durst)	Mash
5 lb (2.3 kg)	US two-row malt (Briess)	Mash
1 lb (454 g)	German Munich (Best)	Mash
12 oz (340 g)	Belgian Caravienne (Dingemans)	Mash
1 oz (28 g)	Czech Saaz 3% whole	FWH
1 oz (28 g)	German Hallertauer 3.5% whole	@ 20
1 oz (28 g)	German Hallertauer 3.5% whole	@ 10
1 oz (28 g)	Czech Saaz 3% whole	@ 5
1 oz (28 g)	US Cascade 5% whole	dry hop
	Wyeast 1271 American Ale II yeast	

Water treatment: RO water treated with ¼ tsp 10% phosphoric acid per 5 gallons

1 tsp CaCl$_2$ in mash

Mash technique:	Hybrid (step and decoction) mash, mashout
Mash rests:	131°F(55°C) 10 minutes
	Pull thick decoction (1/3 of mash), rest at 149°F (65°C) for 15 minutes, 158°F (70°C) for 15 minutes, then boil for 15 minutes. Meanwhile, ramp main mash up to 149°F (65°C) and hold while decoction in progress. Remix to hit 158°F (70°C), then hold for 20 minutes.
	168°F (76°C) 10 minutes
Kettle Volume:	8.5 gallons (32 L)
Boil Length:	90 minutes
Final Volume:	6.5 gallons (25 L)
Fermentation temp:	68–70°F (20–21°C)

Sensory Description: Grainy and bready wheat flavor with moderate bitterness, but the malty richness helps cut that impression. The yeast gives it a slightly fruity quality, while the hops add floral, spicy, and citrusy notes to the flavor and aroma. The dry hopping helps reinforce that this isn't a German beer.

Formulation notes: Uses some Munich malt for body and flavor without the associated sweetness of crystal malt. I like using decoction mashes for wheat beers since I think it improves the flavor and mouthfeel. The US two-row cuts some of the malt flavor and avoids giving it a Pils-like flavor that is more common with the German *weissbiers*. I like mixing classic German and American hops in this beer to provide aromatic complexity without getting overly aggressive.

Variations: Try it the way the recipe suggests first before playing around with variations. You can change the hopping around to suit your tastes; I like using hops with more of a tropical or stone fruit character (e.g., Galaxy, Amarillo, Citra), or mimicking a modern American IPA in terms of hop complexity. You can make darker versions of this by adding some crystal or darker malts during *vorlauf*, but watch out with clashing hop flavors if you use crystal malts. Reducing the gravity can also turn this into a more sessionable summer beer.

NUT BROWN ALE

I don't make this style very often, but it has a fond place in my heart because Newcastle Brown Ale was the first craft beer I liked and it was also the very first beer style I brewed (my one and only kit). The beer style is quite a bit broader than Newcastle represents, so keep an open mind about this beer. Basically, any moderate-strength brownish beer with English flavors that doesn't taste as roasty as a porter would qualify as a brown ale.

Style: English Brown Ale (Classic BJCP Style)

Description: Bready, toasty base with moderate caramel flavor and a touch of chocolate. The malt and bitterness are evenly balanced but the finish stays malty. The yeast gives a light fruitiness.

Batch Size:	6.5 gallons (25 L)	**OG:** 1.045		**FG:** 1.012	
Efficiency: 70%		**ABV:** 4.4%	**IBU:** 18		**SRM:** 18

Ingredients:

6 lb (2.7 kg)	UK Maris Otter (Crisp)	Mash
3 lb (1.4 kg)	UK Golden Promise (Simpsons)	Mash
1 lb (454 g)	Torrified wheat	Mash
12 oz (340 g)	UK Crystal 65 (Crisp)	*Vorlauf*
4 oz (113 g)	UK Crystal 45 (Crisp)	*Vorlauf*
5 oz (142 g)	UK Chocolate (Fawcett)	*Vorlauf*
1 oz (28 g)	UK Goldings 5% whole	@ 60
0.5 oz (14 g)	UK Goldings 5% whole	@ 10
	Wyeast 1318 London III yeast	

Water treatment: RO water treated with ¼ tsp 10% phosphoric acid per 5 gallons
1 tsp CaCl$_2$ in mash

Mash technique: Infusion, mashout, dark grains added at *vorlauf*

Mash rests: 150°F (66°C) 60 minutes
168°F (76°C) 15 minutes

Kettle Volume: 8 gallons (30 L)

Boil Length: 75 minutes

Final Volume: 6.5 gallons (25 L)
Fermentation temp: 68°F (20°C)

Sensory Description: The malt is in control in this beer, but the hops do support it quite well. The crystal and chocolate malt flavors provide the primary flavor, as well as some additional mouthfeel and residual sweetness in the finish. The late hops are restrained and provide a little bit of character without being obtrusive. The fermentation profile is a touch fruity but the yeast leaves a malty impression.

Formulation notes: The English crystal and chocolate malts are very important for this beer, as is some kind of British base malt. I like using some Golden Promise to keep the breadiness of the Maris Otter in check, while the torrified wheat adds a toasty quality.

Variations: Add some UK brown malt (4–8 oz) if you want it to seem like a small porter. This beer can also serve as the base for a darker fruit or spice beer. The beer will seem a bit different if other English yeast strains are used, so it can serve as a decent control when evaluating yeast differences in a maltier beer.

HONEY BROWN ALE

I almost never make this kind of beer, but it's a fairly common request. I made up this batch as a request for a party, and wished I had made a double batch (it ended up being very good). Skipping the honey turns this into a solid English brown ale. A more versatile and practical approach for this beer is to make a double-sized batch with honey being added to only one fermenter (which is the recipe I use here).

Style: Alternative Sugar Beer (New BJCP Style, Experimental)

Description: A split batch producing equal portions of a nut brown ale and a honey brown ale. The honey beer will be stronger than the parameters shown for this recipe (about 5.8%, finishing around FG 1.013).

Batch Size: 11 gallons (42 L)   **OG:** 1.044   **FG:** 1.011
Efficiency: 60%   **ABV:** 4.4%   **IBU:** 26   **SRM:** 23

Ingredients:

14 lb (4.5 kg)	UK Maris Otter (Crisp)	Mash
2.25 lb (1 kg)	German Munich (Durst)	Mash
1 lb (454 g)	German Vienna (Durst)	Mash
1 lb (454 g)	Carapils	Mash
10.5 oz (298 g)	Wheat malt (Durst)	Mash
2.25 lb (1 kg)	UK Dark Crystal 65 (Crisp)	*Vorlauf*
7 oz (198 g)	UK Chocolate (Fawcett)	*Vorlauf*
3.5 oz (99 g)	UK Roasted barley (Crisp)	*Vorlauf*
2 lb (907 g)	Honey	Fermenter 1
1.5 oz (43 g)	UK Challenger 7% pellets	@ 60
1 oz (28 g)	US Centennial 10.3% whole	@ 10
1 oz (28 g)	US Cascade 4.5% whole	@ 1
	Wyeast 1318 London Ale III yeast	

Water treatment: RO water treated with ¼ tsp 10% phosphoric acid per 5 gallons
2 tsp CaCl$_2$ in mash

Mash technique: Infusion, mashout, dark grains added at *vorlauf*, no sparge

Mash rests: 154°F (68°C) 60 minutes
168°F (76°C) 15 minutes

Kettle Volume: 13.5 gallons (51 L)

Boil Length: 90 minutes

Final Volume: 11 gallons (42 L)

Fermentation temp: 68°F (20°C)

Sensory Description: The brown ale is a bit of a throwback since it's similar to a Pete's Wicked Ale, which was basically an English Brown Ale with higher bitterness and classic citrusy finishing hops. The honey beer has a rounder flavor with more body and a sweeter finish with the honey being apparent (but not so much as to suggest a braggot).

Formulation notes: Run off equal amounts into two fermenters and ferment the same, until the *kräusen* begins to fall. Add the honey to one of the fermenters. Don't just dump cold honey in; warm it and stir in an equal volume of the fermenting beer so it combines well (try to avoid aerating it), and then mix the solution into the fermenter. I used Tupelo honey in this recipe, but I use that in most recipes because it tastes so good.

Variations: The quantity of honey is somewhat of a personal preference, so that's where I would experiment. Try varying the quantities and varieties of honey. You might find a match you like better. If you can get your hands on meadowfoam honey, that would pair well with this beer since it adds a vanilla and toasted marshmallow flavor.

AMERICAN AMBER ALE

This is a very broad style that is open to interpretation. It includes strong, hoppy, and bitter west coast red ales, as well as maltier, more caramel traditional examples. I think many of the red ales push into the red IPA territory, so I prefer to make mine a little less bitter. It's still a bitter beer, but it has much more malt to back it up and as a result feels more even.

Style: American Amber Ale (Classic BJCP Style)

Description: Chewy malt complexity with layers of caramel and dark fruit, with a firm bitterness, clean fermentation profile, and a fruity-citrusy hop aroma.

Batch Size: 6.5 gallons (25 L)	**OG:** 1.055	**FG:** 1.016
Efficiency: 70%　**ABV:** 5.2%	**IBU:** 35	**SRM:** 17

Ingredients:

4 lb (1.8 kg)	US two-row (Briess)	Mash
4 lb (1.8 kg)	German Vienna (Best)	Mash
2 lb (907 g)	UK Maris Otter (Crisp)	Mash
1 lb (454 g)	Belgian Aromatic (Dingemans)	Mash
8 oz (227 g)	Belgian Cara 20 (Dingemans)	*Vorlauf*

1.5 lb (680 g)	Belgian Cara 45 (Dingemans)	*Vorlauf*
8 oz (227 g)	CaraMunich III (Weyermann)	*Vorlauf*
4 oz (113 g)	Extra Dark Crystal (Crisp)	*Vorlauf*
2 oz (57 g)	Belgian Special B (Dingemans)	*Vorlauf*
1 oz (28 g)	UK Pale Chocolate (Crisp)	*Vorlauf*
1 oz (28 g)	US Amarillo 8.6% whole	FWH
1 oz (28 g)	US Amarillo 8.6% whole	@ 5
0.5 oz (14 g)	Australian Galaxy 13% pellets	@ 5
0.5 oz (14 g)	Australian Galaxy 13% pellets	@ +10
1 oz (28 g)	US Citra 13.4% whole	dry hop
1 oz (28 g)	US Centennial 10.3% whole	dry hop
	Wyeast 1272 American Ale II yeast	

Water treatment: RO water treated with ¼ tsp 10% phosphoric acid per 5 gallons
1 tsp $CaCl_2$ in mash

Mash technique: Infusion, mashout, dark grains and crystal malts added at *vorlauf*

Mash rests: 156°F (69°C) 60 minutes
168°F (76°C) 15 minutes

Kettle Volume: 8.5 gallons (32 L)

Boil Length: 90 minutes

Final Volume: 6.5 gallons (25 L)

Fermentation temp: 70°F (21°C)

Sensory Description: Toasty, bready base malt with layers of caramel and dark fruit. The finish is chewy and a touch malt sweetness, which enhances the fruity notes from the hops and takes the edge off the bitterness. The fermentation character is clean with a little fruitiness that goes well with the malt and hops.

Formulation notes: It's hard to make a bitter beer that has strong caramel and hop flavors since crystal malts tend to clash with American hop varieties. I prefer to go with the more fruity-tasting Belgian and German crystal malts and pair them with fruity-tasting New World hops. I add the crystal and darker malts during *vorlauf* to reduce harshness, and I use first wort hopping, hop bursting, and a hop stand to increase the hop character without the associated harshness. The hop stand gives it a higher bitterness than estimated.

Variations: You can turn this beer into a brown ale by adding some chocolate malt (not the pale chocolate malt), steeped along with the crystal. I'd use a good UK chocolate like Thomas Fawcett. Eliminating the crystal and darker malts and mashing lower would make a strong pale ale. Scaling the recipe up to around 7% would make an American strong ale, or if you keep going, a rich barleywine. If the crystal malts are too high for your taste, you can use less; I wouldn't try this much crystal malt with a more conventionally-hopped beer.

ATYPICAL ALTBIER

This recipe has an unusual story. In the 1990s, we couldn't get Zum Uerige or other German altbiers in the US, so we had to rely on descriptions we'd read about the style. One homebrewer visited the brewery and claimed to have talked to the brewmaster and gotten the recipe. He described a beer with 90% dark Munich and 10% Aromatic malt, which isn't anywhere close to the actual recipe. It does however make for a very unusual beer. I wouldn't enter this in a competition necessarily, but I love the intense flavors. The malt is like a black hole for hop bitterness; it doesn't seem anywhere near as bitter as calculated.

Style: Altbier (Classic BJCP Style)

Description: Supremely malty with a huge bitterness that is somewhat masked by the intense malt character.

Batch Size: 10.5 gallons (40 L)		**OG:** 1.054	**FG:** 1.012
Efficiency: 75%	**ABV:** 5.6%	**IBU:** 50	**SRM:** 11

Ingredients:

18 lb (8.2 kg)	German Dark Munich (Weyermann)	Mash
2.25 lb (1 kg)	Belgian Aromatic (Dingemans)	Mash
5 oz (142 g)	German Spalt 5.7% whole	@ 60
	Wyeast 1338 European Ale yeast	

Water treatment:	RO water treated with ¼ tsp 10% phosphoric acid per 5 gallons
	2 tsp $CaCl_2$ in mash
Mash technique:	Step Infusion, mashout
Mash rests:	131°F (55°C) 15 minutes
	145°F (63°C) 60 minutes
	155°F (68°C) 20 minutes
	168°F (76°C) 10 minutes
Kettle Volume:	13 gallons (49 L)
Boil Length:	90 minutes
Final Volume:	10.5 gallons (40 L)
Fermentation temp:	Start at 58°F (14°C), allowing to rise to 68°F (20°C) to finish and drop bright. Lager at 40°F (4°C) for 4 weeks, then 32°F (4°C) for 3–4 weeks.

Sensory Description: Very clean fermentation character. Extremely malty, with a richly bread crust flavor that dominates the palate. Apparent IBUs seem lower than calculated. Not necessarily a great *altbier* but an unusual beer with a ton of flavor.

Formulation notes: The malt and hops were very specific in the original recipe, but were eventually debunked when Zum Uerige became available in the US and the label specified the actual ingredients. Spalt hops are very traditional. If you're looking for a modern, authentic *altbier*, try the next recipe. This one is strictly an experimental beer, but it tastes so unusual that it's worth trying. Note that several maltsters make dark Munich malt, but flavors can vary widely. You don't want a *very* dark one, since that will have a much different flavor. I'd stick with the Weyermann Munich II.

Variations: Try scaling it up to make a *doppelsticke*-like beer, which is like a German barleywine. Try for something at about 8.5% ABV with a similar OG and IBU balance.

CLASSIC ALTBIER

I owe the makeup of this recipe to my good friend Keith Kost, a great brewer and fierce competitor who brews a terrific alt. This recipe has won awards at a number of competitions, and Keith often names it, "In Third Place with an Altbier is Keith Kost" to be confusing when awards are announced. I judged this beer for a BJCP exam in Pittsburgh, and I wondered how they managed to get a fresh example of Zum Uerige. Really, it's that good.

Style: Altbier (Classic BJCP Style)

Description: Rich, grainy, bready malt with strong bitterness and clean lager smoothness. The intensity of the malt allows for a high level of bitterness without seeming like an aggressively bitter beer. The dryness and malty flavors make it quite drinkable, which sets it apart from aggressive malty/hoppy beers like American Strong Ales that may appear superficially similar. That's the German secret; well-attenuated, smooth beers are highly drinkable.

Batch Size: 11 gallons (42 L)	**OG:** 1.051	**FG:** 1.012
Efficiency: 75% **ABV:** 5.1%	**IBU:** 53	**SRM:** 16

Ingredients:

11 lb (5 kg)	German Pilsner (Weyermann)	Mash
7 lb (3.2 kg)	German Munich (Weyermann)	Mash
1 lb (454 g)	German Wheat malt (Durst)	Mash
8 oz (227 g)	CaraMunich III (Weyermann)	*Vorlauf*
6 oz (170 g)	Carafa III (Weyermann)	*Vorlauf*
3 oz (85 g)	German Perle 9.1% whole	@ 90
1 oz (28 g)	German Tettnang 3.9% pellets	@ 10
1 oz (28 g)	German Tettnang 3.9% pellets	@ 0
	White Labs WLP029 German Ale/Kölsch yeast	

Water treatment: RO water treated with ¼ tsp 10% phosphoric acid per 5 gallons
0.5 tsp $CaCl_2$ and 0.5 tsp $CaSO_4$ in mash

Mash technique: Decoction, mashout, crystal/dark malts added at *vorlauf*

Mash rests:	Mash in 144°F (62°C); hold for 20 minutes Pull 1/3 thick decoction; boil decoction 15 minutes, continuing to hold main mash Remix, hitting 154°F (68°C); hold for 45 minutes Pull thin portion of mash; boil decoction 10 minutes, continuing to hold main mash Remix, hitting 168°F (76°C); hold for 10 minutes
Kettle Volume:	14.5 gallons (55 L)
Boil Length:	90 minutes
Final Volume:	11 gallons (42 L)
Fermentation temp:	62°F (17°C) 3 days 68°F (20°C) 10 days or until finished 32°F (0°C) lager for two months

Sensory Description: The malt is bready, grainy, and rich, but the overall impression is smooth. The malt richness dries out in the finish and the flavor is clean. The bitterness is strong and noticeable, but the malt does a great job of balancing it. There is a light hop presence at the end that adds some character without being distracting. The color is a light copper, and the beer is very clear. The aftertaste goes on forever with the smooth, rich malt and hop bitterness lingering. Despite the stronger flavors, the attenuation and smoothness makes this very easy to drink. I visited Düsseldorf and tried the most famous examples to help update the BJCP Style Guidelines in 2008, and this beer easily fits in with those fresh examples.

Formulation notes: This makes a double batch: 10 gallons of finished beer suitable for two kegs (you can halve the recipe for a single keg batch). The classic German ingredients are pretty important for the style. Decoction mashing helps bring out the maltiness and smoothness of the beer. Lagering is important for smoothing out the finished beer. One month is the minimum lagering time, but two to three months is better. There is some IBU loss over time, so the beer is a little more aggressive in bitterness knowing that it will be served with some age. The *Kölsch* yeast can produce a little sulfur, but lagering helps reduce that somewhat.

Variations: If trying to mimic the water from Düsseldorf, add more CaSO$_4$ to the mash and reduce the IBUs. Other neutral, attenuative yeast strains would likely work as well. This beer would work as a bottom-fermenting lager using any clean German strain. I think this version would also be a good basis for the stronger *Sticke* alt variant (the "secret" alt brewed stronger and hoppier on special occasions); in that case, I'd scale the recipe up so that the ABV is around 6% and double the late hops.

5 | STRONG ALE RECIPES

"There is no strong beer. Only weak men."

—*Sign at the Anchor Brewing Company*

Like some homebrewers, I developed an early interest in brewing strong beer. Good commercial options weren't always easy to find, and when they were, they were prohibitively expensive. I thought it much better to brew my own and then cellar them to an age when I would enjoy them the most. This is a personal flavor preference, I think; I don't like my strong beers to have a boozy aspect to them, I prefer them to have a velvety maturity like a fine red Bordeaux.

Strong beers present their own challenges. Higher gravity means a bigger mash tun, or using extract, sometimes of unknown composition or age. It also means that you have to understand the limits of fermentation, and the special challenges a higher gravity environment presents to yeast (remember, in higher quantities, alcohol is toxic to yeast just like it is to humans).

Most problems with strong beers can be overcome by mashing for fermentability, not overdoing specialty malt additions, using oxygen, and pitching plenty of healthy yeast. I often repitch yeast from a moderate strength beer for a strong ale, or get a large pitch from a craft brewery.

At home, I have a few kegs set aside for my keeping beers—those higher-gravity brews that I want to bulk age for several years. When the kegs get low, I sometimes will rack to smaller containers (or buy more kegs). If you have the space, bottle-conditioning strong beers is more traditional, and works well. I have more cool storage space for kegs than bottles, so I tend to use kegs.

Whatever storage method you devise, I recommend that you have some way of keeping these big beers around for a while. They almost always taste better with age, and I'd hate for storage considerations (such as lack of availability of kegs or storage space for cases of bottles) to force these beers to be consumed too young. Vintage dating your big beers and keeping them around for special occasions is also fun for you and your beer loving friends.

One final thought: if you know you are going to be aging a strong beer for years before consuming it (such as making a special batch to commemorate a birthday or anniversary), consider increasing the amount of hops used in the recipe (compared to a batch you intend to consume sooner). The bitterness and hop character tends to fade over time, so go a little higher so that you get the right balance as it ages. There is no magic formula for this, unfortunately, as it involves too many variables. Another approach for extending the lifetime of a beer is to take the gueuze approach and blend some of an older batch with a newer batch, which can produce qualities difficult to create in a single batch of beer.

- **Old School Barleywine** – An American style barleywine loosely like Sierra Nevada Bigfoot. Big malt and big hops make this an aggressive style. I won an NHC silver medal with a beer based on this recipe in 2010; it was a blend of five year old beer with a little bit of one year old beer (to freshen the hop aromatics).
- **Belgian Barleywine** – There is no BJCP style for Belgian Barleywine; it's usually found in the Dark Strong Ale category or as a type of *Quad*. This is a concept beer inspired by the strong amber artisanal beer, Bush (Scaldis in the US).
- **English Dark Barleywine** – The classic English style, which favors darker beers. Uses fairly traditional English ingredients but no crystal malts.
- **English Gold Barleywine** – A modern development, golden barleywines are like the classic Thomas Hardy's Ale. However, that

beer hasn't been made since the late 1990s. They brought it back in the 2000s in a different brewery, but the beer wasn't the same. I use that classic beer's style parameters as inspiration this recipe.

- **Golden Promise Barleywine** – An experiment for me, I decided to push the limits of Golden Promise malt and see what I could brew. I guess I didn't reach those limits because I got a delicious English barleywine as a result. This is likely my new favorite, and not modeled after any commercial beer.

- **Nightstalker Barleywine** – My first barleywine, which lasted 14 years before it was finished. I must have learned good bottle filling and capping practices because it wasn't oxidized at all. Bottle-conditioned and stored in a proper cellar environment, it developed many additional layers of flavors and complexity as it aged.

- **Wheatwine** – What do you brew when you need to use up a sack of wheat malt? That's right, a barleywine-strength wheat beer.

- **Old Ale** – A pale, barleywine-style old ale made from pale malt and invert sugar only. Very well-suited to cask aging. Old ales don't have to be dark, and don't need dark fruit flavors. They just have to have to be at least moderately strong and capable of aging well.

- **Winter Warmer** – A moderately strong, dark, chewy beer suitable for shaking off the cold of winter without the power of a barleywine.

- **English Strong Ale** – A broad category covering those beers stronger than a big bitter but smaller than a barleywine. This version is a chestnut-colored strong ale with a powerful hop bite.

- **Malt Liquor** – There are many kinds of strong American beer, and the name *malt liquor* is quote often derided due to its perceived audience. Historically, *Stock Ale* is probably more accurate name, and these days I might try using the somewhat amusing *Imperial Cream Ale* as a description.

- **Strong Scotch Ale** – Also known as Wee Heavy, I provided a recipe for a higher alcohol beer of this style in *Brewing Better Beer*. This version is more modest in strength, which means it's ready to drink sooner. I've also been known to use it as a blending batch for making a braggot (a blend of mead and beer).

OLD SCHOOL BARLEYWINE

I won a silver medal at the 2010 NHC with a five-year old beer based on this recipe. I was using the general balance of Sierra Nevada Bigfoot as a template: a barleywine with a strong malty backbone and a big American hop nose. It's much better when it has several years on it (which is the same opinion I had of Bigfoot when I first started drinking them in the 1990s, even though recent vintages seem more ready to drink).

Style: American Barleywine (Classic BJCP Style)

Description: A classic American barleywine with big malt and big hops, requiring some age to balance. It's a deep amber color. The emphasis on malt is one of the major differentiators between this style and American double IPAs.

Batch Size: 5 gallons (19 L)   **OG:** 1.109   **FG:** 1.033
Efficiency: 70%   **ABV:** 10.2%   **IBU:** 95   **SRM:** 13

Ingredients:

12 lb (5.4 kg)	US two-row (Great Western)	Mash
6 lb (1.4 kg)	UK Maris Otter (Crisp)	Mash
8 oz (227 g)	Belgian Caravienne (Dingemans)	*Vorlauf*
8 oz (227 g)	US Crystal 40	*Vorlauf*
4 oz (113 g)	UK Crystal 65 (Crisp)	*Vorlauf*
2 oz (57 g)	US Crystal 120	*Vorlauf*
2 oz (57 g)	Belgian Special B (Dingemans)	*Vorlauf*
1 lb (454 g)	Orange blossom honey	Boil (@ 0)
1 oz (28 g)	US Cascade 6% whole	FWH
2 oz (67 g)	US Tomahawk 16.8% whole	@ 60
1 oz (28 g)	US Centennial 10.5% whole	@ 15
1 oz (28 g)	US Cascade 6% whole	@ 5
1 oz (28 g)	US Tomahawk 16.8% whole	@ 2
1 oz (28 g)	US Cascade 6% whole	@ 0
1 oz (28 g)	US Centennial 10.5% whole	@ 0
2 oz (57 g)	US Cascade 6% whole dry hop	
1 oz (28 g)	US Centennial 10.5% whole dry hop	
	Wyeast 1272 American Ale II yeast	

Water treatment:	RO water treated with ¼ tsp 10% phosphoric acid per 5 gallons
	2 tsp CaSO$_4$ and 1 tsp CaCl$_2$ in mash
Mash technique:	Infusion, mashout, crystal malts added at *vorlauf*
Mash rests:	152°F (65°C) 90 minutes
	168°F (76°C) 15 minutes
Kettle volume:	6.5 gallons (24 L)
Boil length:	75 minutes
Final volume:	5 gallons (19 L)
Fermentation temp:	68°F (20°C)

Sensory description: Full body with a strong hop character throughout. The late hops are bright and citrusy. Complex bread and caramel base with a moderate fruitiness. Clean fermentation with a strong alcohol punch, this needs some age to let the alcohol and hops come back into balance.

Formulation notes: I don't like using all Maris Otter in American beers since it has such a strongly biscuit flavor, so I cut it with two-row. The crystal malts add complexity. This beer is designed to age so the hops may seem out of balance when it's young (just as the alcohol may seem too forward).

Variations: You can adjust the recipe to try to make it servable at a younger age, but I like the flavors of this kind of beer when it gets several years on it. If you feel that the hops have lost too much over time, blend in some of a newer batch.

BELGIAN BARLEYWINE

I visited the Debuisson brewery in Belgium in 2006, and really enjoyed their Bush beer. Loosely modeled on English barleywines, the Belgium inspired variant is unique. It can get lumped in with Belgian Dark Strong ales, but this doesn't have the strong yeast character of those beers. It's a malt-driven beer primarily, and fairly well attenuated.

Style: Clone Beer (New BJCP Style)

Description: A dry and malty Belgian interpretation of a barleywine. Limited late hopping allows for some yeast character, but it's mostly malt-driven.

Batch Size: 6.5 gallons (25 L)   **OG:** 1.108   **FG:** 1.023
Efficiency: 50%   **ABV:** 11.5%   **IBU:** 44   **SRM:** 17

Ingredients:

18 lb (8.2 kg)	Belgian pale ale (Dingemans)	Mash
2 lb (907 g)	Belgian pils malt (Dingemans)	Mash
3 lb (1.4 kg)	Belgian aromatic (Dingemans)	Mash
8 oz (227 g)	Belgian biscuit malt (Dingemans)	Mash
1 lb (454 g)	Belgian CaraMunich (Dingemans)	*Vorlauf*
12 oz (680 g)	Belgian CaraVienne (Dingemans)	*Vorlauf*
4 oz (113 g)	Belgian Crystal 45 (Dingemans)	*Vorlauf*
2 oz (57 g)	Belgian Special B (Dingemans)	*Vorlauf*
5 lb (2.3 kg)	White beet sugar	Boil
1.25 oz (28 g)	US Tomahawk 16.8% whole	@ 60
0.5 oz (14 g)	Czech Saaz 3% whole	@ 15
0.5 oz (14 g)	Czech Saaz 3% whole	@ 5
	White Labs WLP515 Antwerp Ale yeast	

Water treatment: RO water treated with ¼ tsp 10% phosphoric acid per 5 gallons
1 tsp CaCl$_2$ in mash

Mash technique: Infusion, mashout, crystal malts added at *vorlauf*, no sparge

Mash rests: 152°F (65°C) 60 minutes 168°F (76°C) 15 minutes

Kettle volume: 9 gallons (34 L)

Boil length: 90 minutes

Final volume: 6.5 gallons (25 L)

Fermentation temp: 72°F (22°C)

Sensory description: Malty clean base with an intense richness and restrained caramel. Dry finish, warming, with a light hop character. The yeast profile is fairly clean with just a little bit of Belgian character; don't expect a massive Trappist-like yeast profile.

Formulation notes: My starting concept was a scaled-up Belgian pale ale recipe. I think I used the Pils malt because I ran out of pale; either would work as a base malt. The bittering hops can be anything. I picked what I had on hand that had a high AA%. If I went out to buy hops, I'd probably go for something like Magnum to keep the bitterness even. The Antwerp yeast is fairly clean. The sugar is a must in order to get the attenuation. You can play around with the character malts as well; I was using up small bits of malt with this recipe, so that's why I used so many. Notice the low efficiency because of no sparge, and also note the volume reduction (this beer need a very vigorous boil).

Variations: A good beer to try aging on wood; Debuisson also makes Bush Prestige, which is barrel aged. If you're trying to match the Bush beer closely, lighten up the color; this is darker than their beer (deep copper rather than deep amber). As with most Belgian beers, you can change the character significantly using different yeast. Try Wyeast 1762 Abbey II yeast, White Labs WLP510 Bastogne yeast, or Wyeast 3522 Belgian Ardennes yeast and compare the differences. The beer would probably do well with the Wyeast 1388 Belgian Strong Ale yeast that can bring some apple and pear esters. An attenuative English yeast strain such as Wyeast 1028 London Ale yeast could also be used, particularly if you want to rely mostly on the malt flavors to carry the beer. If you want to make it darker and bring in additional flavors, try substituting Belgian candi syrups or even Lyle's Golden Syrup for some of the white sugar.

ENGLISH DARK BARLEYWINE

A classic English barleywine with a relatively simple grist, but no crystal malt. This beer is like scaled-up pale ale with some dark malt for color adjustment. Not excessively strong, so it should be ready to drink before other, bigger beers. The dark malts add to the stability of the beer, so it ages well.

Style: English Barleywine (Classic BJCP Style)

Description: A straight-forward copper-colored English barleywine that hits the center of the style range, is well-balanced, and features a bready malt flavor with a floral and orange-like hop profile.

Batch Size: 6.5 gallons (25 L)   **OG:** 1.096   **FG:** 1.024
Efficiency: 70%   **ABV:** 9.7%   **IBU:** 52   **SRM:** 17

Ingredients:

20 lb (9.1 kg)	UK Pearl malt (Fawcett)	Mash
1 lb (454 g)	UK Amber malt (Fawcett)	Mash
3 lb (1.4 kg)	Flaked maize	Mash
4 oz (113 g)	Debittered black malt (Dingemans)	*Vorlauf*
1.5 oz (43 g)	UK Goldings 5.5% whole	FWH
1.5 oz (43 g)	UK Challenger 8.2% pellets	@ 60
1 oz (28 g)	Styrian Goldings 4.5% whole	@ 10
2 oz (57 g)	Styrian Goldings 4.5% whole	@ 0
	Wyeast 1028 English Ale yeast	

Water treatment: RO water treated with ¼ tsp 10% phosphoric acid per 5 gallons
1 tsp CaCl$_2$ in mash

Mash technique: Infusion, mashout, dark malt added at *vorlauf*

Mash rests: 149°F (65°C) 60 minutes
168°F (76°C) 15 minutes

Kettle volume: 8.5 gallons (32 L)

Boil length: 90 minutes

Final volume: 6.5 gallons (25 L)

Fermentation temp: 68°F (20°C)

Sensory description: Bready-rich malt base with restrained biscuit flavors, crackery, toast dryness, and a rounded mouthfeel. Floral hop flavor and moderate bitterness with a spicy, orange marmalade-like aroma. Alcohol is noticeable but not intense, and the beer finishes fairly dry with malty but not sweet flavors.

Formulation notes: The base malt variety should be English pale ale type, but try to use something other than Maris Otter (other choices are Pipkin or Halcyon). You are looking for something that still has richness, but is less biscuity than Maris Otter. The amber malt supplies a dry, toasted flavor, while the flaked corn brings some roundness to the mouthfeel. The black malt is for color adjustment and should not add much flavor. Traditional hops and yeast are used; both can be swapped according to personal preferences.

Variations: The amber malt may not be to everyone's liking, as it has a dry, crackery kind of flavor. Substituting a mid-range crystal malt (like a Crystal 55) would give it some caramel notes instead. However, barley-wines usually have plenty of malty richness from their gravity alone. The hops added at knockout could be used as dry hops instead.

ENGLISH GOLD BARLEYWINE

While I prefer dark English barleywines, I've had some tasty golden versions. If you're going to try to make a gold barleywine, there really is only one (ahem) gold standard reference beer: the classic Thomas Hardy's Ale. I tend to not enter this beer in homebrew competitions because most judges expect a darker beer for the style with more specialty malt character. Save this one just for your own enjoyment. Try one on your birthday every year to see how well it is aging. Note that this one takes a large mash tun; it's a real cereal killer.

Style: English Barleywine (Classic BJCP Style)

Description: Uses the style parameters of the original Thomas Hardy's Ale as a starting point and uses mostly traditional English ingredients to create a strong barleywine suitable for long aging. A strong, pale English barleywine without any specialty malts, but suitable for long aging.

Batch Size: 5.25 gallons (20 L)	**OG:** 1.125	**FG:** 1.034
Efficiency: 57% **ABV:** 12.3%	**IBU:** 58	**SRM:** 11

Ingredients:

31 lb (14.1 kg)	UK Maris Otter (Crisp)	Mash
1.5 oz (43 g)	UK Challenger 8.3% pellets	@ 60
1 oz (28 g)	UK Challenger 8.3% pellets	@ 30

1 oz (28 g)	UK Fuggles 4.5% whole	@ 10
1 oz (28 g)	US Crystal 3.2% whole	@ 10
0.5 oz (14 g)	UK Goldings 6% whole	dry hop
0.5 oz (14 g)	German Hallertauer 3% whole	dry hop
	Wyeast 1028 London Ale yeast	

Water treatment:	RO water treated with ¼ tsp 10% phosphoric acid per 5 gallons
	1 tsp CaCl$_2$ and 1 tsp CaSO$_4$ in mash
Mash technique:	Infusion, mashout, no sparge
Mash rests:	149°F (65°C) 90 minutes
	168°F (76°C) 15 minutes
Kettle volume:	8 gallons (30 L)
Boil length:	120 minutes
Final volume:	5.25 gallons (20 L)
Fermentation temp:	68°F (20°C)

Sensory description: Deep gold color. Rich, bready malt aroma and flavor with significant bitterness and a pleasant hop aroma. Quite strong; needs to be aged. More esters develop as it ages.

Formulation notes: I was trying to match the general parameters of Thomas Hardy's Ale but used ingredients that are more commonly available. I'm using some German hops for their fine floral aromatics, which I think helps the overall impression of this beer.

Variations: There are published versions of the actual original recipe online,[1] as well as tips on late era batches (such as using Pipkin malt as the base, with Challenger, Northdown, and Styrian Goldings hops). One ingredient that wasn't available when I formulated this recipe was the yeast, which can now be purchased as the White Labs WLP099 Super High Gravity yeast. Thomas Hardy's Ale had a slightly darker color than my recipe, so if you don't get enough color through the boil, you can add a touch of dark malt in *vorlauf* (that will also help its stability over time). The other parameters of my recipe match late era formulations. Additional special ingredients (such as medium to dark crystal, chocolate malt, extra dark crystal, darker brewing sugars) can add some more color and flavor, but will make a different kind of barleywine.

---

[1] http://barclayperkins.blogspot.com/2013/03/lets-brew-wednesday-eldridge-pope-1967.html

GOLDEN PROMISE BARLEYWINE

After I started testing new recipes with Golden Promise malt, I found myself wondering how far I could push its limits. Could I make a barleywine with only Golden Promise? How would it taste? Delicious, as it turns out. I think this may be my new favorite English barleywine.

Style: English Barleywine (Classic BJCP Style)

Description: A very flavorful English barleywine showcasing the Golden Promise malt, which has a clean bready-malty flavor, accentuated with specialty malts to give hints of caramel, toast, and dark fruit. A wintertime sipper.

Batch Size: 6.25 gallons (24 L)	**OG:** 1.098	**FG:** 1.025
Efficiency: 60%	**ABV:** 9.9%	**IBU:** 36	**SRM:** 20

Ingredients:

25 lb (11.3 kg)	UK Golden Promise (Simpsons)	Mash
2 lb (907 g)	Torrified wheat	Mash
1 lb (454 g)	UK Crystal 45 (Crisp)	*Vorlauf*
12 oz (340 g)	UK Dark Crystal 135 (Hugh Baird)	*Vorlauf*
3 oz (85 g)	UK Pale Chocolate (Crisp)	*Vorlauf*
2 oz (57 g)	UK Challenger 7.2% pellets	@ 60
	Wyeast 1968 London ESB Ale yeast	

Water treatment:	RO water treated with ¼ tsp 10% phosphoric acid per 5 gallons 1 tsp CaCl$_2$ in mash
Mash technique:	Infusion, mashout, dark grains and crystal malts added at *vorlauf*
Mash rests:	149°F (65°C) 60 minutes 168°F (76°C) 15 minutes
Kettle volume:	9 gallons (34 L)
Boil length:	120 minutes
Final volume:	6.25 gallons (24 L)
Fermentation temp:	68°F (20°C)

Sensory description: Reddish-copper color. Malt, fruit, sweet, and caramel aromas. Medium bitterness lets the malt come through strongly. The esters are more like cherries and plums, not dried fruit (at least when young). Caramel and toast flavors from the specialty malts. Thick, chewy, but fully fermented. Finishes malty with some residual sweetness.

Formulation notes: It's all about the Golden Promise malt, so don't substitute. Hops can be anything, really. I picked the 1968 yeast because of its fruity profile, so try that one first. The pale chocolate malt is for color adjustment only. The boil is quite hard, trying to develop additional complex Maillard reaction flavors in the kettle. I used yeast nutrient and Whirlfloc in this beer to encourage a healthy fermentation and to clarify the beer. Abundant oxygen is helpful to keep the yeast healthy and active, as is a very large starter. This yeast can drop out early, so be sure to measure the final gravity and take a tasting; it might need to be roused and/or warmed up near the end of fermentation.

Variations: The bittering hops can be increased and still be well within the style; I would tend to do that if it seems a bit on the sweet side for your palate. I've found that big beers with residual sweetness can continue to slowly attenuate over time if they are conditioned on the yeast. I think this beer is a good candidate for aging in an oak cask, since the tannins from the wood would help balance the malt and provide some dryness, while any toasty, vanilla characteristics from the wood would be welcome. I'd use medium toast Hungarian or French oak. Aging in a barrel that held distilled spirits is also a possibility but I'd hate to overshadow the delicious malt.

NIGHTSTALKER BARLEYWINE

This recipe is a hybrid between English and American barleywine styles. It has the bitterness of an American barleywine, but with English variety finishing hops. I like more even-keel English hops more than the resiny and citrusy American varieties that are often used. I think the balance of this beer is somewhat reminiscent of Anchor Brewing's Old Foghorn. I drink this beer in a Riedel crystal wine glass in cold weather. My experience is that it ages beautifully, and is a good candidate for vintage-dating.

Style: American Barleywine (Classic BJCP Style)

Description: A hybrid barleywine, uses mostly English ingredients but is balanced and bittered like an American barleywine.

Batch Size: 5 gallons (19 L)   **OG:** 1.101   **FG:** 1.028
Efficiency: 75%   **ABV:** 9.8%   **IBU:** 69   **SRM:** 16

Ingredients:

14 lb (6.4 kg)	UK Maris Otter (Crisp)	Mash
8 oz (227 g)	Belgian Aromatic (Dingemans)	Mash
8 oz (227 g)	Carapils	Mash
1 lb (454 g)	UK Crystal 65 (Crisp)	*Vorlauf*
8 oz (227 g)	CaraMunich III (Weyermann)	*Vorlauf*
1 lb (454 g)	Light brown sugar	Boil
1 oz (28 g)	German Magnum 14.2% pellets	@ 60
1 oz (28 g)	UK Challenger 8.5% pellets	@ 30
1 oz (28 g)	UK Fuggles 4.5% whole	@ 10
1 oz (28 g)	US Willamette 4.5% whole	@ 5
2 oz (57 g)	UK Goldings 6% pellets	@ 0
2 oz (57 g)	Styrian Goldings 4.5% whole	dry hop
	Wyeast 1318 London III yeast	

Water treatment: RO water treated with ¼ tsp 10% phosphoric acid per 5 gallons
1 tsp CaSO$_4$ in mash

Mash technique: Infusion, mashout, dark grains added at *vorlauf*

Mash rests: 152°F (67°C) 60 minutes
168°F (76°C) 15 minutes

Kettle volume: 6.5 gallons (25 L)

Boil length: 90 minutes

Final volume: 5 gallons (19 L)

Fermentation temp: 68°F (20°C)

Sensory description: Lovely reddish-copper color, clear, yet with a certain impression of depth, as if looking through a gemstone. Layers of dark and dried fruit, plus earthy and floral hops with a slight orange marmalade character. Quite bitter and malty when young, but the beer ages and balances well, with layered textures and flavors.

Formulation notes: English flavors and American balance work well in this beer. The crystal malts provide some sweetness and body, which will mellow over time. Any minimally-processed brown sugar works; just avoid the fake stuff that is white sugar with molasses added. Look in the organic section of the supermarket for unusual sugars. I bottle-conditioned this beer repitching Wyeast 1028 at bottling, relying on its higher attenuation to help dry out the beer and carbonate it as it aged.

Variations: I sometimes make an all-American hopped version of this beer, but I don't like to use piney or resiny varieties. I like to use Cascade late, sometimes with some Centennial thrown in. I've yet to make it with my favorite New World hop varieties, but I think the ones with tropical fruit or stone fruit characteristics would work well with the malt.

WHEATWINE

Wheatwine is much more than just a barleywine made with wheat. Stan Hieronymus's Brewing with Wheat provides good background on the style and recipe. I used some of this suggestions when formulating this recipe. I had an open sack of wheat malt that I wanted to use up, and this recipe takes a lot of it.

Style: Wheatwine (New BJCP Style)

Description: A full-bodied, dry, wine-like beer with a large fruity component and considerable wheat flavor. Strong and relatively bitter, this beer ages like a good wine.

Batch Size:	6.5 gallons (25 L)	OG: 1.104	FG: 1.018
Efficiency: 70%	ABV: 11.6%	IBU: 51	SRM: 10

Ingredients:

14 lb (6.4 kg)	German wheat malt (Durst)	Mash
3 lb (1.4 kg)	Euro Pils malt (Dingemans)	Mash

3 lb (1.4 kg)	UK Golden Promise (Simpsons)	Mash
1 lb (454 g)	Flaked wheat	Mash
1 lb (454 g)	Honey malt (Gambrinus)	Mash
1 lb (454 g)	Carawheat 60 (Weyermann)	Mash
1.5 lb (680 g)	White table sugar or corn sugar	Boil
1.3 oz(38 g)	German Magnum 14.4% pellets	@ 60
1 oz (28 g)	US Citra 13.4% pellets	@ 5
1 oz (28 g)	NZ Nelson Sauvin 12.5% pellets	@ 1
1 oz (28 g)	NZ Motueka 7.5% pellets @ 0, steep 45 minutes	
	White Labs WLP001 California Ale yeast	

Water treatment:	RO water treated with ¼ tsp 10% phosphoric acid per 5 gallons
	1 tsp $CaCl_2$ in mash
Mash technique:	Step mash, mashout
Mash rests:	104°F (40°C) 10 minutes
	131°F (55°C) 15 minutes
	146°F (63°C) 40 minutes
	158°F (70°C) 15 minutes
	168°F (76°C) 15 minutes
Kettle volume:	8.5 gallons (32 L)
Boil length:	90 minutes
Final volume:	6.5 gallons (25 L)
Fermentation temp:	66°F (19°C)

Sensory description: Deep amber color. Mild grainy, sweet honey aroma with apples, pears, and luscious ripe fruit like peaches and melons. The fruity component is huge; one of the highest ester levels of any beer I've done. Large grainy wheat flavor with medium to medium-high bitterness and noticeable alcohol. This beer needs to be aged to smooth out the alcohol. A clean fermentation profile, with a spicy, fruity, and herbal hoppy finish. Has a full body but is dry, and is chewy but not sweet. This is the kind of beer that should age well, as the grainy notes merge with the bitterness and dryness in the aftertaste and the alcohol and fruit smooth out over time.

Formulation notes: The varied grist provides some additional character. Any continental Pilsner malt would work, like German, Belgian, etc. Using additional forms of wheat to provide extra character seems more appropriate when you're trying to emphasize the wheat qualities of the beer. An intensive step mash helps create more attenuative wort and improves clarity. I was looking for some unusual hop aromatics, with tropical, lush fruit, and white grape notes, so I chose some New Zealand hops to match the fruity Citra. The honey malt adds to the fruit aromatics from the hops. Any clean bittering hop and yeast strain would work; I wouldn't want to bring any more fruit complexity to the mix since it's almost a fruit salad as is. The bitterness estimation doesn't include steeping hop contributions; the actual bitterness level might be higher.

Variations: The hops can be changed to suit your preference, both in terms of finishing hops and the overall level of bitterness Many of these types of beers are oak-aged when produced commercially; I can see how a toasty vanilla flavor from the wood would play well with this beer.

OLD ALE

This is an unusual old ale (to Americans, at least), made with pale malt and invert sugar, and then aged in an oak cask. Compare this recipe with the Throwback Mild recipe (Chapter 6) to what you can do with one malt and one type of sugar. This recipe is based on the Burton Bridge Thomas Sykes Old Ale, a barleywine-like old ale that is a wonderful cask beer and a personal favorite.

Style: Old Ale (Classic BJCP Style)

Description: An old ale designed for an oak cask, with bready malt and toffee sugar flavors that benefit from the tannic oak character that combines with the malt flavors when aging. Proves that not all old ales need to be dark.

Batch Size: 6.5 gallons (25 L)	OG: 1.093	FG: 1.020
Efficiency: 70% ABV: 10.0%	IBU: 50	SRM: 7

Ingredients:

18 lb (4.5 kg)	UK Maris Otter (Fawcett)	Mash
3 lb (1.4 kg)	Lyle's Golden Syrup	Boil
2 oz (57 g)	UK Target 10.5% whole	@ 60
1 oz (28 g)	UK First Gold 8% whole	@ 5
	Wyeast 1099 Whitbread Ale yeast or White Labs WLP017 Whitbread Ale yeast	

Water treatment:	RO water treated with ¼ tsp 10% phosphoric acid per 5 gallons
	1 tsp CaSO$_4$ in mash
Mash technique:	Infusion
Mash rests:	156°F (69°C) 90 minutes
Kettle volume:	9 gallons (34 L)
Boil length:	120 minutes
Final volume:	6.5 gallons (25 L)
Fermentation temp:	64°F (18°C), allowing to rise

Sensory description: Dark gold color, bright, thick and somewhat sweet, with flavors of toffee, vanilla, cream sherry, and honey. Would do well aged in a light to moderate toasted oak cask (Hungarian or French oak).

Formulation notes: A very simple but fairly traditional recipe, showing how much flavor can be derived from few ingredients. If you can't get this yeast, a good alternative is the Wyeast 1335 British II yeast. You want to use enough hops so that the beer doesn't seem too sweet, but avoid too much late hopping as that can get in the way of the oak character. The toffee qualities of the sugar can be melded with the toasty vanilla flavors from the oak, and the tannins from the wood act provide balance and increase dryness in a somewhat malty beer. After the beer comes off the wood, it may need to continue to age to smooth out the tannins from the wood.

Variations: According to the brewery, Thomas Sykes old ale uses only Target hops, so if you are trying to match that beer, stick with the single hop variety. This beer can be served unaged, aged, or aged in an oak cask (or with other suitable oak products, like chips). Playing with different types of wood (sources, forms, toast levels, durations) can be a fun split-batch experiment. I would avoid adding too many other ingredients because you'll miss the main point of seeing how the oak interacts with the base beer. Once you have a combination you like, you can start varying that base beer with additional ingredients. Since many British beers use pale malt and brewer's sugar, this beer can be a template for experimentation with different sugars. You could brew a Burton-like beer by raising the mash temperature to 158°F (70°C), using invert #3 as the sugar, and increasing the bittering hops by 50% or more. Or use a completely different type of sugar (like honey) or flaked maize.

WINTER WARMER

I debated whether to categorize this as a strong beer or an experimental beer; it could go in either place. It's a dark, chewy beer for the cold of winter, but derived some of the dark flavors from Belgian candi syrup. The dark fruit, dried fruit, toffee, dark chocolate and rich sugar flavors from the extra dark candi syrup are all welcome in this style.

Style: British Strong Ale (New BJCP Style, Experimental)

Description: A darker, malty, sweet, and rich beer with a full body and warming alcohol. Has a deep flavor from the Belgian candi syrup.

Batch Size: 6.5 gallons (25 L)		**OG:** 1.060	**FG:** 1.015
Efficiency: 70%	**ABV:** 5.9%	**IBU:** 27	**SRM:** 20

Ingredients:

5 lb (2.3 kg)	UK Maris Otter (Fawcett)	Mash
5 lb (2.3 kg)	UK Mild Ale malt (Pauls)	Mash
1 lb (454 g)	German Munich (Best)	Mash
1 lb (454 g)	Flaked Maize	Mash
2 lb (907 g)	UK Crystal 80 (Crisp)	*Vorlauf*
1 lb (454 g)	D-2 dark candi syrup (darkcandi.com)	Boil
1 oz (28 g)	UK Challenger 7% pellets	@ 60
1 oz (28 g)	UK Goldings 5.5% whole	@ 10
1 oz (28 g)	Styrian Goldings 4.5% whole	@ 0
	Wyeast 1968 London ESB yeast	

Water treatment:	RO water treated with ¼ tsp 10% phosphoric acid per 5 gallons
	1 tsp CaCl₂ in mash
Mash technique:	Infusion, mashout, dark grains added at *vorlauf*
Mash rests:	151°F (66°C) 60 minutes
	170°F (77°C) 15 minutes
Kettle volume:	8.5 gallons (32 L)
Boil length:	90 minutes
Final volume:	6.5 gallons (25 L)
Fermentation temp:	68°F (20°C)

Sensory description: Chewy, somewhat rich and sweet, with deep, dark fruit flavors and lightly warming alcohol. The bitterness is subdued given the level of sweetness and malt flavors. The hops can give some complementary floral and fruity notes as well.

Formulation notes: I'm using a blend of Maris Otter and mild ale malts to get some extra dextrins while still retaining bready notes. The Munich is for extra maltiness, and the flaked maize adds a rounded character. The dark crystal brings caramel and fruity flavors, along with dextrins, and the candi syrup adds complexity through dark sugar and fruit flavors. Since the crystal malt and mild malts are adding dextrins, I mash low so that it isn't excessively full-bodied. I like to use fruity English ale yeast, or one that emphasizes malt flavors, avoiding overly dry and minerally yeasts. Getting some residual sweetness is fine, since it enhances the chewy body and cold-weather sipping nature of the beer.

Variations: If you want a stronger beer, try increasing the amount of candi syrup. Trying different kinds of dark sugars (such as invert #3 or other brands of dark candi syrup) can give bring out different flavors, and might be an educational side-by-side experiment. This could serve as the base for a spiced beer, using the flavors of English Christmas pudding, or similar desserts to take the beer in another direction. Adding extra dark crystal malts or malts such as Special B that bring a raisiny flavor can work well, as can adding some of the dark crystal malts that have dark and/or dried fruit flavors, such as plums.

ENGLISH STRONG ALE

This style is a grab-bag of fairly strong traditional English styles, along with modern variations that don't fit elsewhere. It's mostly a gravity classification for beers that are bigger than the strongest everyday beers and weaker than barleywines. This is a sizeable beer, in the vein of Fuller's 1845, Fuller's Vintage Ale, and Young's Winter Welcome, although not a clone of any of them.

Style: British Strong Ale (New BJCP Style)

Description: This beer is big in both malt and hops, with moderate body and a full finish. It has a bready, toasty malt flavor, is somewhat fruity, and has a fairly strong traditional English hop character.

Batch Size: 6.5 gallons (25 L)   **OG:** 1.079   **FG:** 1.019
Efficiency: 70%   **ABV:** 8.1%   **IBU:** 40   **SRM:** 16

Ingredients:

15 lb (6.8 kg)	UK Maris Otter (Crisp)	Mash
2 lb (907 g)	German Munich (Best)	Mash
1 lb (454 g)	UK Amber malt (Crisp)	Mash
1 lb (454 g)	Belgian CaraVienne (Dingemans)	*Vorlauf*
1 lb (454 g)	UK Crystal 65 (Crisp)	*Vorlauf*
1 oz (28 g)	UK Chocolate malt (Crisp)	*Vorlauf*
1 oz (28 g)	UK Northdown 8% pellets	@ 60
0.5 oz (14 g)	UK Target 10.5% whole	@ 30
1.5 oz (43 g)	UK Bramling Cross 6% whole	@ 10
1 oz (28 g)	UK Goldings 5.5% pellets	@ 1
1 oz (28 g)	UK Northdown 8% pellets	@ 1
	Wyeast 1335 British Ale II yeast	

Water treatment: RO water treated with ¼ tsp 10% phosphoric acid per 5 gallons
1 tsp $CaSO_4$ in mash

Mash technique: Infusion, mashout, dark grains added at *vorlauf*

Mash rests: 154°F (68°C) 60 minutes
170°F (77°C) 15 minutes

Kettle volume:	8.5 gallons (32 L)
Boil length:	90 minutes
Final volume:	6.5 gallons (25 L)
Fermentation temp:	68°F (20°C)

Sensory description: Bready, toasty base malt with dark caramel and deep fruit flavors. Strong bitterness and alcohol balance the malt, and allow for a long, complex aftertaste showing bready, toasty, caramelly malt with a floral, earthy hop and somewhat fruity yeast character.

Formulation notes: Traditional grist, mostly, except for the extra malt pop from the Munich malt. Maris Otter and amber malt carry most of the flavor, while the crystal adds some complexity. The yeast is balanced, allowing the hops to come through with floral, earthy, and herbal notes. The gypsum adds to the dryness.

Variations: The beer can be scaled down to around 6% to make it more accessible but still fit within the style. A variety of hops and character malts can be used to adjust the balance and flavor. The yeast is balanced but a strain that emphasizes another desirable character (fruity, malty, minerally, etc.) could also be used.

MALT LIQUOR

In the 2000s, there was a brief surge of craft-produced malt liquors. At the 2008 AHA Conference, one of the commemorative beers was called an Imperial Cream Ale. I remember tasting something similar at the 2004 conference in Las Vegas, when Bob Kauffman shared a beer he called a Stock Ale (a stronger beer designed for aging). These are all describing the same type of beer: something pale and strong with adjuncts. This version is based on Bob's example and is more in line with the craft versions or historical beers, not the headache-inducing, cheap stuff sold in 40 oz cans.

Style: American Strong Ale (New BJCP Style)

Description: Think of it as a heavily-hopped Imperial Cream Ale that is designed to be aged.

Batch Size: 6.5 gallons (25 L) **OG:** 1.076 **FG:** 1.014
Efficiency: 70% **ABV:** 8.2% **IBU:** 64 **SRM:** 6

Ingredients:

14 lb (6.4 kg)	US two-row (Briess)	Mash
4 lb (1.8 kg)	Flaked maize	Mash
2 oz (57 g)	UK Pale Chocolate (Crisp)	*Vorlauf*
1 lb (454 g)	White table sugar or corn sugar	Boil
1 oz (28 g)	UK Fuggles 4.5% whole	FWH
2 oz (57 g)	US Cluster 7.5% whole	@ 60
1 oz (28 g)	UK Fuggles 4.5% whole	@ 30
1 oz (28 g)	UK Goldings 5.5% whole	@ 15
2 oz (57 g)	UK Goldings 5.5% whole	dry hop
	Wyeast 1056 American Ale yeast	

Water treatment: RO water treated with ¼ tsp 10% phosphoric acid per 5 gallons
1 tsp CaCl₂ in mash

Mash technique: Step mash, mashout, dark grains added at *vorlauf*

Mash rests: 122°F (50°C) 5 minutes
146°F (63°C) 30 minutes
156°F (69°C) 30 minutes
170°F (77°C) 15 minutes

Kettle volume: 8.5 gallons (32 L)
Boil length: 90 minutes
Final volume: 6.5 gallons (25 L)
Fermentation temp: 68°F (20°C)

Sensory description: A strong beer with significant flavor; the corn gives it a rounded flavor but the big bitterness demands respect. English finishing hops give it a pleasant floral aroma.

Formulation notes: The basic recipe is very similar to a cream ale, just brewed to a higher gravity. The dark malt is only for color adjustment, and shouldn't add flavor. Cold conditioning or lagering the beer would improve it, but it can also just be cellared for a long time. I'd wait at least 6 months before trying this.

Variations: If you're up for it, you can switch the flaked maize out for corn grits and perform a cereal mash. Bob's original recipe also used Cluster hops as a FWH addition, but I'm not a fan of their kind of catty and black currant flavor.

SARA BONNYMAN'S ALE

This beer is named after my late maternal grandmother, who taught me an appreciation of all things Scottish. I think she would have liked this beer. It's a classic, strong Scotch ale that I like to serve as is, or sometimes blend with tupelo mead to make a killer braggot or a complex honey beer.

Style: Wee Heavy (Classic BJCP Style)

Description: Strongly malty with restrained bitterness and moderately strong alcohol. A malt-bomb, but still very drinkable.

Batch Size: 6.5 gallons (25 L)	**OG:** 1.087	**FG:** 1.024
Efficiency: 60%　**ABV:** 8.5%	**IBU:** 35	**SRM:** 24

Ingredients:

25 lb (11.3 kg)	UK Golden Promise (Simpsons)	Mash
8 oz (340 g)	UK Roasted Barley	*Vorlauf*
2 oz (57 g)	UK Goldings 5.5% whole	@ 60
1 oz (28 g)	UK Goldings 5.5% whole	@ 30
	Wyeast 1728 Scottish Ale yeast	

Water treatment: RO water treated with ¼ tsp 10% phosphoric acid per 5 gallons
1 tsp $CaCl_2$ in mash

Mash technique:	Infusion, mashout, dark grains added at *vorlauf*, no sparge
Mash rests:	158°F (70°C) 90 minutes
	170°F (77°C) 15 minutes
Kettle volume:	8.5 gallons (30 L)
Boil length:	60 minutes
Final volume:	6.5 gallons (25 L)
Fermentation temp:	59°F (15°C)

Sensory description: Toast and caramel rich malt flavor, full body, warming alcohol with a hint of dryness in the finish. Deep mahogany color. The malt dominates the palate and lasts through the finish, with just enough hops to keep it from being cloying.

Formulation notes: Traditional grist without caramel malts. Classic hops and yeast. Use a no sparge method to get a higher quality malt flavor at the expense of mash efficiency. I use a somewhat thick mash, and then add more water during *vorlauf* while not actually sparging. Turn on the flame under the kettle right before run off so that you caramelize some of the first runnings. I normally run off slowly and rock the kettle (like you swirl wine in a glass) to let more of the new first runnings hit the hot kettle bottom.

Variations: The kettle caramelization isn't as strong as some methods I've used in the past,(like boiling down the first 1 gallon (4 L) of first runnings to 1 quart (1 L)). That process can produce some diacetyl flavors that will taste like butterscotch, and I'm only going for a light scorching of sugars. It shouldn't taste burnt, just a bit caramelly. You can skip this step and add crystal malt if you like, but it will have more of a sugary, sweet flavor. You can use the boiling down method too, b make sure that you hear some sizzling when the sugary wort hits the pan. Use a pot or pan with a large surface area and a heavy bottom. As I described in the introduction, I like to blend this with tupelo mead to make a braggot. The proportions of the two in a blend are not set in stone; try several small glass samples with varying proportions of mead to beer, then pick the one that tastes the best to you, scaling it up to the amount you want to produce. It can also take a little vanilla, and might do well with a short trip through a Scotch whiskey barrel.

6 | DARK BEER RECIPES

"Weather forecast for tonight: dark."

—*George Carlin, comedian*

When judging in competition, I often ask not to judge dark beers because I got tired of the harshness and astringency in many of the beers. That desire to avoid that harshness is what led me to the technique of adding the dark grains during *vorlauf* instead of during the mash. After all, dark grain or malt doesn't really need to be mashed; it's just being steeped to release color and flavor. Keeping the grain material in contact with hot water for an extended period of time doesn't add any value, but can add astringency to the beer unless handled carefully.

The beers grouped in this section could have been listed with the everyday beers, strong ales, and in other places. However, since they all tend to share that same technique for handling dark grain, I grouped them together. I think it helps illustrate how the late dark grain addition technique is best used.

- **Irish Stout** – There is more to Irish stout than Guinness. While a great beer, it's also ubiquitous. Some of the other Irish stouts like Beamish, Murphy's, and (my favorite) O'Hara's use a different grist with more complexity. While I could make a simple Guinness clone, I prefer the layered flavors and slightly lower bitterness of the other brands.

- **Dark Mild** – Dark mild has long been a favorite style of mine. I took a trip to the UK in 1998 with the primary purpose of investigating this style. Since then I've been investigating all the variations. Some people collect stamps; I collect mild recipes. I'm including five of my favorites to show the wide range of the style: Simplicity Mild, Complexity Mild, NHC Mild, GABF Mild and Cask Mild.

- **Throwback Mild** – Would you believe a beer with 25% crystal malt would taste good? It does if you use the right malts in conjunction. This is a historical beer you can still find today if you look hard, or if you are visiting Birmingham, England.

- **Modern London Porter** – This is probably my favorite porter, reminiscent of a Fuller's London Porter. It relies on English brown malt; don't bother trying to make this beer without that it (it won't taste the same).

- **Robust English Porter** – Some people say that English porters use chocolate malt, stouts use roasted barley, and American porters use black malt. That's not true at all. Without diving into the history, this Robust Porter recipe is an English porter that uses traditional ingredients.

- **American Porter** – American versions of porter tend to be darker, stronger, and often have a more prominent roast character (at least in modern versions). I'm including two different versions that use different types of dark malts and grains to achieve that roast character.

- **American Brown Ale** – There are many different interpretations of this broad style. Many modern versions aren't overly bitter; those that are, start to push into the IPA territory. In my recipes, I go easy on the hops and choose varieties carefully so as to not clash with the malt.

- **Dunkelweizen** – One of my favorite flavor combinations is the caramel and slightly chocolate malt flavor along with the banana and spice of a *dunkelweizen*. Maybe it reminds me of a dessert, but I find that it has much more exciting than a hefeweizen.

- **Weizenbock** – If I like dunkelweizen, you can well imagine that I love *weizenbock*. All the same flavors but with more intensity.

I made a smoked version of this beer that took a gold medal at the 2008 NHC.

- **Danzig** – In *Brewing Better Beer*, I provided a recipe that was in the style of Carnegie Porter; this one is more like a Sinebrychoff Porter.
- **Jamaican Eclipse** – Dark, sweet, and strong, it's counterintuitive that this beer style would be popular in the hot weather of the Caribbean and other parts of the globe (but it is).
- **Imperial Stout** – Three different variations (Katherine the Strong Imperial Stout, Ferret and Trouer Ley Imperial Stout, and the Dirty Dozen) are presented, all with different goals. One of the broadest styles there is, I could have included a dozen different recipes and none would have been the same.

IRISH STOUT

Not all Irish Stout is like Guinness Draught. While it is certainly a classic, it's also fairly different than other stouts from Ireland. Most have more complexity to them than the simple pale malt, flaked barley, roasted barley recipe of Guinness. This recipe is more representative of some of the other versions.

Style: Irish Stout (Classic BJCP Style)

Description: More in the style of some of the stouts from Cork or Carlow than those from Dublin.

Batch size: 6.5 gallons (25 L)	**OG:** 1.046	**FG:** 1.013
Efficiency: 75%　**ABV:** 4.4%	**IBU:** 33	**SRM:** 39

Ingredients:

7.25 lb (2.3 kg)	UK Pale Ale malt	Mash
1.75 lb (794 g)	UK Flaked Barley	Mash
6 oz (170 g)	Carapils	Mash
12 oz (340 g)	UK Crystal 80	*Vorlauf*
12 oz (340 g)	UK Roasted Barley	*Vorlauf*
6 oz (170 g)	Debittered black malt	*Vorlauf*
1.3 oz (37 g)	UK challenger 8.5% pellets	@ 60
	Wyeast 1028 London Ale yeast	

Water treatment:	RO water treated with ¼ tsp 10% phosphoric acid per 5 gallons
	1 tsp $CaCl_2$ in mash
Mash technique:	Infusion, mashout, dark grains added at *vorlauf*
Mash rests:	154°F (68°C) 70 minutes
	168°F (76°C) 15 minutes
Kettle volume:	8 gallons (30 L)
Boil length:	75 minutes
Final volume:	6.5 gallons (25 L)
Fermentation temp:	64°F (18°C)

Sensory description: A clean coffee-like roast flavor with moderate bitterness. The flavors are clean and distinct, but don't taste excessively roasted or aggressively bitter. The crystal malt gives it a bit of residual sweetness that helps smooth the finish as well but the roasted barley does lend dryness to the aftertaste.

Formulation notes: Because it uses crystal malt and black malt, this beer differs from Guinness. It's also less bitter, which adds to the drinkability.

Variations: Try a little English chocolate malt for even more complexity. Push the beer up to the 6–6.5% range to make an extra stout. If you want more of roast bite, use regular black malt, not the debittered type.

SIMPLICITY MILD

I'm always on the lookout for a great tasting mild since they are so sessionable. When I saw a 3.1% version on the menu at the Yellow Springs Brewery, I knew I had to try it, as that's the kind of strength it would be traditionally in the UK. I was surprised when brewmaster Jeffrey McElfresh told me it uses only three malts, since his beer packed so much flavor. This recipe shows how much you can do with a few well-chosen ingredients that deliver the exact flavors you desire.

Style: Dark Mild (Classic BJCP Style)

Description: A spot on dark mild that would be welcome at any English pub in the midlands. Fortunately I can get it at my local brewpub in Yellow Springs, Ohio, where the beer is called *Kerfuffle*.

Batch size: 6.5 gallons (25 L) **OG:** 1.036 **FG:** 1.012
Efficiency: 75% **ABV:** 3.1% **IBU:** 15 **SRM:** 20

Ingredients:

7 lb (3.2 kg)	UK Maris Otter (Fawcett)	Mash
12 oz (340 g)	UK Crystal 65–75 (Fawcett)	*Vorlauf*
7 oz (198 g)	UK Chocolate (Fawcett)	*Vorlauf*
0.5 oz (14 g)	UK Target 8.1% pellets	@ 60
	Wyeast 1968 London ESB yeast	

Water treatment: RO water treated with ¼ tsp 10% phosphoric acid per 5 gallons
0.5 tsp $CaCl_2$ and 0.5 tsp $CaSO_4$ in mash

Mash technique: Infusion, mashout, dark grains added at *vorlauf*

Mash rests: 158°F (70°C) 60 minutes
168°F (76°C) 15 minutes

Kettle volume: 8 gallons (30 L)

Boil length: 60 minutes

Final volume: 6.5 gallons (25 L)

Fermentation temp: 66°F (19°C)

Sensory description: Dextrinous, chewy, but with a rich chocolate flavor. Has a fruity and lightly caramel supporting layer with low bitterness. Served with low carbonation and at cellar temperature, takes the drinker straight to England. At 3.1% ABV, very easy to drink over a long period.

Formulation notes: The Fawcett chocolate malt is the key to this recipe. I've seen it used in other dark beers, and it really has a classic chocolate flavor without harsh notes. It's a 325–400L chocolate malt.

Variations: It would be fun to experiment with this recipe to try malts from different suppliers to see how much they impact the flavor profile of the final beer. Varying the proportions in this recipe would be another interesting exercise to see how flavor and balance can be influenced by the percentages of individual grist components.

COMPLEXITY MILD

This recipe has seven malts and grains to produce layers of flavor. It's a different type of mild, with less emphasis on the chocolate flavor.

Style: Dark Mild (Classic BJCP Style)

Description: A toasty, bready mild with caramel and light chocolate flavor and a chewy body.

Batch size: 6.5 gallons (25 L)   **OG:** 1.033   **FG:** 1.010
Efficiency: 70%   **ABV:** 3.1%   **IBU:** 18   **SRM:** 16

Ingredients:

6 lb (2.7 kg)	UK Golden Promise (Simpsons)	Mash
12 oz (340 g)	UK Torrified Wheat	Mash
4 oz (113 g)	Aromatic malt (Dingemans)	Mash
8 oz (227 g)	UK Crystal 55	*Vorlauf*
8 oz (227 g)	UK Crystal 80	*Vorlauf*
4 oz (113 g)	UK Crystal 135	*Vorlauf*
3 oz (85 g)	UK Chocolate (Fawcett)	*Vorlauf*
1 oz (28 g)	UK Goldings 5.5% whole	@ 60
	White Labs WLP005 British Ale yeast	

Water treatment:	RO water treated with ¼ tsp 10% phosphoric acid per 5 gallons
	1 tsp CaCl$_2$ in mash
Mash technique:	Infusion, mashout, dark grains added at *vorlauf*
Mash rests:	152°F (66°C) 60 minutes
	170°F (77°C) 25 minutes
Kettle volume:	8 gallons (30 L)
Boil length:	75 minutes
Final volume:	6.5 gallons (25 L)
Fermentation temp:	68°F (20°C)

Sensory description: Malt-forward with a bready, toasty, caramel, and chocolate flavor profile. The bitterness is low and there is no late hop character, so the beer remains malty. A moderate fruity character enhances the darker malt flavors.

Formulation notes: I find the challenge of milds to be in balancing the maltiness of the grist with the character of the yeast. In this recipe, I'm using malts that provide bready and toasty flavors with layers of caramel and dark fruit. The fresh chocolate flavor tops it off. The yeast is somewhat malty and fruity, and adds a pleasant character to the beer. I mash low so that it doesn't seem too sweet; I'm getting body and sweetness from the crystal malts so I don't need to mash higher.

Variations: Since mild is a small beer, it's pretty easy to do a double-sized batch and use it for yeast experiments. I've tried Wyeast 1318, 1968, 1469, 1335, 1028, and others with good luck. I've often thought of 1318 as great mild yeast, but you have to be careful of getting too malty with the grist since the yeast is also malty. I like 1469, but it is fairly minerally. Once when I did a split batch with 1318 and 1469, I actually liked a 2:1 blend of the two batches much better than either individually.

NHC MILD

This recipe comes to me from my friend Dan George, who has won multiple NHC medals with this beer. The low alcohol level is unusual, even for a mild.

Style: Dark Mild (Classic BJCP Style)

Description: A lower gravity and lower bitterness mild that packs significant flavor into a small beer, making it highly sessionable.

Batch size: 5 gallons (19 L)	**OG:** 1.034	**FG:** 1.015
Efficiency: 55% **ABV:** 2.5%	**IBU:** 15	**SRM:** 24

Ingredients:

7 lb (3.2 kg)	UK Maris Otter (Crisp)	Mash
1 lb (454 g)	UK Crystal 75 (Simpsons)	*Vorlauf*
6 oz (170 g)	UK Chocolate malt (Fawcett)	*Vorlauf*

1 oz (28 g)	Carafa II malt (Weyermann)	*Vorlauf*
0.5 oz (14 g)	UK Goldings 5.5% whole	@ 60
0.25 oz (7 g)	UK Goldings 5.5% whole	@ 15
Wyeast 1968	London ESB yeast	

Water treatment:	RO water treated with ¼ tsp 10% phosphoric acid per 5 gallons
	0.5 tsp CaSO$_4$ in mash, 0.5 tsp CaSO$_4$ in boil
Mash technique:	Infusion, mashout, dark grains added at *vorlauf*, no sparge
Mash rests:	154°F (68°C) 60 minutes
	170°F (77°C) 15 minutes
Kettle volume:	6.5 gallons (25 L)
Boil length:	75 minutes
Final volume:	5 gallons (19 L)
Fermentation temp:	68°F (20°C)

Sensory description: Very easy drinking beer, with chocolate, toffee, and bready malt, a lightly floral hop flavor, and a soft fruity palate. Has enough body to not seem watery, but finishes malty.

Formulation notes: The no sparge technique increases the malt flavor, which helps in this small beer. The deep toffee and chocolate flavors pair well against the bready base malt. The yeast brings a fruity note that always goes well with chocolate.

Variations: The alcohol level can be increased to make it a more normal strength mild; target around 3.3%, either by scaling the recipe up or decreasing the final gravity. This recipe has low attenuation (56%); a more normal (70%) attenuation for this yeast would take this down to 1.010, producing a 3.2% ABV beer—perfectly normal for a mild. If it seems a bit too sweet, try it again with a touch of black malt or roasted barley (about 1.5 ounces, or 1% of the grist).

GABF MILD

I tasted this beer while at the 2014 GABF; it was a pro-am entry from my friend and fellow club member James Henjum. It's a bigger mild by UK standards. I drank quite a few of these at the GABF, one ounce at a time.

Style: Dark Mild (Classic BJCP Style)

Description: A beer that would be called a *strong mild* in the UK, features a toasty, bready, nutty character.

Batch size: 6.5 gallons (25 L)	**OG:** 1.041	**FG:** 1.013
Efficiency: 70% **ABV:** 3.7%	**IBU:** 20	**SRM:** 18

Ingredients:

7.75 lb (3.5 kg)	UK Maris Otter (Crisp)	Mash
10 oz (283 g)	UK Golden Promise (Simpsons)	Mash
4 oz (113 g)	CaraPils malt	Mash
12 oz (340 g)	UK Crystal 55 (Simpsons)	*Vorlauf*
9 oz (255 g)	UK Crystal 135 (Baird)	*Vorlauf*
5 oz (142 g)	UK Pale chocolate (Crisp)	*Vorlauf*
0.5 oz (14 g)	Debittered black malt (Dingemans)	*Vorlauf*
1.2 oz (28 g)	UK Fuggles 4.5% whole	@ 60
0.3 oz (14 g)	UK Fuggles 4.5% whole	@ 30
	Wyeast 1335 British Ale II yeast	

Water treatment:	RO water treated with ¼ tsp 10% phosphoric acid per 5 gallons
	0.5 tsp CaCl$_2$ and 0.5 tsp CaSO$_4$ in mash
Mash technique:	Infusion, mashout, dark grains added at *vorlauf*
Mash rests:	154°F (68°C) 60 minutes
	170°F (77°C) 15 minutes
Kettle volume:	8 gallons (30 L)
Boil length:	60 minutes
Final volume:	6.5 gallons (25 L)
Fermentation temp:	68°F (20°C)

Sensory description: Bready, toasty, and nutty malt flavors with caramel and toffee. Very restrained roast characteristics. Medium-bodied with a malty finish. Superb balance and drinkability.

Formulation notes: Blending of base malts for added complexity, bringing in some toasty notes to go with the strong bready flavors. The darker malts are nutty and lightly roasted, lacking a strong punch of burnt flavor. The yeast profile is balanced, allowing the malt to be the star. Hops added primarily for bitterness.

Variations: For a more chocolate-focused beer, replace some or all of the pale chocolate malt with regular chocolate malt (Fawcett would be my first choice).

CASK MILD

Many English dark beers get their color and flavor from brewing sugars, either in addition to or instead of specialty grains. This beer makes good use of invert #3 sugar, and also includes some corn, a common adjunct in English brewing. Unusual in many homebrewed milds, this one is dry-hopped, which smells lovely when served from a cask.

Style: Dark Mild (Classic BJCP Style)

Description: Unusual for homebrewers, but a fairly typical English dark beer with adjuncts. A chance for homebrewers to try brewing with some less standard ingredients.

Batch size: 6.5 gallons (25 L)	**OG:** 1.033	**FG:** 1.009
Efficiency: 70% **ABV:** 3.1%	**IBU:** 21	**SRM:** 19

Ingredients:

5.5 lb (2.5 kg)	UK Mild ale malt (Fawcett)	Mash
8 oz (227 g)	Flaked maize	Mash
1 lb (454 g)	UK Crystal 80 (Baird)	*Vorlauf*
4 oz (113 g)	UK Crystal 135 (Baird)	*Vorlauf*
2 oz (57 g)	Carafa III Special (Weyermann)	*Vorlauf*

12 oz (340 g)	Invert Sugar #3	Boil
1 oz (28 g)	UK Goldings 5.5% whole	@ 60
0.5 oz (14 g)	UK WGV 6.5% pellets	@ 5
0.5 oz (14 g)	UK Goldings 5.5% whole	dry hop
	Wyeast 1335 British Ale II yeast	

Water treatment:	RO water treated with ¼ tsp 10% phosphoric acid per 5 gallons
	0.5 tsp $CaCl_2$ and 0.5 tsp $CaSO_4$ in mash
Mash technique:	Infusion, mashout, dark grains added at *vorlauf*
Mash rests:	152°F (67°C) 60 minutes
	170°F (77°C) 25 minutes
Kettle volume:	8 gallons (30 L)
Boil length:	60 minutes
Final volume:	6.5 gallons (25 L)
Fermentation temp:	68°F (20°C)

Sensory description: Dark beer with ruby highlights. Dark caramelized sugar, dark fruit, and other complex flavors. Moderately bitter, but the varied dark fruit and dark sugar flavors are most prominent on the palate.

Formulation notes: Mild malt for dextrins, corn for a rounded sweetness, crystal malts for flavor contributions, and the invert sugar for color and deep caramelized sugar flavors. The yeast is one of the more balanced strains, and is a good all-around choice Dry hopping this beer provides an extra fresh floral note that comes out well when served on cask at cellar temperature.

Variations: English brewing sugars produce complex flavors that are difficult to reproduce using just malts (licorice notes are virtually impossible). An approximation of the invert sugar can be made with 329 g of Lyle's Golden Syrup and 11 g of good-quality blackstrap molasses (select a molasses that tastes like dark licorice, not like bitter, burnt sugar).

THROWBACK MILD

On a trip to England in 1998, I had a chance to try Sarah Hughes Dark Ruby Mild, and have been trying to recreate it ever since. Roger Protz's Real Ale Almanac had enough clues in it to put together a template recipe. This recipe matches the framework parameters but I'm still searching for the perfect crystal malt for the dark fruit flavor profile. This recipe is a lot like the Sarah Hughes beer, but not an exact clone.

Style: English Strong Ale (New BJCP Style)

Description: A stronger 1921 mild from the Birmingham area in England. Fruity, malty, and quite a bit stronger than modern milds, it relies solely on dark crystal malt for flavor and color.

Batch size: 6.5 gallons (25 L) **OG:** 1.058 **FG:** 1.014
Efficiency: 70% **ABV:** 5.9% **IBU:** 24 **SRM:** 22

Ingredients:

11 lb (5 kg)	UK Maris Otter (Fawcett)	Mash
3.7 lb (1.7 kg)	UK Crystal 77 (Crisp)	*Vorlauf*
0.8 oz (23 g)	UK Challenger 7.2% pellets	@ 60
0.75 oz (21 g)	UK Goldings 5.9% whole	@ 15
	Wyeast 1968 London ESB yeast	

Water treatment: RO water treated with ¼ tsp 10% phosphoric acid per 5 gallons
1 tsp CaCl$_2$ in mash

Mash technique: Infusion, mashout, crystal malt added at *vorlauf*

Mash rests: 154°F (68°C) 60 minutes
168°F (76°C) 15 minutes

Kettle volume: 8.5 gallons (30 L)

Boil length: 90 minutes

Final volume: 6.5 gallons (25 L)

Fermentation temp: 68°F (20°C)

Sensory description: Clear, with a deep reddish hue. Has a dark fruity and malty sweet palate but tastes attenuated. Medium-low bitterness in the balance.

Formulation notes: I know 25% crystal malt seems insane, but this really does work. The crystal malt is the key ingredient for the recipe, and is the basis for experimentation. I don't think I've yet found a perfect match, but I'm also relying on my tasting notes and flavor memory from a visit to the brewery nearly two decades ago. The parameters for color will seem dark, but it will be a very dark reddish color, not black. A fruity yeast enhances the flavor profile, so if you make a change, go with something that produces fruit flavors. I think the Fuller's yeast is a good choice because other than fruitiness, it's relatively clean and isn't highly attenuative.

Variations: Every time I make this recipe, I use a different crystal malt so I can compare the flavors. It seems the darker I go, the better it is, as long as I don't start getting the burnt sugar flavors that also bring bitterness. You need at least a British 75–85°L crystal malt; those around the 90–120°L range are likely to give the most intense flavors but they may be too strong. The flavor profile of British dark crystal malts vary widely by the maltster, so some experimentation is needed. If you think you've nailed it, be sure to tell me what you used so I can give it a try.

MODERN LONDON PORTER

This is one of the recipes I put together while promoting Brewing Better Beer. I served it at the NHC conference in Seattle and it was a big hit. One of the main points I was making at the time was that great dark beer could be made essentially the same great pale ale is made.

Style: English Porter (Classic BJCP Style)

Description: A modern English porter with a great chocolate flavor and the unmistakable brown malt taste that epitomizes the style.

Batch size: 6.5 gallons (25 L)		OG: 1.054	FG: 1.016
Efficiency: 70%	ABV: 5.1%	IBU: 20	SRM: 31

Ingredients:

9 lb (4.1 kg)	UK Maris Otter (Fawcett)	Mash
1 lb (454 g)	German Munich (Best)	Mash
1.5 lb (680 g)	UK Brown malt (Crisp)	Mash
1.75 lb (794 g)	UK Crystal 65 (Crisp)	*Vorlauf*
12 oz (340 g)	UK Chocolate malt (Fawcett)	*Vorlauf*
1.5 oz (43 g)	UK Fuggles 4% whole	@ 60
0.75 oz (21 g)	UK Goldings 5% whole	@ 10
	Wyeast 1968 London ESB yeast	

Water treatment:	RO water treated with ¼ tsp 10% phosphoric acid per 5 gallons
	1 tsp CaCl$_2$ in mash
Mash technique:	Infusion, mashout, dark grains added at *vorlauf*
Mash rests:	153°F (67°C) 60 minutes
	168°F (76°C) 15 minutes
Kettle volume:	8 gallons (30 L)
Boil length:	75 minutes
Final volume:	6.5 gallons (25 L)
Fermentation temp:	66°F (19°C)

Sensory description: Delicious balance. The brown malt adds so much complexity, and is that *missing flavor* that you can taste in beers like Fuller's London Porter. The crystal malt gives it a higher finishing gravity and richer body, while the Munich pumps up the maltiness. Combined, those malty, sweet flavors help balance the bready, toasty, and roasty notes from the base malt, brown malt, and chocolate malt. Lightly fruity, soft floral hop flavor, supportive bitterness in a malt-forward beer.

Formulation notes: I like to use UK-sourced ingredients since they have the authentic flavors that are important to the style (particularly the brown and chocolate malts). If you can't get brown malt, make a different recipe; this just won't be the same without it. The Munich malt is optional. I use it to get extra maltiness without additional sweetness. If you want even more maltiness, try Aromatic malt. If you are trying for a purist recipe, delete it and go all English. The yeast choice is Fuller's strain, which I think gives a clean malt flavor with a restrained fruity accent.

Variations: The flavors from the UK malts (especially brown malt) can vary a bit by maltster, so compare various products from maltsters like Crisp, Fawcett, Baird, and Simpsons. I was shooting for a beer like Fuller's, so I used their yeast; other fruity, malty English strains (such as White Labs WLP037 Yorkshire Square yeast) would work as well and might also make a delicious alternative.

ROBUST ENGLISH PORTER

Quite different from the caramel and chocolate porters you often find today, this recipe brings out the flavors of old school porters using traditional British ingredients.

Style: English Porter (Classic BJCP Style)

Description: A style that pays homage to English porters from an earlier era that had bigger dark malt flavor.

Batch size: 6.5 gallons (25 L)	**OG:** 1.052	**FG:** 1.014
Efficiency: 75% **ABV:** 5.1%	**IBU:** 37	**SRM:** 37

Ingredients:

9.25 lb (4.2 kg)	UK Golden Promise (Simpsons)	Mash
2 lb (907 g)	UK Brown Malt (Fawcett)	Mash
1 lb (454 g)	UK Black Malt (Simpsons)	*Vorlauf*
4 oz (113 g)	UK Crystal 135 (Baird)	*Vorlauf*
0.75 oz (21 g)	UK Northdown 8.5% pellets	@ 60
1 oz (28 g)	UK Fuggles 5% whole	@ 30
1 oz (28 g)	UK Goldings 5.5% whole	@ 10
	Wyeast 1187 Ringwood Ale yeast	

Water treatment: RO water treated with ¼ tsp 10% phosphoric acid per 5 gallons
1 tsp $CaCl_2$ in mash

Mash technique: Infusion, mashout, dark grains and crystal malt added at *vorlauf*

Mash rests:	154°F (68°C) 60 minutes
	168°F (76°C) 15 minutes
Kettle volume:	8 gallons (30 L)
Boil length:	75 minutes
Final volume:	6.5 gallons (25 L)
Fermentation temp:	66°F (19°C)

Sensory description: Roast, bitter, and fruity with bread and toast base notes and the big flavor of brown and black malts. Light hop flavor adds some complexity.

Formulation notes: Be careful with this yeast! Give it plenty of oxygen and make sure it completely finishes or it can throw a significant amount of diacetyl. Taste it before you rack it; it might need additional time on the yeast to clean up. Raise the temperature to 72°F (22°C) for a few days if needed. However finicky, it gives a unique (and very British) fruity quality. The use of pale, brown, and black malts to produce a porter is very classic formulation, while the extra dark crystal malt provides a touch of additional complexity.

Variations: If the black malt is too strong for your taste, try debittered black malt instead, or cold steep it; that will produce a very different beer since the black malt carries much of the flavor. If you have issues with the yeast, feel free to substitute any good English ale yeast. I like the fruitiness from the yeast, but hate diacetyl.

ROBUST PORTER

This is a fairly typical traditional robust porter, with an emphasis on the flavors of the specialty malts. The bitterness and strength are not too high, which allows the malt flavors to stand out. Uses a combination of English and American ingredients to both pay homage to the history of the style while putting a bit of a New World spin on it.

Style: American Porter (Classic BJCP Style)

Description: A modern American porter with the classic chocolate and roasty, burnt dark malt flavors, and some caramel sweetness to help take the edge off the finish. Lightly fruity with some spicy and citrusy hop aromatics.

Batch size: 6.5 gallons (25 L) **OG:** 1.056 **FG:** 1.014
Efficiency: 70% **ABV:** 5.7% **IBU:** 27 **SRM:** 42

Ingredients:

9.5 lb (4.3 kg)	US two-row (Briess)	Mash
2 lb (907 g)	UK Maris Otter (Crisp)	Mash
1.25 lb (567 g)	US Crystal 60	*Vorlauf*
1 lb (454 g)	UK Chocolate malt (Crisp)	*Vorlauf*
9 oz (255 g)	UK Black malt	*Vorlauf*
1.0 oz (28 g)	Northern Brewer 8% whole	@ 60
1 oz (28 g)	Northern Brewer 8% whole	@ 5
0.75 oz (21 g)	US Sterling 7% whole	@ 0
0.5 oz (14 g)	US Cascade 4.5% whole	@ 0
	Wyeast 1272 American Ale II yeast	

Water treatment:	RO water treated with ¼ tsp 10% phosphoric acid per 5 gallons
	1 tsp CaCl$_2$ in mash
Mash technique:	Infusion, mashout, dark grains added at *vorlauf*
Mash rests:	154°F (68°C) 60 minutes
	170°F (77°C) 15 minutes
Kettle volume:	8.5 gallons (32 L)
Boil length:	90 minutes
Final volume:	6.5 gallons (25 L)
Fermentation temp:	66°F (19°C)

Sensory description: Lightly fruity profile with a light bready and caramel base under a dark chocolate finish. The beer is substantial and has a fuller body, but the dryness from the dark malts provides balance. A light spicy, citrusy hop finish adds some complexity.

Formulation notes: I didn't want the base malt to have too much of a bready flavor, so I use mostly US two-row. The dark malts and crystal malts are added late to keep the harshness down. I use classic American citrusy hops for the aroma but want to avoid that in the flavor since I think it can clash with the dark malts. I think the English dark malts have a smoother, less harsh quality, and a more potent taste than American versions, so I prefer them.

Variations: Sometimes I make this as a single-hop beer with all Northern Brewer, trying for an Anchor Porter like profile. The hop profile can be traditional English as well, using Fuggles and Goldings in any combination. I also have made this with all New World hops, favoring the tropical and stone fruit hops, like Amarillo, Galaxy, and Citra. Ahtanum is another good choice for a late hop, with its floral, citrus profile. If you want to experiment with cold-steeping grains, this is a good recipe to use; just steep the dark malts overnight, strain, and then add the liquid to the last 5 minutes of the boil.

AMERICAN PORTER

American porters have a stronger character than modern English porters (which is true for most American adaptations of traditional English styles). The challenge in making this style is to not have overly burnt flavors dominate, and not have the hops clash with the dark malts. This one uses roasted barley instead of black malt, and the hopping includes some orange and apricot flavors.

Style: American Porter (Classic BJCP Style)

Description: Interesting in between type of porter that uses many traditional English ingredients but is more recognizable in balance today to the American style.

Batch size: 6.5 gallons (25 L)		OG: 1.060	FG: 1.014
Efficiency: 75%	ABV: 6.1%	IBU: 34	SRM: 36

Ingredients:

13 lb (5.9 kg)	US two-row	Mash
1 lb (454 g)	UK Crystal 77 (Crisp)	*Vorlauf*

12 oz (340 g)	UK Chocolate malt (Fawcett)	*Vorlauf*
6 oz (170 g)	UK Roasted Barley	*Vorlauf*
2 oz (57 g)	UK Fuggles 4.5% whole	FWH
0.75 oz (21 g)	US Amarillo 8.6% whole	@ 10
1 oz (28 g)	Styrian Goldings 4.5% whole	@ 5
1 oz (28 g)	Styrian Goldings 4.5% whole	dry hop
	White Labs WLP001 California ale yeast	

Water treatment:	RO water treated with ¼ tsp 10% phosphoric acid per 5 gallons
	1 tsp CaCl$_2$ in mash
Mash technique:	Infusion, mashout, dark grains added at *vorlauf*
Mash rests:	154°F (68°C) 60 minutes
	170°F (77°C) 15 minutes
Kettle volume:	8 gallons (30 L)
Boil length:	75 minutes
Final volume:	6.5 gallons (25 L)
Fermentation temp:	64°F (18°C)

Sensory description: Balanced roast with a bready base malt, slightly fruity fermentation character, and earthy hops. Moderately strong with a dry finish, malty and roast aftertaste, and balanced bitterness.

Formulation notes: Fairly straightforward composition, featuring mostly English ingredients. The base malt and yeast are more neutral than an English version, which lets the specialty malts and hops be prominent. The hop flavor is higher on this version, with the first wort hops providing a woody, earthy note, while the later hops give more apricot and orange notes(which I think plays well with the chocolate and light coffee character). Strength and body are on the higher side. The dry hopping is optional, but I fresh hop character as an extra aroma dimension.

Variations: I also like using noble hops as the late finishing hops instead of the Styrians; I sometimes use Tettnanger, Halltertauer, or some of the US versions such as Vanguard or Santiam. If you really want to stand out as an American style, you can also use classic hops like Cascade and Centennial late. I normally use Cascade at knockout instead of the 5 minute addition and dry hop with Centennial. With fairly simple grist, this beer is also a good baseline for matching other beer flavors to source ingredients. Look for the deep caramel, chocolate, and coffee flavors and adjust the quantities based on what you prefer. I would adjust each of those specialty grains no more than 50% up or down as you experiment. I think this beer is also good with a lower bitterness level (in the mid 20s). I tend to mash a couple degrees lower when making aversion with lower bitterness (like 151°F/66°C). I've also made a more session strength version of this, reducing everything proportionally to be a 4% ABV beer and omitting the dry hopping altogether. A stronger 7% version is also good; I sometimes make that version to age.

AMERICAN BROWN ALE

There is disagreement on the standard flavor profile for American Brown Ale. Homebrewers seem to think it's a Brown IPA, but commercial craft brewers often treat it almost like a dark American lager. I think there is a happy medium: a beer with a rich malty profile with chocolate and caramel flavors, that is still moderately bitter with a noticeable late hop character.

Style: American Brown Ale (Classic BJCP Style)

Description: American ingredients get a little bit of international help to balance chocolate and caramel flavors with a stronger hop character. Clean base malt with caramelly and chocolate flavors, with a fruity and spicy hop character.

Batch size: 6.5 gallons (25 L) **OG:** 1.056 **FG:** 1.014
Efficiency: 70% **ABV:** 5.5% **IBU:** 28 **SRM:** 25

Ingredients:

10 lb (4.5 kg)	US two-row (Briess)	Mash
2 lb (907 g)	German Munich (Best)	Mash
1 lb (454 g)	US Crystal 60	*Vorlauf*
8 oz (227 g)	US Crystal 40	*Vorlauf*
8 oz (227 g)	UK Chocolate malt (Fawcett)	*Vorlauf*

2 oz (57 g)	Carafa II Special (Weyermann)	*Vorlauf*
1 oz (28 g)	US Vanguard 5% whole	FWH
0.5 oz (14 g)	Australian Galaxy 13% pellets	@ 15
1 oz (28 g)	US Sterling 7% whole	@ 5
	Wyeast 1272 American Ale II yeast	

Water treatment:	RO water treated with ¼ tsp 10% phosphoric acid per 5 gallons
	1 tsp CaCl$_2$ in mash
Mash technique:	Infusion, mashout, dark grains added at *vorlauf*
Mash rests:	151°F (66°C) 60 minutes
	170°F (76°C) 15 minutes
Kettle volume:	8.5 gallons (32 L)
Boil length:	90 minutes
Final volume:	6.5 gallons (25 L)
Fermentation temp:	66°F (19°C)

Sensory description: Caramel and chocolate flavors initially with a neutral malt backbone. The light fruity, spicy, and floral hop aroma and flavor complement and support the malt. Neutral fermentation profile allows the malt and hops to shine through. The moderate bitterness is noticeable but doesn't overwhelm the malt flavors.

Formulation notes: I stay with the more neutral-tasting American ingredients for base malts and crystal, while letting the English chocolate malt stand out. To keep the malt from clashing with the hops, I'm using American versions of noble hops with a little bit of Galaxy fruitiness. The yeast is slightly fruity, but relatively clean, so it shouldn't provide much additional character.

Variations: Dry hopping using one of the late hop varieties (Galaxy or Sterling), or a classic American hop like Cascade would work well in this beer. I'd keep the dry hop addition light (0.5 oz/14 g) to let the dark malt character come through in the aroma. I think this beer could carry some honey flavor too; maybe swap out 3 lb (1.4 kg) of the base malt for an equal weight of clean, floral honey of your choice. Add the honey in the last 5 minutes of the boil and stir to mix.

DUNKELWEIZEN

My wife likes wheat beers, so I usually have at least one around. I prefer the yeast character of these beers when they are young and all the flavors are very fresh. I like to drink dunkelweizen in cool weather; it tends to remind me of autumn.

Style: Dunkles Weissbier (Classic BJCP Style)

Description: German dark wheat beer with caramel and light chocolate flavors along with a slightly rich malt base and the signature banana and clove yeast character. Lightly hopped and highly carbonated, this is as tasty as it is refreshing.

Batch size: 6.5 gallons (25 L) **OG:** 1.051 **FG:** 1.012
Efficiency: 70% **ABV:** 5.1% **IBU:** 12 **SRM:** 17

Ingredients:

7 lb (3.2 kg)	German wheat malt (Durst)	Mash
3 lb (1.4 kg)	German Pils malt (Durst)	Mash
12 oz (340 g)	German Munich (Weyermann)	Mash
8 oz (227 g)	Caramel Wheat 60 (Weyermann)	*Vorlauf*
1 lb (454 g)	CaraMunich III (Weyermann)	*Vorlauf*
6 oz (170 g)	Carafa I Special (Weyermann)	*Vorlauf*
1 oz (28 g)	German Hallertauer 4.1% whole	@ 60
	Wyeast 3068 Weihenstephan Wheat yeast	

Water treatment: RO water treated with ¼ tsp 10% phosphoric acid per 5 gallons
1 tsp CaCl$_2$ in mash

Mash technique: Hybrid step and double decoction mash, mashout, dark grains added at *vorlauf*

Mash rests: 113°F (45°C) 10 minutes
131°F (55°C) 5 minutes
Pull thick decoction, rest at 149°F (65°C) for 20 minutes, boil 10 minutes
Remix to hit 149°F (65°C)
149°F (65°C) 20 minutes

Pull thick decoction, rest at 158°F (70°C) for 10 minutes, boil for 10 minutes
168°F (76°C) 15 minutes

Kettle volume: 8.5 gallons (32 L)
Boil length: 90 minutes
Final volume: 6.5 gallons (25 L)
Fermentation temp: 62°F (17°C)

Sensory description: Beautiful deep brown color. Low bitterness. Banana and light chocolate in the nose. Caramel, chocolate, and wheat flavor with light banana and spice.

Formulation notes: I've built upon one of my *hefeweizen* recipes by going from a single to a double decoction, and adding in several additional malts for flavor and color purposes (Munich for malty flavor and richness, CaraMunich and caramel wheat for flavor, and Carafa for color adjustment). I like decoction mashes with wheat beers since it seems to improve the mouthfeel. The rest at 113°F (45°C) is to help increase the clove quality.

Variations: The mash schedule is somewhat complicated. It can be simplified if desired. A single decoction could be used; use a step mash technique to hit the same temperature rests until you get to 149°F (65°C), and then do a decoction and complete the existing recipe. A step mash or single infusion mash program could be used as well, but the mouthfeel might not seem quite as smooth and soft. If I'm making this for cold weather, I might swap out some or all of the Pils malt for Vienna or Munich malt, and the Carafa I for Carafa Special II.

WEIZENBOCK

Weizenbock *is a great winter beer since it has rich flavors, is higher in alcohol, and lower in bitterness. It seems to be a bit more stable than other wheat beers, so you can actually age it if you want. I've made several variations of this style, but this latest iteration incorporates suggestions from Rodney Kibzey, who won the Samuel Adams Longshot competition with this style. He suggested the yeast variety, which works very well with this beer.*

Style: *Weizenbock* (Classic BJCP Style)

Description: A strong, dark wheat beer that uses a wide variety of European specialty malts and a decoction mash.

Batch size: 6.5 gallons (25 L)	**OG:** 1.084	**FG:** 1.020
Efficiency: 75% **ABV:** 8.6%	**IBU:** 19	**SRM:** 18

Ingredients:

8 lb (3.6 kg)	German wheat malt (Durst)	Mash
6 lb (2.7 kg)	German Vienna malt (Durst)	Mash
2 lb (907 g)	Dark wheat malt (Weyermann)	Mash
1.5 lb (680 g)	Belgian Aromatic malt (Dingemans)	Mash
1.5 lb (680 g)	Caramel wheat malt (Weyermann)	*Vorlauf*
4 oz (113 g)	Chocolate wheat malt (Weyermann)	*Vorlauf*
1 oz (28 g)	German Perle 8% whole	@ 60
	White Labs WLP380 Hefeweizen IV yeast or Wyeast 3638 Bavarian Wheat yeast	

Water treatment:	RO water treated with ¼ tsp 10% phosphoric acid per 5 gallons 1 tsp CaCl₂ in mash
Mash technique:	Hybrid step and decoction mash, mashout, dark grains added at *vorlauf*
Mash rests:	131°F (55°C) 15 minutes 144°F (62°C) 15 minutes Pull thick decoction, heat to 158°F (70°C) for 30 minutes, boil 10 minutes

	Remix, hit 158°F (70°C), rest 10 minutes
	168°F (76°C) 15 minutes
Kettle volume:	8.5 gallons (32 L)
Boil length:	90 minutes
Final volume:	6.5 gallons (25 L)
Fermentation temp:	62°F (17°C)

Sensory description: Rich malty, toasty, and bready base with nutty and caramel overtones, and supplemental banana flavors. Fairly strong and full-bodied, with fruity notes developing over time.

Formulation notes: Similar to dunkelweizen, this beer has German specialty wheats for flavor. Vienna and Aromatic malt increase the malty base. The yeast brings in a bit extra fruitiness, while the decoction mash adds to the mouthfeel. Do not oxygenate.

Variations: This is a big *weizenbock;* it can also be made lower in strength, around 6.5%. A rest at 113°F (45°C) can be added if additional clove is desired (but I don't think it's necessary in this beer).

DANZIG

Baltic Porter is a wide-ranging style, but too many homebrewers brew it as if it were an imperial-strength American porter. Baltic porters should have a refined, smooth roast more like that in a schwarzbier than the more aggressive roast typical of American porters. The roast without burnt *quality is fairly important, as is a complexity of base malt and deep fruity esters. This beer has the general balance of a Sinebrychoff, but isn't a clone. So why would I name it after a city in Poland if I'm inspired by a beer from Finland? Hint: Maybe because I was naming it after a heavy metal band?*

Style: Baltic Porter (Classic BJCP Style)

Description: A strong, smooth dark lagered porter with a roasty and chocolatey but not burnt dark malt profile, supported by a complex mix of dark fruit and deep bready flavors.

Batch size: 6.5 gallons (25 L)   **OG:** 1.069   **FG:** 1.016
Efficiency: 70%   **ABV:** 7.1%   **IBU:** 44   **SRM:** 45

Ingredients:

10.5 lb (4.8 kg)	German Munich (Weyermann)	Mash
3 lb (1.4 kg)	German Vienna malt (Best)	Mash
1 lb (454 g)	Dark Munich malt (Weyermann)	Mash
1.5 lb (680 g)	CaraMunich II (Weyermann)	*Vorlauf*
1.5 lb (680 g)	Carafa III (Weyermann)	*Vorlauf*
1 oz (28 g)	German Magnum 14.4% pellets	@ 60
0.5 oz (14 g)	Czech Saaz 4% pellets	@ 20
	Wyeast 2124 Bohemian Lager yeast	

Water treatment: RO water treated with ¼ tsp 10% phosphoric acid per 5 gallons
1 tsp $CaCl_2$ in mash
Mash technique: Infusion, mashout, dark grains added at *vorlauf*
Mash rests: 151°F (66°C) 60 minutes
170°F (77°C) 15 minutes
Kettle volume: 8.5 gallons (32 L)
Boil length: 90 minutes
Final volume: 6.5 gallons (25 L)
Fermentation temp: 57°F (14°C)

Sensory description: Bready, toasty base malts with dark fruit and chocolate flavors. Strong bitterness and alcohol allow this to be aged (it picks up a more interesting fruit character as it mellows and the alcohol subsides). Smooth with a malty, roast finish.

Formulation notes: I'm going more for the balance and smooth chocolate, roast flavor profile of a Sinebrychoff porter, so I hit the ABV and IBU levels with a dark color. I'm using the same general ingredients they do, but I ferment it as a lager since it does seem so smooth. It can be fermented as an ale as well, perhaps using the Wyeast 1084 Irish Ale yeast at 68°F (20°C).

Variations: I could see doing a single-step *hochkurz* decoction mash with these base malts. I've also done these types of beers as fruit beers, blending in compatible dark and/or dried fruits that match the underlying esters (such as cherries, plums, or even figs).

JAMAICAN ECLIPSE

Tropical stouts match foreign-type stouts in strength, but without the strongly roasted and burnt component and with significantly less bitterness. Some have fairly high esters. The lower bitterness makes them seem sweet (as can a higher proportion of crystal malts); many commercial examples are sweetened post-fermentation. It seems kind of counter-intuitive that these would taste good in the hot weather of the tropics, but they do. They must be served quite cold.

Style: Tropical Stout (New BJCP Style)

Description: A traditional Caribbean stout recipe that is easy to tailor to your personal taste preferences.

Batch size: 6.5 gallons (25 L)	**OG:** 1.075	**FG:** 1.013
Efficiency: 70% **ABV:** 8.2%	**IBU:** 25	**SRM:** 42

Ingredients:

9 lb (4.1 kg)	US six-row malt	Mash
4.5 lb (2 kg)	US two-row malt	Mash
1 lb (454 g)	US Crystal 90	*Vorlauf*
4 oz (113 g)	UK Chocolate malt (Crisp)	*Vorlauf*
4 oz (113 g)	UK Black malt	*Vorlauf*
12 oz (340 g)	UK Roasted Barley	*Vorlauf*
2 lb (907 g)	Corn sugar	Boil
1.7 oz (48 g)	UK Goldings 5.9% whole	@ 60
	Wyeast 2124 Bohemian Lager yeast	

Water treatment:	RO water treated with ¼ tsp 10% phosphoric acid per 5 gallons 1 tsp CaCl$_2$ in mash
Mash technique:	Infusion, mashout, dark grains added at *vorlauf*

Mash rests:	158°F (70°C) 60 minutes
	170°F (77°C) 15 minutes
Kettle volume:	8 gallons (30 L)
Boil length:	75 minutes
Final volume:	6.5 gallons (25 L)
Fermentation temp:	59°F (15°C), then lager at 32°F (0°C) for 3 weeks

Sensory description: Roasty and chewy with low bitterness and moderate sweetness. The roast character has depth, combining chocolate and toffee flavors without harshness, while the yeast character adds some fruitiness. Full-bodied and higher in alcohol, although the sweeter flavors tend to mask it fairly well.

Formulation notes: This is a fairly generic recipe that allows for variation. The base malts are traditional, but can be varied between six-row and two-row. Corn sugar is simply added to increase the gravity. The crystal malt can be US or UK in the 80–120°L range. The roast, black, and chocolate malts can be varied in any proportion; use the husked varieties to provide some bite since the percentage isn't that high. The beer is fermented as a warmer lager, and then undergoes a short, cold lager before serving. Typically, the beer is sweetened and darkened with proprietary syrups. A simple sugar syrup at serving time might be best since almost anything a homebrewer would use would either ferment or bring unwanted additional flavors (such as lactose, caramels, brewing sugars, etc.).

Variations: If you think of this as a Jamaican stout, how about adding in some Jamaican spices? You can add a bit of allspice for an accent, or go whole hog (or should it be whole goat?) with Jamaican jerk or curry seasonings. The sweetness and richness of the beer can balance smoky or spicy additions. If you want to be both goofy and inauthentic at the same time, you can use Italian coffee syrup flavorings to provide sweetness at serving.

KATHERINE THE STRONG IMPERIAL STOUT

This is an older recipe I put together to celebrate the birth of my daughter. We drank some of it after her christening, which was held during an ice storm that made the town look like the inside of a snow globe. I remember drinking it while listening to Metallica's eponymous black album, which seemed both appropriate for the beer and jarringly disconnected from the outside world. Funny how you can tie a beer to important memories.

Style: Imperial Stout (Classic BJCP Style)

Description: An American version of imperial stout with a big chocolate flavor and a hoppy, bitter finish.

Batch size: 5 gallons (19 L)	**OG:** 1.086	**FG:** 1.022
Efficiency: 70% **ABV:** 8.6%	**IBU:** 67	**SRM:** 74

Ingredients:

12 lb (5.4 kg)	UK Maris Otter (Crisp)	Mash
8 oz (227 g)	Flaked Barley	Mash
1 lb (454 g)	US Crystal 60	*Vorlauf*
8 oz (227 g)	US Crystal 80	*Vorlauf*
4 oz (113 g)	US Crystal 120	*Vorlauf*
8 oz (227 g)	Belgian Special B (Dingemans)	*Vorlauf*
12 oz (340 g)	UK Chocolate malt (Fawcett)	*Vorlauf*
1 lb (454 g)	UK Roasted Barley	*Vorlauf*
8 oz (227 g)	UK Black malt	*Vorlauf*
1 oz (28 g)	UK Goldings 5.5% whole	FWH
1 oz (28 g)	US Chinook 10.5% whole	@ 60
1 oz (28 g)	US Centennial 10.3% whole	@ 15
1 oz (28 g)	US Willamette 4.5% whole	@ 5
1 oz (28 g)	US Chinook 10.5% whole	dry hop
0.5 oz (14 g)	UK Fuggles 4.5% whole	dry hop
	Wyeast 1084 Irish Ale yeast	

Water treatment: RO water treated with ¼ tsp 10% phosphoric acid per 5 gallons

	1 tsp CaCl₂ in mash
Mash technique:	Infusion, mashout, dark grains and crystal malts added at *vorlauf*
Mash rests:	152°F (67°C) 60 minutes
	170°F (77°C) 15 minutes
Kettle volume:	6.5 gallons (25 L)
Boil length:	75 minutes
Final volume:	5 gallons (19 L)
Fermentation temp:	68°F(20°C)

Sensory description: Roasty and hoppy with a strong mocha component to the roast. The late hops are earthy, woody, and piney. Full-bodied and chewy, with caramel, toffee sweetness underneath. Strong alcohol and hop levels allow this one to be aged for a long time.

Formulation notes: Layers of crystal malt provide some additional sweetness and balance to the roast, chocolate, and coffee flavors of the dark malts. Strong hopping provides some heavy bitterness. The piney Chinook hops go well with the roast as an aroma, but I would avoid using them as a flavor addition because their resiny character can clash with the dark malts.

Variations: I think it would be fun to omit the late hops and add a couple vanilla beans (or just 1 to 2 Tbsp of good-quality vanilla extract, or to taste) to this beer. The vanilla and chocolate character would be a good match, but only if the piney hop notes weren't in the way of the aroma.

FERRET AND TROUSER LEG IMPERIAL STOUT

This recipe comes from my friend Jay Wince, who was an award-winning homebrewer before becoming a GABF-medaling craft brewer at Weasel Boy Brewing Company (where he calls this recipe "Anastasia RIS"). I love this recipe because it's so simple. Who would believe you could get such complexity in a style like this with only three ingredients in the grist? I've brewed this recipe several times, including several variations on the main theme.

Style: Imperial Stout (Classic BJCP Style)

Description: An English-style Imperial Stout that derives its flavors from very specific ingredients, and ages nicely.

Batch size: 6.5 gallons (25 L)   **OG:** 1.086   **FG:** 1.027
Efficiency: 70%   **ABV:** 8.0%   **IBU:** 73   **SRM:** 82

Ingredients:

18 lb (8.2 kg)	US two-row (Great Western)	Mash
2 lb (907 g)	UK Chocolate malt (Fawcett)	*Vorlauf*
2 lb (907 g)	UK Roasted Barley (Fawcett)	*Vorlauf*
1.8 oz (28 g)	US Tomahawk 16.8% whole	@ 60
0.5 oz (14 g)	US Centennial 8.5% whole	@ 10
0.5 oz (14 g)	US Centennial 8.5% whole	@ 0
	Wyeast 1318 London Ale III yeast	

Water treatment: RO water treated with ¼ tsp 10% phosphoric acid per 5 gallons
1 tsp CaCl₂ in mash

Mash technique: Infusion, mashout, dark grains added at *vorlauf*

Mash rests: 152°F (67°C) 60 minutes
170°F (77°C) 15 minutes

Kettle volume: 8 gallons (30 L)

Boil length: 75 minutes

Final volume: 6.5 gallons (25 L)

Fermentation temp: 68°F (20°C), letting rise to 73°F (23°C)

Sensory description: Deep black color with a strong roast flavor that has chocolate and coffee components. The bitterness is high, which gives it a bittersweet finish like dark chocolate. Light but noticeable late hop character with a citrusy, floral quality. Rich and full-bodied, this beer ages very well.

Formulation notes: A very simple recipe with a high percentage of roasted grains and malts. The base malt is neutral, so the dark malts and grains carry all the flavor. Fawcett malt is the key; their grains aren't as highly roasted as some other maltsters, so they can be used in higher proportions without bringing additional harshness. The yeast is another key choice, along with the fermentation temperature. This yeast can be driven warmer without bringing harsh alcohols or off flavors. This beer can be ready quickly, but it also ages well with all that dark grain present; Jay won his GABF gold with a version that was 10 months old.

Variations: I've made this as a 1.070 foreign stout as well. The most interesting thing I did with one batch was to turn it into a chocolate imperial stout for a retirement party. Someone asked for a beer similar to Southern Tier Choklat, so I decided to play with flavoring an existing beer rather than brewing a new one. I soaked 4 oz (113 g) of cocoa nibs in crème de cacao, dissolved some Penzey's Dutch cocoa in crème de cacao, let both steep for several days, and then strained. I blended that with the beer, and also added a small bottle of chocolate extract and a splash of real vanilla extract. I stirred in about 8 oz (227 g) of lactose, too. It was a very chocolate beer, and worked amazingly in vanilla stout floats. I think a bottle of Godiva chocolate liqueur would also work well, as long as it's the clear version not the one that's milky like Bailey's Irish Cream (I think anything like that would curdle in the beer). At the brewery, Jay also ages his in a bourbon barrel. Be careful with any wood aging since there is a lot of dark malt, and the tannins from the wood can add astringency.

THE DIRTY DOZEN

As a contrast to the previous recipe, here is an Imperial Stout with a complex grist; there are twelve different components in the mash. Many imperial stouts have tremendous complexity and this is one way of getting that character.

Style: Imperial Stout (Classic BJCP Style)

Description: A stronger, chewier, more intensely flavored imperial stout that derives its layers of flavors from a complex list of ingredients.

Batch size: 6.5 gallons (25 L)	**OG:** 1.098	**FG:** 1.025
Efficiency: 70% **ABV:** 9.9%	**IBU:** 67	**SRM:** 102

Ingredients:

12 lb (5.4 kg)	UK Golden Promise (Simpsons)	Mash
2 lb (907 g)	German Munich (Best)	Mash
1 lb (454 g)	Dark Munich malt (Weyermann)	Mash
1 lb (454 g)	Belgian Aromatic malt (Dingemans)	Mash
1 lb (454 g)	German Vienna malt (Best)	Mash
2 lb (907 g)	UK Brown malt (Crisp)	Mash
8 oz (227 g)	Flaked Oats	Mash
2 lb (907 g)	UK Roasted Barley (Pauls)	*Vorlauf*
1 lb (454 g)	UK Chocolate malt (Fawcett)	*Vorlauf*
2 lb (907 g)	Carafa III Special (Weyermann)	*Vorlauf*
8 oz (227 g)	CaraMunich III (Weyermann)	*Vorlauf*
8 oz (227 g)	UK Crystal 135 (Baird)	*Vorlauf*
2 oz (57 g)	German Magnum 11% pellets	@ 90
1 oz (28 g)	US Sterling 7% pellets	@ 30
2 oz (57 g)	US Sterling 7% pellets	@ 0
2 oz (57 g)	UK Fuggles 4.5% whole	dry hop
	Wyeast 1335 British Ale II yeast	

Water treatment:	RO water, no acid added
	1 tsp $CaCl_2$ in mash and 1 tsp $CaCl_2$ in boil
Mash technique:	Step mash, mashout, dark grains added at *vorlauf*
Mash rests:	131°F (55°C) 15 minutes
	144°F (62°C) 50 minutes
	158°F (70°C) 50 minutes
	170°F (77°C) 15 minutes
Kettle volume:	8.5 gallons (32 L)
Boil length:	90 minutes
Final volume:	6.5 gallons (25 L)
Fermentation temp:	68°F(20°C)

Sensory description: Deep toasty, bready, and malty base with strongly roasted flavors, moderately high bitterness, and a light fruity background. Rich and chewy body, with a malty, roasty finish. Spicy, earthy hop character. Ages well.

Formulation notes: A beer designed to age. Has high hopping and alcohol with significant dark malts. Uses a very malty base similar to some Belgian beers. The strong roast and deep caramel flavors have to punch through the rich bready, toasty, malt base. The flavors need some time to meld and the alcohol needs to mellow a touch, so age this one for at least a year.

Variations: For an even richer malt base, this beer can be decocted using similar rest temperatures. Dry hopping with varieties known for a tropical fruit character might add another layer of complexity.

7 | LAGER RECIPES

"Some British drinkers think, wrongly, that lager is not beer."

— *Michael Jackson*, Michael Jackson's Beer Companion

I don't make lagers too frequently because they require significant time investment after brew day, and I have to plan my equipment availability carefully to maintain temperature control throughout the entire process. When I do make a lager, I really want it to have that clean flavor profile and smooth mouthfeel so characteristic of the style. There is nothing more disappointing than a lager that has been rushed through so fast that it has a rough profile, sulfury flavors, or a green beer[1] taste. I can forgive a big ale that is served too young more so than a lager, because the brewer has finished with the ale; it's now only a matter of cellaring. But a young lager is incomplete, and the brewer has not finished his job. Don't go to the trouble of brewing a lager if you aren't going to follow proper lagering practices, as a large portion of the character of the beer comes from the storage process.

---

[1] *Green beer* refers to post-primary fermentation beer that has not been sufficiently conditioned and matured (it doesn't have anything to do with St. Patrick's Day). Green beer tends to be hazy, and is not considered ready to drink. It has immature flavors that have not yet melded together, and may have noticeable yeast fermentation byproducts still present (acetaldehyde, diacetyl, various sulfur compounds, etc.) as well as the taste of yeast that has not yet been separated from the beer. One of the main goals of lagering is to transform green beer into stable, mature beer, suitable for consumption.

The process for brewing a lager is not the same as brewing an ale except using a cooler fermentation temperature. There is more to the overall process, and some additional brewing considerations that must be taken into account. Before we get to the recipes, I want to summarize my method; it works for homebrewers and uses some more traditional techniques. After that I'll contrast my method with modern German commercial lagering practices, which may contain some steps you'll want to incorporate into your method. The recipes in this chapter generally use the first method, but feel free to adjust them accordingly if you're more comfortable with something closer to the second method.

When I brew a lager, I always make a large yeast starter (1–2 L, typically), use oxygen, and typically pitch on the cold side, maybe 46–48°F (8–9°C). I take care not to have the starter at a temperature warmer than the wort, since this can shock the yeast. I usually ferment at 50–52°F (10–11°C) in a carboy. When the *kräusened* has fallen, I rack to a keg, and start lowering the temperature by 1–2°F a day (0.6–1.1°C). I lager at 33°F (1°C) for 1 week per 1°P of starting gravity (a traditional German method). I use a pressure-activated relief valve on the keg to keep pressure from building up. When lagering is complete, I check the clarity and fine with gelatin if necessary before racking to a serving keg (where I typically force carbonate the beer). Most of the time, the extended lagering period has caused the yeast to naturally flocculate, and I just carefully rack without fining.

Modern German commercial breweries use an accelerated lagering process for economic reasons, which is performed in a cylindroconical vessel that is used for both fermentation and conditioning. Pitching occurs at 43–45°F (6–7°C) and the temperature is allowed to rise to 46–48°F (8–9°C) during fermentation. After two days at the highest temperature, the beer is slowly cooled to 37–39°F (3–4°C), then transferred to another vessel. At this point, the beer still has about 1–1.5°P (4 to 6 gravity points) of extract remaining. The beer is *kräusened* with 5–10% actively fermenting yeast at low to high *kräusen* (the percentage is measured by volume of green beer), and then slowly cooled and lagered at 30°F (-1°C) for at least a week (but less than 5 weeks). This process can also be performed without cooling the beer before racking; an optional diacetyl rest may be added if necessary. Either way, the process involves careful temperature control and measurement of gravity during the fermentation process.

Kräusening the beer improves the flavor and foam, helps the beer attenuate, and speeds the conditioning process by cleaning up the fermentation byproducts faster. When conducted in a closed vessel, it can also carbonate the beer. *Kräusening* is a very common practice in modern German breweries. At the homebrew scale of approximately 5 gallons (19 L), 5–10% of the volume translates to 1 to 2 quarts (roughly 1 to 2 L) or the size of the original yeast starter I recommended. *Kräusening* might seem like repitching your yeast, but be sure to separate out the primary fermentation yeast first (and possibly repitch it into a new batch of beer).

I have a few tips for brewing lager beers based on my experiences as well as my personal preferences:

- **Yeast strain selection** – I've seen a lot of otherwise good beers hobbled by a poor choice of yeast. I don't like strains that produce a lot of sulfur; they tend to make the beers, well, stink. It's best to avoid known large sulfur producers.
- **Cooling to lager temperature** – You need to slowly reduce the temperature of your beer after primary fermentation so that you don't crash the yeast. A sudden cold temperature shock can stun the yeast and cause them to flocculate; they can't do their job lagering if they're lying dormant on the bottom of the fermenter.
- **Lagering temperature** – Lagering works much better at colder temperatures. It makes a huge difference in how long it takes to lager a beer at 32°F (0°C) than at 38–40°F (3–4°C), and it seems to produce a noticeable difference in smoothness. A good target range for lagering is 30–33°F (-1–1°C).
- **Pressure relief** – Allow pressure to escape during lagering to vent sulfur and other scrubbed-out volatiles. If you are using a carboy, use an airlock; if you are using a keg, vent it regularly or use a pressure-sensitive relief valve.

FIXING A SULFURY LAGER

If you do wind up with a lager that has too much sulfur in it and you need to serve it soon, you can scrub the sulfur out of the beer using CO_2. Chill the keg, carbonate it well, then warm the keg (for me that means putting it in a chest freezer with a temperature control, then removing it). Rapidly release the gas from the keg. Repeat this process *three or four times. The escaping CO_2 will take some of the sulfur with it. Even doing this just once can improve your beer.*

The following is a broad collection of some of my favorite lager styles from around the world. OK, maybe not from *all* around the world; this selection does have a strong emphasis on German styles (but for good reason).

- **Dark American Lager** – Wait! Don't skip over this one. My version has cranked the flavor up about as high as you can go while staying within style. It's a very drinkable, roasty, smooth lager with low bitterness and a dry finish.
- **Nothing but Vienna** – A SMaSH beer with Vienna malt and Sterling hops. Want to see what Vienna malt tastes like? Here you go.
- **Mexican Vienna** – The Vienna style was carried into Mexico by immigrants. It changed a bit (OK, a lot) over the years, but retains some tie to its original roots in this amber adjunct lager.
- **Czech Dark Lager** – Just added to the BJCP Style Guidelines, this old style is finally getting some respect. I show my adoration with two different recipes for what the Czechs call *tmavé pivo*.
- **Dunkel** – How do you go all-in with malt on a dark lager from Munich? Load it up with dark Munich malt; then decoct it.
- **Helles** – How can a style so simple be so hard to brew? It's hard to find good examples, but you can produce a great version of this golden lager from Munich if you're willing to use good quality ingredients.
- **Maibock** – Think all *bocks* feature nothing but malt? This pale *bock* has a surprising spicy hop character to go along with all that Pils malt deliciousness.
- **Traditional Oktoberfest** – The classic amber Märzenbier is no longer the signature beer at the Munich festival but is still very recognizable to US consumers. Now it exists primarily as an export beer, and as a target that few American craft brewers are able to hit.
- **Modern Oktoberfest** – The modern golden festbier served at Oktoberfest, designed to be easier to drink in large quantities than the traditional amber version. A fun case study to compare this beer to the *helles* and the *maibock*.

- **Rauchbock** – A smoked dark amber *bockbier* from Germany with a rich malt profile to balance the smoked malt character.
- **Schwarzbier** – A traditional black lager from Franconia. The black IPA of Germany. Not really, but can you think of a better way to get people to brew this style?
- **Traditional Bock** – Not all big malty German lagers need to be *doppelbocks*. Try a slightly smaller, more drinkable version for a change. This style is the original *bockbier* style from Einbeck, sometimes called Ur-Bock (original *bock*) or dunkles *bock* (dark bock).
- **Blonde doppelbock** – Not all *doppelbocks* are dark; some are golden in color. The malt profile of this recipe isn't as deeply rich, but it's still pretty intense.

DARK AMERICAN LAGER

I got excited about trying to make this style after trying a version at a book signing in New York City. Lee Jacobson brought a beer for me to try, and told me it was a dark American lager. I thought, "Cool, I don't try those very often." It was very good, so I asked about the recipe. He kind of got a sheepish look on his face and said, "it's a cream ale with Sinamar." I totally respect that move; he made a great beer in an unorthodox way. My kind of beer. What's that got to do with this beer? Nothing really, except that it inspired me to come up with my own version.

Style: International Dark Lager (New BJCP Style)

Description: A lawn mower beer for night? A very easy to drink summer beer with low bitterness and a chocolate and caramel malt richness unusual in many more pedestrian commercial examples. The yeast further enhances the malty richness.

Batch size: 6.5 gallons (25 L)	OG: 1.049	FG: 1.012
Efficiency: 70% ABV: 4.9%	IBU: 14	SRM: 25

Ingredients:

7 lb (3.2 kg)	US 2-row (Briess)	Mash
2 lb (907 g)	Euro Pilsner malt (Dingemans)	Mash
1 lb (454 g)	Flaked corn	Mash
1 lb (454 g)	Flaked rice	Mash
12 oz (340 g)	Carafa II Special (Weyermann)	*Vorlauf*
8 oz (227 g)	Cara 45 (Dingemans)	*Vorlauf*
1 oz (28 g)	US Vanguard 4.6% whole	@ 70
	White Labs WLP833 German Bock yeast	

Water treatment:	RO water treated with ¼ tsp 10% phosphoric acid per 5 gallons
	1 tsp CaCl$_2$ in mash
Mash technique:	Infusion, mashout, dark grains added at *vorlauf*
Mash rests:	147°F (64°C) 60 minutes
	168°F (76°C) 15 minutes
Kettle volume:	8.5 gallons (32 L)
Boil length:	90 minutes
Final volume:	6.5 gallons (25 L)
Fermentation temp:	50°F (10°C) primary
	34°F (1°C) lager

Sensory description: Restrained roast, super smooth. Malty with low bitterness. Very well layered. Malt supports roast nicely. Like a schwarzbier without the bitterness. Medium body, dry finish. Light coffee-like character with zero harshness. Mild caramel richness in background. Very well balanced. Definitely a regular drinking beer that should be popular in almost any crowd.

Formulation notes: Don't rush the lagering; it makes a big difference with this yeast. I go with some extra flavor European malts for more interest than straight American two-row with specialty malts. I'm trying for big flavor, but al trying to maintain the balance of the style by going light on the bittering hops. The yeast is non-traditional for this style, but I like the added flavor and malt-forward balance it gives.

Variations: This beer is pretty easy to adjust to your taste preferences. Add or remove hops, dark malts, or caramel malts. You can easily increase bitterness or vary the gravity. If you want something more neutral, swap in American ingredients for the European ones, and use a yeast strain with less character.

NOTHING BUT VIENNA

Using all Vienna malt, this recipe packs a lot in the flavor department. A double decoction mash increases the color, maltiness, and efficiency (of the malt conversion, not of your brew day).

Style: Vienna Lager (Classic BJCP Style)

Description: A recipe with one type of malt and hops, creates a smooth, toasty, malty, and balanced lager.

Batch size: 6.5 gallons (25 L) **OG:** 1.052 **FG:** 1.013
Efficiency: 75% **ABV:** 5.2% **IBU:** 22 **SRM:** 6

Ingredients:

12 lb (5.4 kg)	German Vienna malt (Weyermann)	Mash
1.2 oz (34 g)	US Sterling 6.2% whole	@ 60
	Wyeast 2206 Bavarian lager yeast	

Water treatment:	RO water treated with ¼ tsp 10% phosphoric acid per 5 gallons
	1 tsp CaCl$_2$ in mash
Mash technique:	Double decoction mash
Mash rests:	144°F (62°C) 20 minutes
	Pull thick decoction, rest 15 minutes at 158°F (70°C), then boil 20 minutes.
	Remix to hit 154°F (68°C), rest 20 minutes.
	Pull thick decoction, then boil 20 minutes.
	Remix to hit 170°F (77°C), rest 5 minutes.
Kettle volume:	8.5 gallons (30 L)
Boil length:	90 minutes
Final volume:	6.5 gallons (25 L)

Fermentation temp: 50°F (10°C) 2 weeks

32°F (0°C) 13 weeks

Sensory description: Rich toasty malt palate with balanced bitterness, clean fermentation character, and a smooth finish. The body is medium and has a slightly creamy texture, but still seems fully attenuated. The taste is slightly malt forward with the bitterness rising towards the finish to meet it, while the aftertaste is balanced and clean.

Formulation notes: The decoction is important for color development; the beer should be at least a golden-amber color. There are no late hops in this beer, but some could easily be added for extra complexity. A half ounce (14g) at 5 minutes would work. Since this recipe includes nothing but Vienna malt, it's a good beer to use to compare the flavors from different maltsters.

Variations: I once made this as a double batch with another homebrewer and miscalculated the volumes. We wound up with 1.063 wort. Fermented out, it was described by one judge as "malty as hell" but well-attenuated with a smooth palate and deceptive alcohol presence. I found that I could sometimes enter it as a *maibock* and have it do well. The bittering hops can be bumped up if you like, and some late hops can also be used (maybe try a hop burst or first wort hopping) to make this a SMaSH beer. It could even be brewed as a pseudo-lager using a neutral ale yeast followed by cold conditioning. I'm not sure I'd enter that in competition, but I'd certainly drink it.

MEXICAN VIENNA

Vienna lagers originated in Austria in the first half of the 1800s, and were brought to Mexico by European immigrants in the late 1800s. These beers survive today, although they have been radically changed into modern American (or International) adjunct lagers. Cuauhtémoc makes a winter seasonal beer called Noche Buena *(Good Night, or Christmas Eve) that is basically a strong Vienna made with some adjuncts. The beer is labeled as* 'estilo Bock' (bock *style), which might be a bit misleading unless it's looked at solely as an indicator of strength. This recipe is inspired by that flavorful beer and sits at the absolute upper end of the BJCP International Amber Lager style.* Nochebuena *is also the name of the Poinsettia flower in Mexico, and that flower appears on the beer's label.*

Style: International Amber Lager (New BJCP Style)

Description: Toasty malt with caramel, mild richness, moderate bitterness, and a dry finish with slight corn sweetness.

Batch size: 6.5 gallons (25 L)	**OG:** 1.058	**FG:** 1.015
Efficiency: 70% **ABV:** 5.8%	**IBU:** 25	**SRM:** 16

Ingredients:

8 lb (3.6 kg)	US two-row (Briess)	Mash
3 lb (1.4 kg)	German Vienna malt (Best)	Mash
12 oz (340 g)	Belgian Aromatic malt (Dingemans)	Mash
1.5 lb (680 g)	Flaked maize	Mash
4 oz (113 g)	Carafa III Special (Weyermann)	*Vorlauf*
4 oz (113 g)	US Crystal 120°L malt	*Vorlauf*
1 lb (454 g)	US Crystal 40°L malt	*Vorlauf*
1 oz (28 g)	Styrian Goldings 4.5% whole	@ 60
1 oz (28 g)	Styrian Goldings 4.5% whole	@ 30
0.5 oz (14 g)	Styrian Goldings 4.5% whole	@ 10
0.5 oz (14 g)	Styrian Goldings 4.5% whole	@ 1
	White Labs WLP940 Mexican Lager yeast	

Water treatment: RO water treated with ¼ tsp 10% phosphoric acid per 5 gallons
1 tsp $CaCl_2$ in mash

Mash technique:	Infusion, mashout, dark grains added at *vorlauf*
Mash rests:	152°F (67°C) 60 minutes
	168°F (76°C) 15 minutes
Kettle volume:	8.5 gallons (32 L)
Boil length:	90 minutes
Final volume:	6.5 gallons (25 L)
Fermentation temp:	50°F (10°C) primary
	32°F (0°C) lager 14 weeks

Sensory description: Toast and caramel malt backbone with moderate bitterness and a slightly sweet corn adjunct character. Clean fermentation profile with a little malty sweetness in the finish and a light hop character.

Formulation notes: There isn't much information about this beer on the brewery's web site, except that it's a 5.9% beer and uses Styrian Goldings hops. The base malt and maize are traditional for adjunct beers. I could taste a richer flavor than just those alone, yet it isn't as malt-rich as beers with all continental ingredients. I can taste the toasty malt, caramel, and corn, and the yeast profile reminds me of a Corona, so I chose ingredients accordingly.

Variations: If you want to make a more upscale version of this beer, substitute more flavorful malts for the US varieties (German Pilsner malt for US two-row, Caramunich II for US C-40, UK Extra Dark Crystal for the US C-120). To get a beer more in the center of the International Amber Lager style, reduce the strength and bitterness to 5% and 18 IBUs.

CZECH DARK LAGER

Czech Dark Lager is like a hoppier Munich dunkel, often with a sweeter finish. Many different versions exist, so we'll start off with a recipe for a traditional 12° beer. Czech beers are normally referred to by their strength (starting gravity in degrees Plato, so a 12°P beer is 1.048) and their color. So this beer is a 12° tmavý ležák (dark lager) beer.

Style: Czech Dark Lager (New BJCP Style)

Description: This version of Czech Dark Lager relies on more highly kilned base malts with some caramelly and chocolatey specialty malts. It has the sweet balance of the older traditional versions.

Batch size: 5.5 gallons (21 L)	**OG:** 1.048	**FG:** 1.012
Efficiency: 75%	**ABV:** 4.8%	**IBU:** 18	**SRM:** 22

Ingredients:

6 lb (2.7 kg)	German Vienna malt (Weyermann)	Mash
2 lb (907 g)	German Munich malt (Weyermann)	Mash
8 oz (227 g)	Dark Munich malt (Weyermann)	Mash
8 oz (227 g)	Caramunich II (Weyermann)	*Vorlauf*
8 oz (227 g)	Carafa II Special (Weyermann)	*Vorlauf*
0.65 oz (18 g)	Czech Saaz 3.6% pellets	FWH
0.65 oz (18 g)	Czech Saaz 3.6% pellets	@ 60
0.65 oz (18 g)	Czech Saaz 3.6% pellets	@ 0
	White Labs WLP802 Czech Budejovice Lager yeast	

Water treatment:	RO water treated with ¼ tsp 10% phosphoric acid per 5 gallons
	1 tsp CaCl₂ in mash
Mash technique:	Step mash, mashout, dark grains added at *vorlauf*
Mash rests:	131°F (55°C) 15 minutes
	147°F (64°C) 30 minutes
	158°F (70°C) 30 minutes
	170°F (77°C) 15 minutes
Kettle volume:	7 gallons (26 L)
Boil length:	60 minutes
Final volume:	5.5 gallons (21 L)
Fermentation temp:	50°F (10°C) 2weeks
	32°F (0°C) 12 weeks

Sensory description: Malty, rich, toasty, and bready with mild caramel and light roast flavor, somewhat sweet tasting in the balance due to moderately low bitterness. Medium-full body. Restrained but noticeable spicy hop aroma and flavor.

Formulation notes: When using fully-modified malts, a step mash works as a substitute (although most Czech brewers still use the traditional decoction mash). The base malts should provide a toasty and rich malty base with the specialty malts adding some caramel and chocolate flavors. The floor-malted Bohemian Pilsner malt from Weyermann can be used instead of the Vienna malt, particularly if a decoction mash is used. Saaz hops are traditional, so try to use those. Sterling would be a good US-produced substitute.

Variations: Can be made in various strengths; if modifying, choose strength based on whole numbers when expressed in degrees Plato (1.044, 1.048, 1.052, 1.057, etc.). The balance can be adjusted to suit tastes; if you want to adjust caramel flavors, change the amount of Caramunich. If you want more malty richness, increase the dark Munich. If you want to make this as a decoction mashed beer, you can use the a single decoction *hochkurz* style at the same rest temperatures, pulling the decoction while resting at 145°F (63°C). This version represents the more traditional balance of the style, with a more sweet impression. Modern examples are often drier, have a higher bitterness (to give a somewhat bittersweet flavor), and more late hops. To brew one of these, increase the IBUs to around 30, and double the last hop addition.

HERE'S LOOKING AT U

U Flek *is the best known Czech Dark Lager. This recipe is based on the general parameters of that beer as well as notes taken from brewery visits. It's offered as a contrast to the other Czech Dark Lager recipe to help illustrate the range of the style; it's a 13°P beer, which would be called a* tmavé speciální pivo *(special dark beer, or simply a special) in the Czech Republic.*

Style: Czech Dark Lager (New BJCP Style)

Description: This version is stronger than the previous example, and has a Pils malt base with some darker grains for color. It uses a double decoction mash and has more bitterness. Smooth palate with a creamy texture, rich bready and caramelly flavors with a mild, clean roasted character.

Balanced bitterness with a spicy fresh hop flavor and aroma that blends well with the deep malt character.

Batch size: 6.5 gallons (25 L)   **OG:** 1.052   **FG:** 1.014
Efficiency: 70%   **ABV:** 5.1%   **IBU:** 28   **SRM:** 28

Ingredients:

6.5 lb (2.9 kg)	German Pilsner malt (Weyermann)	Mash
4 lb (1.8 kg)	German Munich malt (Weyermann)	Mash
2 lb(907 g)	Caramunich III (Weyermann)	*Vorlauf*
10 oz(283 g)	Carafa III Special (Weyermann)	*Vorlauf*
1 oz(28 g)	Czech Saaz 3% whole	FWH
1.9 oz(54 g)	Czech Saaz 3% whole	@ 60
1 oz(28 g)	Czech Saaz 3% whole	@ 5
	Wyeast 2124 Bohemian Lager yeast	

Water treatment: RO water treated with ¼ tsp 10% phosphoric acid per 5 gallons
1 tsp $CaCl_2$ in mash

Mash technique: Hybrid step and double decoction, mashout, dark grains added at *vorlauf*

Mash rests: 99°F (37°C) 10 minutes
127°F (53°C) 15 minutes
Pull decoction, rest at 145°F (63°C) for 15 minutes, 163°F (73°C) for 15 minutes, boil 15 minutes, remix
145°F (63°C) 15 minutes
Pull decoction, rest at 163°F (73°C) for 15 minutes, boil 15 minutes, remix
163°F (73°C) 15 minutes
170°F (77°C) 20 minutes

Kettle volume: 8.5 gallons (32 L)
Boil length: 90 minutes
Final volume: 6.5 gallons (25 L)
Fermentation temp: 50°F (10°C) 2 weeks
32°F (0°C) 13 weeks

Sensory description: Rich base malt with an impression of sweetness, malt lingering into finish. Medium body, lightly creamy, with a balanced bitterness. Mild spicy-peppery hop flavor and aroma.

Formulation notes: Try the Weyermann floor-malted bohemian pilsner malt if you can't find undermodified Czech pilsner malt. I haven't tried the Weyermann Carabohemian malt yet, but I'm curious to see how it would work as a replacement for the Caramunich III. The first low-temperature rest can be omitted if fully modified malt is used. Use a thin mash to reduce the changes of scorching.

Variations: Stronger version can be made; I'm fond of the 14°P (1.057) version. To scale up this recipe, add more Munich malt to make up the gravity differences. It's OK to go up to 1:1 in Pils:Munich if you'd like. Scale up the bittering hops to keep the same IBUs. For a slightly roasted version, use the normal Carafa malt, not the dehusked special.

DUNKEL

This recipe won best of show in a local competition. When I asked the brewer, Darren Link, for the recipe, he laughed and reminded me that I had helped him formulate it a year earlier. I had given him some general advice on key ingredients, and he took it the rest of the way. Darren has since become a professional craft brewer, so I think his innate brewing skill had something to do with it, too. This is my version of Darren's recipe using a different mash schedule. I'll have to see if he's rebrewed his so we can compare them side-by-side.

Style: Munich Dunkel (Classic BJCP Style)

Description: Rich malty intensity in a dark brown lager from Munich.

Batch size: 6.5 gallons (25 L)   **OG:** 1.049   **FG:** 1.012
Efficiency: 70%   **ABV:** 4.9%   **IBU:** 21   **SRM:** 20

Ingredients:

11 lb (5 kg)	Dark Munich malt (Weyermann)	Mash
8 oz (227 g)	Melanoidin malt (Weyermann)	Mash
6 oz (170 g)	Carafa II Special (Weyermann)	*Vorlauf*
1.4 oz (40 g)	German Tettnang 4.7% whole	@ 60
	White Labs WLP833 German Bock yeast	

Water treatment: RO water treated with ¼ tsp 10% phosphoric acid per 5 gallons
1 tsp CaCl$_2$ in mash

Mash technique: Step mash with decoction, mashout, dark grains added at *vorlauf*

Mash rests: 133°F (56°C) 5 minutes
147°F (64°C) 20 minutes
158°F (70°C) 30 minutes
Pull off most of the thin liquid and save; bring to a boil slowly, stirring constantly; boil the thick part of the mash gently for 30 minutes, stirring constantly. Add the thin part of the mash back in and remix.
166°F (75°C) 20 minutes

Kettle volume: 8.5 gallons (32 L)

Boil length: 90 minutes

Final volume: 6.5 gallons (25 L)

Fermentation temp: 50°F (10°C) for 2 weeks, then lager at 32°F (0°C) for 6 weeks.

Sensory description: Rich maltiness with dark toasted bread flavor. Smooth lager character with gently supporting bitterness. Clean fermentation profile with a strongly malty aftertaste. Alcohol not noticeable.

Formulation notes: This beer takes a few special ingredients. I love the dark Munich malt (Weyermann Munich II) in this recipe, since it has the rich bread crust flavor the style needs. I bump up the maltiness with Melanoidin malt, and adjust the color with Carafa Special II. The yeast is from Ayinger, and has a richly malty profile with low sulfur. Alternative yeasts are Wyeast 2124 or Saflager 34/70. The decoction mash adds to the malty smoothness, and it lagers sufficiently to sand off any sharp edges.

Variations: The same beer can be brewed with a straight infusion mash at 154°F (68°C) [that's what Darren did]. It won't be quite as malty or smooth, but it will still be great (it did, after all, win a best of show). This is around a 12°P beer, but it can be made at an export strength (13–14°P) instead, or can be taken up to 18°P (for a *doppelbock*). I sometimes do a version that is 94% dark Munich and 6% Caramunich III (at 1.052 and 22 IBUs) that ends up being very much like Ayinger.

HELLES

This is a subtle style where ingredient quality matters. The malt bill is the star, but the hops and yeast shouldn't be overlooked. The yeast enhances the malt-forwardness, while the hops provide a gentle balance, and a barely detectable but pleasantly floral flavor.

Style: Munich Helles (Classic BJCP Style)

Description: A pale German lager that has an abundance of Pils malt flavor with a moderate body, supportive bitterness, and a malty finish. The relatively dry finish makes it easy to drink in quantity.

Batch size: 6.5 gallons (25 L)	**OG:** 1.048	**FG:** 1.011
Efficiency: 70% **ABV:** 4.9%	**IBU:** 17	**SRM:** 4

Ingredients:

10 lb (4.5 kg)	German Pils malt (Weyermann)	Mash
1.5 lb (680 g)	German Munich (Best)	Mash
4 oz (113 g)	Belgian Aromatic malt (Dingemans)	Mash
2 oz (57 g)	CaraPils malt	Mash
0.25 oz (7 g)	US Vanguard 5.4% whole	FWH
0.75 oz (21 g)	US Vanguard 5.4% whole	@ 60
	White Labs WLP833 German Bock yeast	

Water treatment: RO water treated with ¼ tsp 10% phosphoric acid per 5 gallons
0.75 tsp $CaCl_2$ and 0.25 tsp $CaSO_4$ in mash

Mash technique:	Step mash, mashout
Mash rests:	131°F (55°C) 10 minutes
	145°F (63°C) 40 minutes
	158°F (70°C) 20 minutes
	168°F (76°C) 10 minutes
Kettle volume:	8.5 gallons (32 L)
Boil length:	90 minutes
Final volume:	6.5 gallons (25 L)
Fermentation temp:	50°F (10°C) 2 weeks
	32°F (0°C) 13 weeks

Sensory description: Malty with a smooth, clean Pils flavor. Clear golden color. The finish remains malty with the bitterness just propping up the malt. There is a light hint of floral hops present that adds complexity.

Formulation notes: I like using mostly Pils malt for this style (it can and often is made with all Pils malt). I pump this up with some Munich, just to emphasize the malt. The Carapils® provides just a touch of dextrins so it has body (without having to mash too high). The Vanguard hops are Hallertauer-like, and are usually fresher in my local shop. The *bock* yeast is great for malty beers, and is a low sulfur producer.

Variations: I've made this as a no-sparge beer as well, which changes the intensity of malt flavor. A single decoction would work as well, but I wouldn't boil for more than 5 to 10 minutes to avoid it getting too dark. It can be brewed smaller or larger; the one I present is fairly common. I sometimes like to make an 11°P (1.044) beer for more sessionable occasions. If done as a single infusion mash, go with a rest at 150°F (66°C). Wyeast 2124 would be a good alternative yeast, and makes for a slightly drier beer.

MAIBOCK

Brewed to celebrate the coming of Spring, and to shake off the winter chill, maibock *is a pale, malty style that is stronger than average but not as numbing as some of the deep winter beers. When thinking of* bock *beer, many people think very malty with low bitterness. That's true for the darker versions, but their paler brothers have more hop character and bitterness since they lack the depth of flavor from the dark malts. As a result, many people seem surprised by the hop character they find in a fresh* maibock. *Compare this beer to the* helles, *the* festbier, *and the blonde* doppelbock *to help illustrate how similar ingredients can be varied to produce different styles.*

Style: Helles Bock (Classic BJCP Style)

Description: A fairly strong pale malty German lager with the clean fermentation profile you'd expect in a German beer, but with a rich pale malt base and a spicy hop aroma and flavor.

Batch size: 6.5 gallons (25 L)   **OG:** 1.065   **FG:** 1.014
Efficiency: 70%   **ABV:** 6.7%   **IBU:** 29   **SRM:** 7

Ingredients:

9 lb (4.1 kg)	German Pils malt (Weyermann)	Mash
4 lb (1.8 kg)	German Vienna malt (Best)	Mash
2 lb (907 g)	German Munich (Best)	Mash
1 lb (454 g)	Belgian Aromatic malt (Dingemans)	Mash
0.5 oz (14 g)	German Tettnang 4.5% whole	FWH
0.5 oz (14 g)	German Magnum 14.4% pellets	@ 60
0.5 oz (14 g)	German Tettnang 4.5% whole	@ 5
0.5 oz (14 g)	German Tettnang 4.5% whole	@ 0
	White Labs WLP833 German Bock yeast	

Water treatment: RO water treated with ¼ tsp 10% phosphoric acid per 5 gallons
1 tsp CaCl$_2$ in mash

Mash technique: Hybrid step and single decoction, mashout

Mash rests: 131°F (55°C) 10 minutes
145°F (63°C) 15 minutes

	Pull decoction, heat to 158°F (70°C) for 20 minutes, boil 10 minutes, remix
	158°F (70°C) 30 minutes
	170°F (77°C) 10 minutes
Kettle volume:	8.5 gallons (30 L)
Boil length:	90 minutes
Final volume:	6.5 gallons (25 L)
Fermentation temp:	48°F (9°C) 2 weeks
	32°F (0°C) 16 weeks

Sensory description: Rich malt base with a clean lightly bready malt flavor in a burnished gold-colored beer. Medium-bodied with a firm bitterness and spicy hop character, this strong beer is not only delicious but very easy to drink. The clean fermentation profile lets the malty richness shine through; deep bready and toasty flavors provide an accent to the richly malty backbone. Finishes malty and full with the bitterness providing balance.

Formulation notes: The base of most pale malty German lagers is Pilsner malt, and this beer is no exception. I like to use some Vienna and Munich malt to add extra richness and increase the color. I like using Tettnanger hops since they have a stronger and spicier quality than Hallertauer. The Ayinger-derived yeast strain works really well in malty beers; Wyeast 2124 Bohemian Lager would be another great choice. I'm using a *hochkurz* single decoction to add to the smoothness and maltiness of the beer. If this is too much for you, use a step mash or a single infusion mash around 154°F (68°C).

Variations: *Bock* beers are traditionally in the OG range of 1.064 to 1.072, so you can make it stronger if you like. I went to the lower side since I'm providing a blond *doppelbock* recipe as well. This beer can be scaled to the strength of a *doppelbock* if you want to see what more hops would be like in that style, but I think most expect *doppelbocks* to be malty first and foremost. If you want to cut back the hops in this recipe to match those expectations, go right ahead. But I think the extra hops add to the enjoyment of this beer. This same beer can be made as an all-Pils malt beer as well; I would use the Wyeast 2124 yeast in that version to help get a lower finishing gravity.

TRADITIONAL OKTOBERFEST

The traditional beer served at Oktoberfest in Munich until the 1990s, when it was largely replaced by what is called Festbier in the BJCP Guidelines. By German regulation, only beers brewed by large breweries within the city limits of Munich can be called Oktoberfestbier. Märzenbier (or March beer) is a more generic name, and it implies that it was brewed in March and lagered over the summer to be served in the fall at Oktoberfest and other occasions.

Style: Märzen (New BJCP Style)

Description: A malty amber German lager known to most in the US as Oktoberfest beer. This recipe pushes the limits on maltiness; my goal was to see how far I could go and not have it taste like a *bock*.

Batch size: 6.5 gallons (25 L)   **OG:** 1.060   **FG:** 1.014
Efficiency: 70%   **ABV:** 6.1%   **IBU:** 22   **SRM:** 11

Ingredients:

3 lb (1.4 kg)	German Pils malt (Best)	Mash
5 lb (2.3 kg)	German Vienna malt (Durst)	Mash
4 lb (1.8 kg)	German Munich (Weyermann)	Mash
1 lb (454 g)	Dark Munich malt (Weyermann)	Mash
1 lb (454 g)	Melanoidin malt (Weyermann)	Mash
8 oz (227 g)	Belgian Aromatic malt (Dingemans)	Mash
4 oz (113 g)	Caramunich III malt (Weyermann)	*Vorlauf*
0.7 oz (20 g)	Hallertauer Tradition 6.8% pellets	@ 60
1 oz (28 g)	German Hallertauer 4.3% whole	@ 20
	White Labs WLP833 German *bock* yeast	

Water treatment: RO water treated with ¼ tsp 10% phosphoric acid per 5 gallons
1 tsp CaCl$_2$ in mash

Mash technique: Infusion, mashout, crystal malt added at *vorlauf*

Mash rests: 152°F (67°C) 60 minutes
168°F (76°C) 15 minutes

Kettle volume: 8 gallons (30 L)

Boil length: 60 minutes

Final volume: 6.5 gallons (25 L)
Fermentation temp: 50°F (10°C) 2 weeks
                        33°F (1°C) 3 months

Sensory description: Beautiful deep reddish-amber color that is clear. Rich malty aroma. Clean lager character. Medium-full body. Rich malt and light hop flavor. Medium to medium-low bitterness. Dry but full finish. The malt has a rich depth to it, intensely malty with a toasty character. Lightly warming and with bready and toasty overtones, this still isn't a *bock* but is heading that way.

Formulation notes: The base of Pils, Vienna, and Munich malts is fairly typical. The addition of the extra malt bomb ingredients (Dark Munich, Aromatic, Melanoidin) is for that malt punch and deeper flavor that many homebrewers (and judges) find so elusive. I avoided a decoction with this recipe since I'm deriving so much flavor from the malt itself. The Ayinger yeast is a great choice for a malty beer, and it produces very little sulfur. Cold lagering smooths it out. It's very important to clear the yeast and give it time to condition; it makes a much smoother and cleaner product.

Variations: I was looking to produce a beer that would judge well in competition, not necessarily something that is a close match to modern German examples that are a bit drier, and not so richly malty. If trying for a drier version, lower both the OG and FG, keeping the ABV about the same or slightly lower. Other yeast would work as well; Wyeast 2124 Bohemian Lager is a good alternative.

MODERN OKTOBERFEST

Most Americans think an Oktoberfest beer is amber and malty. That's how they used to be, but the beer that's been served at Oktoberfest in Munich since around 1990 is this golden version. It was originally developed as a less heavy and more drinkable alternative to the traditional Oktoberfest beer, which is now represented in the BJCP Style Guidelines as the Märzen style. This style can be called an Oktoberfestbier, *a* Festbier, *or a* Wiesn. *The name* Wiesn *comes from Theresienwiese, the meadow where Princess Therese married Crown Prince Ludwig in 1810. The Munich Oktoberfest celebration commemorates this event, and is held on the same grounds.*

Style: Festbier (New BJCP Style)

Description: A golden Oktoberfest-style beer that is bigger and richer than a *helles*, but not really as full-bodied and malty as a *maibock*.

Batch size: 6.5 gallons (25 L)	**OG:** 1.057	**FG:** 1.011
Efficiency: 70% **ABV:** 6.1%	**IBU:** 20	**SRM:** 4

Ingredients:

10 lb (4.5 kg)	German Pils malt (Best)	Mash
2.25 lb (1 kg)	German Munich malt (Best)	Mash
1.75 lb (794 g)	German Vienna malt (Best)	Mash
1.3 oz (37 g)	German Hallertauer 5% whole	@ 60
0.5 oz (14 g)	German Hallertauer 5% whole	@ 5
	Wyeast 2124 Bohemian Lager yeast	

Water treatment:	RO water treated with ¼ tsp 10% phosphoric acid per 5 gallons
	1 tsp $CaCl_2$ in mash
Mash technique:	Step mash, mashout
Mash rests:	131°F (55°C) 10 minutes
	146°F (63°C) 40 minutes
	158°F (70°C) 20 minutes
	168°F (76°C) 10 minutes
Kettle volume:	8.5 gallons (32 L)

Boil length: 90 minutes
Final volume: 6.5 gallons (25 L)
Fermentation temp: 50°F (10°C) 2 weeks
33°F (1°C) 14 weeks

Sensory description: Medium gold color and medium body, with a clean and smooth German lager character. Well attenuated but malty, with a soft mouthfeel and excellent drinkability. Supportive bitterness in the malt-forward beer. Not heavy at all.

Formulation notes: Straight-forward German lager all the way. Classic German ingredients. Mostly Pils malt to keep it drinkable; if there was too much Munich malt it would start tasting like a *bock*. Lagered for 14 weeks.

Variations: This beer could be decocted, but I would boil for no more than 5 minutes to keep color development at a minimum. Some versions finish drier and have slightly more bitterness, so you could also target a final gravity of 1.008 with 27 IBUs, and then double the finishing hops.

RAUCHBOCK

One of the best rauchbiers *I've had the pleasure to judge was brewed by Randy Scorby who won Best of Show at the AHA NHC in 2011. This is a stronger version inspired by his recipe. Since I knew that Schlenkerla makes both a* Rauchbier *Märzen and a* Rauchbier Urbock, *I knew a cranked up version could work.*

Style: Classic Style Smoked Beer (Experimental)

Description: Rich, malty, strong German lager with a moderately smoky character.

Batch size: 6.5 gallons (25 L)   **OG:** 1.064   **FG:** 1.018
Efficiency: 70%   **ABV:** 6.2%   **IBU:** 23   **SRM:** 16

Ingredients:

10 lb (4.5 kg)	Rauchmalz (Weyermann)	Mash
2 lb (907 g)	German Munich (Weyermann)	Mash
1 lb (454 g)	Dark Munich malt (Weyermann)	Mash
1 lb (454 g)	Melanoidin malt (Weyermann)	Mash
8 oz (227 g)	Belgian Aromatic (Dingemans)	Mash
1 lb (454 g)	German CaraRed (Weyermann)	*Vorlauf*
8 oz (227 g)	Caramunich III (Weyermann)	*Vorlauf*
3 oz (85 g)	Carafa II Special (Weyermann)	*Vorlauf*
2 oz (37 g)	German Tettnanger 4% whole	@ 60
0.5 oz (8.5 g)	German Tettnanger 4% whole	@ 5
	Wyeast 2124 Bohemian Lager yeast	

Water treatment:	RO water treated with ¼ tsp 10% phosphoric acid per 5 gallons
	1 tsp CaCl$_2$ in mash
Mash technique:	Step mash, mashout, crystal and dark grains added at *vorlauf*
Mash rests:	131°F (55°C) 10 minutes
	152°F (67°C) 60 minutes
	158°F (70°C) 15 minutes
	168°F (76°C) 15 minutes
Kettle volume:	8 gallons (30 L)
Boil length:	60 minutes
Final volume:	6.5 gallons (25 L)
Fermentation temp:	50°F (10°C) 2 weeks
	33°F (1°C) 3 months

Sensory description: Smoky flavor and aroma but with a strong bready, malty base and subdued hopping. Clean lager character allows the pairing of smoke and rich malt to take place unobtrusively. The smoke is the dominant character but it isn't overwhelming, which makes the beer more approachable. The malty finish helps take some of the edge off the smoke as well.

Formulation notes: Rich German malts for that rich *bock* flavor pair well with the quintessential smoked malt. The darker crystal malts give it a little sweetness and fruitiness to take the edge off the smoke and increase drinkability. The dark malt is just for color adjustment. Spicy hops add to the smoke. The yeast is the classic German lager variety, and one of my favorites for *bocks*. WLP833 German Bock would also work, particularly if you want the beer to be more malty and sweet in the finish.

Variations: Why stop at a *bock?* Take it to the strength of a *doppelbock* (OG 1.072), which is actually closer to Schlenkerla's version (1.070, 6.5%, 100% *Rauchmalz*). A decoction mash could also be used with this beer; the added richness shouldn't be a problem. You could also increase the smoke by increasing the proportion of *rauchmalz*, but that depends entirely on your taste. Home-smoked malt is an interesting variation for those who have the means to do so, but then the type of wood comes in to play too.

SCHWARZBIER

I find that many homebrewers misunderstand this style. When judging in competition, I often get examples that taste more like porters made with lager yeast than true schwarzbiers. It's important that the roast comes through but that it not be burnt.

Style: Schwarzbier (Classic BJCP Style)

Description: This is in the Schwarzpils style with stronger bitterness and hop character than many examples. It matches the reported Köstritzer specs from 1993, making it a Cold War version. Modern versions aren't quite as bitter; if you brew this for competition, reduce the IBUs to around 27.

Batch size: 6.5 gallons (25 L)	**OG:** 1.050	**FG:** 1.013
Efficiency: 70% **ABV:** 4.9%	**IBU:** 34	**SRM:** 37

Ingredients:

10 lb (4.5 kg)	German Pils malt (Weyermann)	Mash
12 oz (340 g)	Belgian Aromatic (Dingemans)	Mash
8 oz (227 g)	Caramunich III (Weyermann)	*Vorlauf*
1 lb (454 g)	Carafa III Special (Weyermann)	*Vorlauf*
4 oz (113 g)	Carafa II Special (Weyermann)	*Vorlauf*

1 oz (28 g)	German Hallertauer 5% whole	FWH
1 oz (28 g)	German Hallertauer 5% whole	@ 60
0.5 oz (14 g)	German Hallertauer 5% whole	@ 10
1 oz (28 g)	German Hallertauer 5% whole	@ 2
	Wyeast 2206 Bavarian Lager yeast	

Water treatment: RO water treated with ¼ tsp 10% phosphoric acid per 5 gallons
1 tsp CaCl$_2$ in mash

Mash technique: Step mash, mashout, crystal malt dark grains added at *vorlauf*

Mash rests: 131°F (55°C) 10 minutes
146°F (63°C) 60 minutes
158°F (70°C) 15 minutes
168°F (76°C) 15 minutes

Kettle volume: 8.5 gallons (32 L)

Boil length: 90 minutes

Final volume: 6.5 gallons (25 L)

Fermentation temp: 50°F (10°C) 2 weeks
32°F (0°C) 13 weeks

Sensory description: Strongly roasted flavor without any harshness or burnt flavors. Moderately high bitterness and a noticeable floral hop flavor and aroma. The hop character will fade over time. The beer is medium-bodied and smooth, with a dry finish. The hop bitterness is clean and supportive of the roasted malt flavors.

Formulation notes: The most important ingredient in this beer is the Carafa Special III malt. Dehusked, debittered dark malts give the roasty flavors without the associated burnt characteristics. The Aromatic malt isn't very traditional, but I was looking for some added malt richness to support the roast. I use a fairly high percentage of Pils malt since I want the beer to be dry and not have a large Munich-like flavor (which I think is out of place in commercial examples from Germany). I'm using a step mash and an attenuative but clean lager yeast because I want it to be a dry beer. If you want a maltier finish, try WLP833 German *bock* lager yeast or Wyeast 2124 Bohemian Lager yeast.

Variations: It's a fun though experiment to contrast this beer with the Czech dark lager styles, as well as the Munich *dunkel*. This beer is decidedly hoppier with more of the roasted character and less Munich and crystal malts. If you want to make something a little closer to most current commercial examples, you can back off the Carafa Special III, decrease the IBUs to the mid- to upper-20s, and increase the Caramunich. Some prefer a bigger Munich malt character, so you can have up to equal parts Pils malt and Munich malt. The beer will be much maltier than commercial examples, but very good regardless.

TRADITIONAL BOCK

It seems that everyone likes the maltiness of a doppelbock, but for me, I like a slightly smaller beer with the same flavors and increased drinkability. A traditional dark bock fills that bill.

Style: Dunkles Bock (Classic BJCP Style)

Description: A stronger (17°P) dark German lager with rich malty flavors of deeply toasted bread crusts with light caramel accents.

Batch size: 6.5 gallons (25 L) **OG:** 1.068 **FG:** 1.016
Efficiency: 70% **ABV:** 6.9% **IBU:** 26 **SRM:** 15

Ingredients:

10 lb (4.5 kg)	Dark Munich malt (Weyermann)	Mash
6.5 lb (2.9 kg)	Munich malt (Best)	Mash
8 oz (227 g)	Caramunich III (Weyermann)	*Vorlauf*
1 oz (28 g)	Carafa III Special (Weyermann)	*Vorlauf*
2 oz (57 g)	German Hallertauer 5% whole	@ 60
	White Labs WLP833 German Bock yeast or Wyeast 2124 Bohemian Lager yeast	

Water treatment: RO water treated with ¼ tsp 10% phosphoric acid per 5 gallons
1 tsp CaCl$_2$ in mash

Mash technique:	Step mash, double decoction, mashout, dark grains added at *vorlauf*
Mash rests:	131 F (55C) 10 minutes
	149°F (65°C) 60 minutes
	Pull 1/3 thick decoction, boil 15 minutes, remix
	158°F (70°C) 15 minutes
	Pull thin decoction, boil 5 minutes, remix
	168°F (76°C) 15 minutes
Kettle volume:	8.5 gallons (32 L)
Boil length:	90 minutes
Final volume:	6.5 gallons (25 L)
Fermentation temp:	48°F (9°C), then lager at 32°F (0°C) for 4 months

Sensory description: A richly malty beer that retains drinkability with supportive bitterness. Dark bread crusts, toast, and a little dark fruit flavor make the beer complex without being heavy or full-bodied.

Formulation notes: The rich flavors of dark Munich malt are what gives this beer its characteristic flavor, but the intensity is tempered a bit with light Munich malt. Try as you may, it just doesn't really taste as malty if you use nothing but light Munich. Trying to compensate by adding crystal malts and such could give it more color and flavor, but it would tend to have a sweeter instead of maltier flavor.

Variations: An infusion mash at 154°F (68°C) would work, but some additional color malt might be needed.

BLONDE DOPPELBOCK

This beer is a paler version of the more common doppelbock, *which should have a starting gravity of at least 18°P (1.072). In general, when there are pale and dark versions of the same style, the paler versions are a little drier and hoppier than the darker ones. That's true here as well; the beer shouldn't come across as sweet as a* doppelbock *can sometimes be.*

Style: Doppelbock (pale) (New BJCP Style)

Description: Basically this style is a scaled up *helles bock* with a stronger malt presence and a touch fewer hops to allow the malt to be even more prominent in the balance.

Batch size: 6.5 gallons (25 L)	**OG:** 1.078	**FG:** 1.018
Efficiency: 70%	**ABV:** 7.9%	**IBU:** 24	**SRM:** 7

Ingredients:

11 lb (5 kg)	German Pils malt (Best)	Mash
3 lb (1.4 kg)	German Vienna malt (Best)	Mash
3 lb (1.4 kg)	German Munich (Weyermann)	Mash
8 oz (227 g)	Melanoidin malt (Weyermann)	Mash
8 oz (227 g)	Carahell malt (Weyermann)	*Vorlauf*
0.6 oz (17 g)	German Magnum 14.4%	pellets @ 90
0.5 oz (14 g)	German Hallertauer 4.5%	whole @ 5
	White Labs WLP833 German Bock yeast	

Water treatment:	RO water treated with ¼ tsp 10% phosphoric acid per 5 gallons 1 tsp CaCl₂ in mash
Mash technique:	Step mash, mashout, crystal malt added at *vorlauf*
Mash rests:	131°F (55°C) 15 minutes 145°F (63°C) 30 minutes 158°F (70°C) 30 minutes 168°F (76°C) 20 minutes
Kettle volume:	8.5 gallons (30 L)
Boil length:	90 minutes
Final volume:	6.5 gallons (25 L)
Fermentation temp:	50°F (10°C) 2 weeks 32°F (0°C) 20 weeks

Sensory description: Deep golden color. Rich bready, toasty, and malty aroma with a chewy, malty finish. Warming alcohol. Very light hops late. Clean fermentation profile.

Formulation notes: A richer, more full-bodied and stronger *maibock*. The *bock* yeast helps make this a malty beer. Enough hops present to keep it from seeming overly sweet.

Variations: *Doppelbocks* can go very high in gravity. You could take it to the extreme by trying to make something similar to an EKU 28, but you'd have to have a very high starting gravity of about 1.112 (28°P).

8 | FAVORITE BELGIAN RECIPES

"Belgium is the Disneyland of the beer world."

—*Charlie Papazian*, The Complete Joy of Homebrewing

If I could choose only one country in which to drink beer, it would have to be Belgium. I've been there several times, and the experience never gets old. The people a very friendly and take genuine pride in their beer culture. The first time I visited, a stern-looking customs agent took my passport and asked, "business or pleasure?" I thought about it for a second and said, "Beer." He immediately smiled, and he said, "That's the best reason!"

In the United States, we like to think we've made great strides in educating service professionals and consumers about beer. But in Belgium, beer seems to be in their collective DNA. Not only do the Belgians want to serve you a great beer, they want to serve it to you in the proper glass. Not just the proper type of glass either, but a logo glass from the brewery (preferably for the exact beer).

I once found myself in a tiny hotel bar in a very small town in Belgium. It was so small that they had only eight beers available, but the selection was very well chosen. When I saw they had the St. Bernardus 12, I ordered it immediately. The owner apologized and said that all those glasses were in use, and asked if I would like to wait. She of course meant that she didn't have any of the logo glasses that specific beer available, not that she didn't have any glassware. When I asked if I could get the beer in a similar, albeit not-branded chalice, she shot me a pained look. So I had an Orval while waiting for the correct glass. And yes, both beers were delicious and an international incident was avoided.

The thing I like best about Belgian beers is that they are so drinkable. They tend to be well-attenuated, which makes them dry and nicely drinkable. The Belgians call this *digestible* and say that even strong beers shouldn't upset your stomach. Combine this digestibility with large flavor profiles, and you have a recipe for great beers you can enjoy at any time of the year.

When Americans ask me about trying to find rare and expensive Belgian beers, I advise them to save their money for a plane ticket to Belgium. The beers are much cheaper there, the food is great, and the scenery is beautiful (and the chocolate isn't bad either).

The following recipes are inspired by some of my favorite beers from Belgium, many of which I only discovered or sampled fresh while in the country. My goal is to make beer inspired by or as a tribute to these great beers, not something that is an exact replica. Belgians admire and value creativity, and don't expect all breweries to be producing beers that taste the same.

- **Heather** – I put this recipe together when making a beer for my friend Heather, whose favorite beer is Leffe Blond. It's a traditional Belgian Blond ale that's smaller and less aggressive than a *tripel*.
- **The Big O** – This is a reimagining of Orval as a stronger beer. Many people have successfully made beer similar to a standard Orval, and I've tasted Orval's lower alcohol beer, but I haven't heard of them trying a stronger version (thus this recipe)
- **Belgian Dark Strong** – One of my favorite styles, this style is very broad with many different interpretations. I've made several versions, including some that are inspired by Westveterlen and Rochefort. This one is more like St Bernardus 12, which is probably my favorite example that is commonly available in the US.
- **Am I Blue?** – To show the range of the style, I made a version inspired by Chimay Blue. It's drier and spicier than the other maltier Belgian Dark Strong recipe.

- **The Forbidden Beer** – Hoegaarden makes a beer that I don't normally see imported in the US: *Verboden Vrucht* (forbidden fruit). It's a fruity, sweet, malty, and fairly strong beer.
- **The Gnome** – A visit to Brasserie d'Achouffe inspired me to try to make a La Chouffe-like strong artisanal blonde ale that's wicked dry with a light spritz of coriander freshness.
- **Bière de Garde** – This beer style can come in different colors and strengths, but I prefer the average strength amber to brown versions the best since it has more nuanced flavors to go with the malty balance of the beer.
- **Odds and Ends Saison** – I'm kind of picky about *saisons*, so I resisted making them until I felt I had figured them out. Discussions with my fellow club member Steve Fletty helped me finally take the plunge, and this recipe is the delicious result.
- **Dubbel** – This was the first all-grain beer I brewed, as I had wanted to make a *dubbel* but couldn't find the right kind of extracts. Now. Fortunately, we have more extract options available. I present two versions of this recipe, the Traditional Homebrew Dubbel version where the flavor primarily comes from specialty grains, and the Modern Homebrew Dubbel where the syrups drive the flavor profile.
- **Flanders Red** – I don't make very many (intentionally) sour beers, but I've always appreciated the balance in this style. As more and more commercial examples go sweet, I like to stay with the drier, more sour version.
- **Alison** – In *Brewing Better Beer*, I gave my recipe for a *tripel* inspired by La Rulles Tripel. This one is like the prototypical Westmalle Tripel, and uses classic ingredients.

HEATHER

Sometimes I'll name a beer after a friend if that person really likes the beer, or if they do something amusing while drinking the beer. My friend Heather really likes Leffe Blond, so I created this for her after researching the style using ingredient information and style parameters from Stan Hieronymus's Brew Like a Monk *(and information from the brewery itself).*

Style: Belgian Blond Ale (Classic BJCP Style)

Description: Well balanced and moderately strong, this beer has a rounded malt palate with moderate bitterness and yeast character. It's kind of like a smaller, less aggressive *tripel* that is enjoyable on a wider range of occasions.

Batch Size: 6.5 gallons (25 L)   **OG:** 1.063   **FG:** 1.013
Efficiency: 75%   **ABV:** 6.6%   **IBU:** 25   **SRM:** 7

Ingredients:

12 lb (4.5 kg)	Belgian Pils malt (Dingemans)	Mash
12 oz (340 g)	Belgian Aromatic malt (Dingemans)	Mash
1 lb (454 g)	Flaked maize	Mash
1 lb (454 g)	Belgian Caravienne (Dingemans)	*Vorlauf*
1.4 oz (40 g)	Czech Saaz 6% whole	@ 60
1 oz (28 g)	German Hallertauer 3.3% whole	@ 10
1 oz (28 g)	Styrian Goldings 4.9% pellets	@ 5
	Wyeast 3787 Trappist High Gravity yeast	

Water treatment: RO water treated with ¼ tsp 10% phosphoric acid per 5 gallons
1 tsp $CaCl_2$ in mash

Mash technique: Step mash, mashout, crystal malt added at *vorlauf*

Mash rests: 131°F (55°C) 15 minutes
146°F (63°C) 40 minutes
158°F (70°C) 15 minutes
168°F (76°C) 15 minutes

Kettle volume: 8.5 gallons (32 L)
Boil length: 90 minutes
Final volume: 6.5 gallons (25 L)
Fermentation temp: 67°F (19°C), letting rise as necessary to fully attenuate

Sensory description: Soft, rounded malt with characteristic Pils malt flavor. Moderate bitterness, relatively dry finish (but not bone dry). There is some noticeable hop character, and the yeast can be a bit spicy. Light esters add additional layers. The aftertaste is balanced with some clean, bready, grainy malt and a light impression of sweetness from the corn.

Formulation notes: When using 3787 yeast, it's been my experience that you can't constrain the fermentation temperature too much or it will stall. I tend to let the yeast rise as it wants to until it finishes. I keep the beer at a constant ambient temperature, because I know it will heat up as it gets going. Rising temperatures help yeast finish, especially the attenuative Belgian strains. I've made this beer with sugar instead of corn, but I didn't like it as much. I think the flavor peaks at about 3–4 months of age; it can be a little rough when young. Give this yeast some time to clean up and allow the beer to condition to develop its best flavors. Dingemans Caravienne seems to have been recently renamed Cara 20, but you may see both names used.

Variations: I like the beer the way it is, so I would leave it alone if trying to nail the style. If you are experimenting, you could add more late hops, or make it the basis for a fruit beer. Sometimes, if I want to play up the orange and lemon flavors, I'll add a few drops of orange oil and lemon oil to the beer. Be careful though; citrus oil is potent and a little goes a long way.

THE BIG O

I don't make very many Brett beers, but Orval is one of my favorites. The photo of me on the back of the book was taken at the café just outside the brewery, and I'm enjoying one of their beers at peak condition. However, I didn't want to try to clone the beer; I've had many examples where that was done, and I've worked with many brewers on the particulars after I took detailed notes at the brewery. I wanted to see how it would taste if I made a scaled up version instead.

Style: Brett Beer (New BJCP Style, Experimental)

Description: You might call this an Orval Extra, a 1.074 beer instead of the normal 1.059 beer. Orval doesn't make a commercial beer of this strength (or name), so this was an experiment. It is a bitter but malty beer with noticeable alcohol strength, a leathery *Brett* character, and a dry finish.

Batch Size: 6.5 gallons (25 L)   **OG:** 1.074   **FG:** 1.004
Efficiency: 90%   **ABV:** 9.2%   **IBU:** 32   **SRM:**

Ingredients:

5 lb (2.3 kg)	Belgian Pils malt (Dingemans)	Mash
4 lb (1.8 kg)	Belgian Pale ale malt (MFB)	Mash
1.5 lb (680 g)	UK Maris Otter (Crisp)	Mash
1.75 lb (794 g)	Belgian Caravienne (Dingemans)	Mash
1.5 lb (680 g)	White beet sugar	Boil
1 oz (28 g)	Styrian Goldings 2.1% whole	FWH
1 oz (28 g)	Hallertauer Tradition 4.5% whole	FWH
1 oz (28 g)	Styrian Goldings 2.1% whole	@ 5
1 oz (28 g)	Hallertauer Tradition 4.5% whole	@ 5
1 oz (28 g)	Styrian Goldings 2.1% pellets	dry hop
1 oz (28 g)	Hallertauer Tradition 4.5% pellets	dry hop
	White Labs WLP510 Bastogne yeast, primary fermentation	
	White Labs WLP644 Brett Brux Trois, pitched after racking to secondary	

Water treatment:	RO water treated with ¼ tsp 10% phosphoric acid per 5 gallons
	1 tsp $CaSO_4$ and 0.5 tsp $CaCl_2$ in mash; same salts in the boil
Mash technique:	Step infusion
Mash rests:	145°F (63°C) 45 minutes
	161°F (72°C) 30 minutes
Kettle volume:	8.5 gallons (32 L)
Boil length:	90 minutes
Final volume:	6.5 gallons (25 L)
Fermentation temp:	60°F (16°C), letting rise to no more than 72°F (22°C)

Sensory description: Leathery aroma with mild hops and moderate fruit like plums. Moderately high bitterness with a dry finish. Medium-high floral, earthy hops and a leathery *Brett* flavor. Noticeable alcohol; needs to age to smooth out. The *Brett* almost makes it seem like it's been aged on wood.

Formulation notes: The recipe was based on my brewery visit notes, as well as information from Stan Hieronymus' *Brew Like a Monk*. The brewery is shooting for 96% attenuation after the *Brett* is done, and thinks the beer peaks in flavor at about 6 months. Note that this recipe has 90% mash efficiency, which is unusual (I wonder if I incorrectly measured base grains; it might be safer to scale the recipe to match your system efficiency). The brewery blends three unnamed pale base malts, so I picked ones that I thought would taste good together (the Maris Otter adds a light biscuity note). The beer ferments to completion with the primary yeast strain, is racked, dry-hopped, racked again, and then the *Brett* is pitched. Orval uses *Brettanomyces Bruxellensis* (White Labs WLP650 equivalent), but I decided to try this other *Brett* strain more commonly used for 100% *Brett* fermentations to see the differences (more fruit, less funk). I bulk conditioned it at room temperature in the fermenter for 6 months on the *Brett* before racking and kegging. This beer was dry-hopped for 3 weeks, which seems like a long time but is the duration I was told on the brewery tour.

Variations: If you want to make this as a standard strength Orval clone, shoot for the following parameters: OG 1.059, FG 1.008, ABV 6.8%, SRM 7.5, IBU 35 (basically brew this exact recipe with 70% mash efficiency). Use the same mash schedule and conditioning. The grain bill and hop varieties are correct, although I'm using my own hopping schedule. The beer is definitely dry-hopped, so never leave that step out. *Brett Bruxellensis* is traditional.

BELGIAN DARK STRONG

People often ask me about my favorite style of beer. That's pretty much an impossible question for any beer geek, but if I had to pick a top five, this style would certainly be on the list. It's my favorite cold weather beer, with all the malt complexity and strong alcohol. There is a huge range to this style, with many interesting and delicious variations. I like to cellar these beers for several years since they always seem to improve with age. I wasn't specifically trying to match the St. Bernardus 12 flavor profile or replicate its grist; I just wanted to try out a beer with a different balance than the other Belgian Dark Strongs I typically brew.

Style: Belgian Dark Strong Ale (Classic BJCP Style)

Description: Malty and rich, but dry and easy to drink. I like the balance of St. Bernardus 12, so I created a recipe with the same gravity and bitterness.

Batch Size: 6.25 gallons (24 L)	**OG:** 1.090	**FG:** 1.014
Efficiency: 70% **ABV:** 10.2%	**IBU:** 22	**SRM:** 24

Ingredients:

11 lb (4.5 kg)	Belgian Pils malt (Dingemans)	Mash
2 lb (907 g)	German Munich (Best)	Mash
2 lb (907 g)	Dark Munich (Weyermann)	Mash
1 lb (454 g)	Belgian Aromatic (Dingemans)	Mash
1 lb (454 g)	Cara 45 (Dingemans)	*Vorlauf*
2 oz (57 g)	UK Chocolate malt (Crisp)	*Vorlauf*
1 lb (454 g)	White beet sugar	Boil
1 lb (454 g)	BR amber sugar darkcandi.com	Boil
1 lb (454 g)	D-2 Syrup darkcandi.com	Boil
1 oz (28 g)	Czech Saaz 6% whole	@ 60
1 oz (28 g)	Styrian Goldings 3.8% pellets	@ 10
0.5 oz (14 g)	Czech Saaz 6% whole	@ 5
	Wyeast 3787 Trappist High Gravity yeast	

Water treatment: RO water treated with ¼ tsp 10% phosphoric acid per 5 gallons
1 tsp $CaCl_2$ in mash

Mash technique: Step mash, mashout, crystal and dark grains added at *vorlauf*

Mash rests: 142°F (61°C) 40 minutes
158°F (70°C) 20 minutes
168°F (76°C) 15 minutes

Kettle volume: 8.5 gallons (32 L)

Boil length: 90 minutes

Final volume: 6.25 gallons (24 L)

Fermentation temp: 64°F (18°C)

Sensory description: At two months old, this was amazingly drinkable. Malty and rich, with a caramel, vanilla, and dark fruit flavor. Lightly spicy with a dry finish and malty aftertaste. Warming alcohol but the malt helped balance it. As the beer dried out, the alcohol became more forward, but then mellowed again with age.

Formulation notes: Has much of the standard malt that I use in *dubbels* and dark strongs, but adjusted to the gravity and bitterness of St. Bernardus 12. I also used some of the newer sugars (dark syrup and soft brown sugar) for Belgian beers, which worked well.

Variations: Would likely make a delicious *dubbel* if brewed to 6.5–7% strength. Could also work well as a spiced beer. Many spice variations are possible; I'd like to try cinnamon and vanilla (with a little cinnamon oil and good-quality vanilla extract, added to taste).

AM I BLUE?

When a friend from work retired, he asked if I could brew four beers for his retirement party. Normally that would be too much, but he told me about it a year in advance, and I knew I would be testing recipes for the book. He asked for a strong Belgian ale like a Chimay Blue, so I created a recipe in that style using the general parameters from the brewery as a reference.

Style: Belgian Dark Strong Ale (Classic BJCP Style)

Description: A dry, fruity, and peppery interpretation of the Belgian Dark Strong ale style, with a lean malt character and high attenuation.

Batch Size: 6.5 gallons (25 L)	**OG:** 1.078	**FG:** 1.011
Efficiency: 70% **ABV:** 9.0%	**IBU:** 31	**SRM:** 20

Ingredients:

12 lb (5.4 kg)	Belgian pale ale (Dingemans)	Mash
1 lb (454 g)	German dark Munich (Weyermann)	Mash
1 lb (454 g)	Aromatic malt (Dingemans)	Mash
1 lb (454 g)	Torrified wheat	Mash
2 oz (57 g)	Debittered black malt	*Vorlauf*
1 lb (454 g)	D-90 candi syrup candisyrup.com	Boil
1 lb (454 g)	D-45 candi syrup candisyrup.com	Boil
1 lb (454 g)	White beet sugar	Boil
0.6 oz (17 g)	German Magnum 14.4% pellets	@ 60
0.3 oz (7 g)	Hallertauer Tradition 6.8% pellets	@ 15
0.5 oz (14 g)	US Vanguard 4.2% whole	@ 5
0.5 oz (14 g)	US Vanguard 4.2% whole	@ 1
	Wyeast 1214 Belgian Abbey yeast	

Water treatment:	RO water treated with ¼ tsp 10% phosphoric acid per 5 gallons
	1 tsp CaCl$_2$ in mash
Mash technique:	Step mash, mashout, dark grains added at *vorlauf*
Mash rests:	131°F (55°C) 15 minutes
	144°F (62°C) 45 minutes
	158°F (70°C) 30 minutes
	168°F (76°C) 15 minutes
Kettle volume:	8.5 gallons (32 L)
Boil length:	90 minutes
Final volume:	6.5 gallons (25 L)
Fermentation temp:	62°F (17°C)

Sensory description: Beautiful reddish-brown color, perfectly clear. Ripe banana, plums, and moderate alcohol. Dry, fruity, and peppery. The alcohol smooths out over time with cellar conditioning.

Formulation notes: The Chimay yeast can produce objectionable levels of banana and solvent if fermented too warm, so start it at the listed fermentation temperature, letting it rise to finish. The dark malt is for color adjustment and to increase stability. I had the US hops on hand, so I used them; they are Hallertauer substitutes (use those if you can get them fresh).

Variations: Not everyone likes this yeast, so feel free to substitute another Belgian strain such as Wyeast 1762 Belgian Abbey II or Wyeast 3522 Belgian Ardennes. Wyeast 3787 Trappist High Gravity would be fine, but I tend to use that yeast in most of my other Belgian strong beers so I was looking for a change. Swapping yeast strains will change the character quite a bit, so don't tell people it's like Chimay.

THE FORBIDDEN BEER

I remember first trying this beer in an outdoor café in Belgium as they prepared for an evening event in the main square. They were testing the sound system by blasting out Pink Floyd's Comfortably Numb. I can't really think of a better song to be listening to while sipping on a fruity, malty, sweet, and strong beer like Hoegaarden's Verboden Vrucht (forbidden fruit). I don't know the recipe of the commercial beer, so I'm just trying to make something that has the same overall feel and style numbers. The yeast drives much of the profile of this beer.

Style: Clone Beer (New BJCP Style)

Description: *Verboden Vrucht* is malty and sweet with a large fruity impression and low bitterness. It doesn't contain any real fruit or spices, but gets those flavors from the yeast and the malt. It's a unique beer that seems like a cross between a *witbier*, a *dubbel*, and a *weizenbock*.

Batch Size: 6.25 gallons (24 L)		**OG:** 1.077	**FG:** 1.015
Efficiency: 70%	**ABV:** 8.2%	**IBU:** 22	**SRM:** 21

Ingredients:

7 lb (3.2 kg)	German wheat malt (Best)	Mash
4 lb (1.8 kg)	German Munich malt (Best)	Mash

3 lb (1.4 kg)	Belgian Pils malt (Dingemans)	Mash
1 lb (454 g)	Belgian Aromatic (Dingemans)	Mash
1 lb (454 g)	Flaked Maize	Mash
4 oz (113 g)	Honey malt (Gambrinus)	Mash
8 oz (227 g)	Belgian CaraVienne (Dingemans)	*Vorlauf*
8 oz (227 g)	Caramel Munich 60 (MFB)	*Vorlauf*
12 oz (340 g)	Caramel Munich 80 (MFB)	*Vorlauf*
4 oz (113 g)	Special B malt (Dingemans)	*Vorlauf*
4 oz (113 g)	Chocolate malt (Dingemans)	*Vorlauf*
1 oz (28 g)	German Hallertauer 3.3% whole	FWH
0.5 oz (14 g)	US Amarillo 8.6% pellets	FWH
1 oz (28 g)	US Amarillo 8.6% pellets	@ 0
	Wyeast 3463 Forbidden Fruit yeast	

Water treatment: RO water treated with ¼ tsp 10% phosphoric acid per 5 gallons

1 tsp CaCl$_2$ in mash

Mash technique: Infusion, mashout, crystal malts added at *vorlauf*

Mash rests: 150°F(66°C) 60 minutes

168°F (76°C) 15 minutes

Kettle volume: 8.5 gallons (32 L)

Boil length: 90 minutes

Final volume: 6.5 gallons (25 L)

Fermentation temp: 68°F (20°C)

Sensory description: Strongly fruity, with dark and dried fruit flavors supported by bready, caramel malt. The bitterness is restrained, so the fruity notes and malt flavors come through unimpeded. The hops provide stone fruit dimensions, while there is a honey-like accent to the malt. The finish is fruity, malty, and sweet. The alcohol can be noticeable when younger, but the malt and sweetness tends to mask it a bit.

Formulation notes: The first goal is to hit the right strength and color, then work on the flavor contributions and overall balance. Bittering hops should be kept low to allow the malt and fruity yeast to take the lead. Specialty grains and hops were selected for their aromatic and flavor contributions (compatible fruity notes primarily). Pay special attention to the volume reduction; this beer needs a hard, rolling boil. The steeping hops give it some more bitterness than estimated. The yeast is a must for this recipe; it's the signature strain for this beer, as you can tell by the name.

Variations: This beer can be spiced. Pick something like the classic *witbier* pairing of orange peel and coriander seeds, or come up with your own choice for spices that will work with fruity, sweet, and malty.

THE GNOME

Brasserie d'Achouffe is located in the wooded hills of the Ardennes in Belgium, in the general area where the Battle of the Bulge was fought in World War II. The name of the brewery comes from chouffe, the local word for gnome, which is the logo and mascot of the company. This recipe is inspired by their flagship beer, La Chouffe. It is not as strong or bitter as the devil-themed Golden Strong Ales, but it is drier and higher in alcohol than Belgian blond ales like Leffe.

Style: Clone Beer (New BJCP Style)

Description: La Chouffe is a strong Belgian artisanal ale, with a golden-amber color and a bit of lemony coriander to accent the yeast.

Batch Size: 6.5 gallons (25 L)	**OG:** 1.066	**FG:** 1.008
Efficiency: 70% **ABV:** 7.8%	**IBU:** 21	**SRM:** 10

Ingredients:

15 lb (6.8 kg)	Belgian Pils malt (Dingemans)	Mash
1 lb (454 g)	Amber candi sugar	Boil
0.5 oz (14 g)	Styrian Goldings 4.5% whole	FWH
1 oz (28 g)	Styrian Goldings 4.5% whole	@ 60
0.5 oz (14 g)	Czech Saaz 3% whole	@ 15
0.5 oz (14 g)	Czech Saaz 3% whole	@ 5
0.4 oz (11 g)	Coriander seeds, crushed	@ 0
	Wyeast 3522 Belgian Ardennes yeast	

Water treatment:	RO water treated with ¼ tsp 10% phosphoric acid per 5 gallons
	0.5 tsp $CaCl_2$ and 0.5 tsp $CaSO_4$ in mash
Mash technique:	Step mash, mashout
Mash rests:	144°F (62°C) 30 minutes
	154°F (68°C) 30 minutes
	168°F (76°C) 15 minutes
Kettle volume:	8.5 gallons (32 L)
Boil length:	90 minutes
Final volume:	6.5 gallons (25 L)
Fermentation temp:	75°F (24°C)

Sensory description: Pleasantly fruity (banana, citrus) with a light hop taste. Deep gold to light amber color. Moderately strong bitterness with a very dry finish. Light spicy, lemony finish.

Formulation notes: I used the rock candi sugar, not the syrups, because I was looking for color and fermentability but not much flavor. If you substitute, be sure to adjust the color to the darker shade noted. The coriander adds a light lemony note. The 3522 yeast strain is from the Achouffe brewery, and it can take a warm fermentation. The higher temperature will bring out more aromatic notes. High attenuation is critical for the style. Don't go too high on the bitterness since the high attenuation will make it seem more bitter.

Variations: Since this is such a simple beer, you could use it as the base for experimentation. Adding darker malts will bring in additional flavors, as will using other spices of your choosing. Make it once as is before varying it to suit your taste.

BIÈRE DE GARDE

The name of this style means beer to store or a keeping beer. It comes from the north of France, generally around the Lille area. It is widely misunderstood outside of France because of the condition of their exported beers. The style doesn't have a musty, cellar-like quality; that is something that comes from dried-out corks used in old bottles. Some imported examples seem fruity due to oxidation. This version has some of those malty and fruity flavors since many judges have become accustomed to those flavors in the style, but please don't intentionally oxidize the beer.

Style: *Bière de Garde* (brown) (Classic BJCP Style)

Description: Smooth, malty, fruity, and fairly strong with a moderate bitterness and a malty finish.

Batch Size: 6.5 gallons (25 L)		**OG:** 1.068	**FG:** 1.012
Efficiency: 70%	**ABV:** 7.4%	**IBU:** 22	**SRM:** 21

Ingredients:

6 lb (2.7 kg)	Belgian Pale Ale malt (MFB)	Mash
6 lb (2.7 kg)	German Vienna malt (Durst)	Mash
1 lb (454 g)	Belgian Aromatic malt (Dingemans)	Mash
12 oz (340 g)	German Wheat malt (Durst)	Mash
6 oz (170 g)	Honey malt (Gambrinus)	Mash
4 oz (113 g)	Belgian Biscuit malt (Dingemans)	Mash
1 lb (454 g)	CaraMunich III (Weyermann)	*Vorlauf*
1 lb (454 g)	UK Crystal 80 (Crisp)	*Vorlauf*
8 oz (227 g)	Belgian CaraVienne (Dingemans)	*Vorlauf*
2 oz (57 g)	Special B malt (Dingemans)	*Vorlauf*
2 oz (57 g)	Carafa III Special malt (Weyermann)	*Vorlauf*
1.33 oz (38 g)	Czech Saaz 5.8% pellets	@ 60
1 oz (28 g)	German Hallertauer 4.3% whole	@ 5
	Wyeast 2206 Bavarian Lager yeast	

Water treatment:	RO water treated with ¼ tsp 10% phosphoric acid per 5 gallons
	1 tsp $CaCl_2$ in mash
Mash technique:	Infusion, mashout, dark grains added at *vorlauf*
Mash rests:	149°F (65°C) 60 minutes
	168°F (76°C) 15 minutes
Kettle volume:	8.5 gallons (30 L)
Boil length:	90 minutes
Final volume:	6.5 gallons (25 L)
Fermentation temp:	60°F (16°C) 2 weeks
	40°F (4°C) cold condition for 4 months

Sensory description: Caramel malt flavor and fruity esters with restrained bitterness. The finish is malty, fruity, and slightly sweet—as much from the lower bitterness as the fruity esters. Smooth and clean with warming alcohol.

Formulation notes: A very malty beer with layers of crystal-type malts and specialty grains. The Carafa is just for color adjustment, not flavor. I'm sticking with a simple infusion mash because I'd like it to retain a little extra residual sweetness. If you want to speed up the lagering, store at near-freezing temperature instead and reduce the storage time to 2 months.

Variations: Can be made with a single decoction mash to increase maltiness and smoothness. If you want it even maltier, try the Wyeast 2124 Bohemian Lager yeast. The beer can be made a little smaller, and the percentage of crystal malts can be reduced. The beer is made with a warm-fermented lager yeast to keep it smooth and to increase the fruity profile. It can be made as an ale using the White Labs WLP515 Antwerp Ale yeast, or possibly the Wyeast 3522 Ardennes Ale yeast (if kept cool). Those yeasts will be a bit spicier and have more of a classic 'Belgian' fruit character than the warmer-fermented lager yeast.

ODDS AND ENDS SAISON

My friend Steve Fletty makes some of the best saisons I've ever tasted. He's experimented with different yeast strains and specialty grains, and I've helped him evaluate the differences. When I interviewed him for an article I was writing on saisons, he happily shared all that he had learned. I tried to take some of his best ideas and use them in a creation of my own. This one features rye as the specialty grain, Pacific Jade hops (lemon rind and black pepper flavors), and uses the Farmhouse yeast strain.

Style: Saison (standard, pale) (Classic BJCP Style)

Description: A *saison* using a variety of base malts along with sugar and rye. I called it my odds and ends beer because I was using up some mostly empty sacks of grain and figured this style would take advantage of that complexity.

Batch Size: 6.25 gallons (24 L)	**OG:** 1.055	**FG:** 1.008
Efficiency: 70% **ABV:** 6.5%	**IBU:** 31	**SRM:** 5

Ingredients:

5.25 lb (2.4 kg)	US six-row (Briess)	Mash
1.25 lb (1.1 kg)	UK Golden Promise (Simpsons)	Mash
2.5 lb (227 g)	Belgian Pale ale malt (MFB)	Mash
2 lb (907 g)	Czech Pils malt	Mash
2 lb (907 g)	US Flaked Rye	Mash
1 lb (454 g)	White beet sugar	Boil
0.5 oz (14 g)	Styrian Goldings 3.8% pellets	FWH
0.5 oz (14 g)	NZ Pacific Jade 14.2% pellets	FWH
0.5 oz (14 g)	Styrian Goldings 3.8% pellets @ 0, 20 minute steep	
0.5 oz (14 g)	NZ Pacific Jade 14.2% pellets @ 0, 20 minute steep	
	Wyeast 3726 Farmhouse Ale yeast	

Water treatment:	RO water treated with ¼ tsp 10% phosphoric acid per 5 gallons
	0.5 tsp $CaCl_2$ and 0.5 tsp $CaSO_4$ in mash
Mash technique:	Infusion, mashout
Mash rests:	149°F (65°C) 60 minutes

	168°F (76°C) 10 minutes
Kettle volume:	8 gallons (30 L)
Boil length:	75 minutes
Final volume:	6.25 gallons (24 L)
Fermentation temp:	73°F (20°C)

Sensory description: Medium gold color, white head. Initial grainy, bready malt taste with a spicy, and bitter finish. Medium-high bitterness. Dry (but not bone dry) finish. Earthy, spicy, and peppery hop flavor lingers into finish. Lemon rind and black pepper, but with a grainy-bready malt aftertaste. Medium-light body. The fruity, spicy flavors come out more as it warms.

Formulation notes: I was using up partial sacks of malt for this beer, so feel free to use whatever you have on hand. Try to use at least half six-row, though. I loved the description of the Pacific Jade hops (smooth bitterness, herbal, fresh citrus, crushed black pepper) and thought it sounded exactly like something to use in a *Saison*. I picked a hop schedule that lets me emphasize aroma and flavor. I used a straight infusion mash, but might try a more intensive step mash schedule next time to try to get it a little drier. I thought 1.008 was good until I got 1.002 with another method (see the *Tom Fitzpatrick's Last Saison* recipe). This beer needs to be highly carbonated (I force carbonate in a keg).

Variations: Steve has worked with other specialty grains including wheat, oats, and spelt. In our side-by-side tasting, we liked rye the best. Flaked rye was used here, but malted rye can also be used. The Farmhouse (Blaugies) yeast strain was used in this batch, but the French Saison (Wyeast 3711) is also good. Any collection of base malts can be used, but Steve likes to use at least some six-row for that extra grainy flavor. Steve prefers Turbinado sugar, although I used white sugar in this batch. Spicing a *saison* is always an option, but I like to be able to evaluate the flavor contributions of the grains, hops, and yeast before experimenting with additions. Some ideas for spice additions include star anise, black pepper, ginger, orange peel, sage, thyme, coriander seeds, cumin, green peppercorns, and pink peppercorns. Don't use all of them at once! Pick flavor combinations that suit your taste preferences and experiment to determine amounts that work for you. When testing these kinds of combinations, I make a tea of the spices by steeping them in boiling water for a few minutes then straining the liquid (just like making tea). Taste the cooled tea and see if you like the balance. Once satisfied with the spice ratio, blend the tea with a small sample of beer to determine what dosing level is pleasing to your palate. It's all very subjective. My advice is to look for a background flavor first since you can always add more.

TRADITIONAL HOMEBREW DUBBEL

This Belgian dubbel *was my first all-grain beer. I wanted to brew something I couldn't really make as an extract beer (at least in the 1990s). I went through several revisions, trying different balances and tweaks, yeasts and malts, but have returned to this recipe as the one I like the best. I enjoy drinking this one the most, and it does well in competitions. It represents the kind of recipe that you'd use if you were making the beer without access to the specialty sugar syrups available today. Specialty malts each add a flavor element and balancing those components is always a challenge.*

Style: Belgian Dubbel (Classic BJCP Style)

Description: This beer is a malty, dark, moderately strong Trappist ale with fruity and spicy yeast character complementing the rich malt, caramel and dark fruit flavors from the malt.

Batch Size: 6.5 gallons (25 L)	**OG:** 1.064	**FG:** 1.014
Efficiency: 70% **ABV:** 6.7%	**IBU:** 22	**SRM:** 17

Ingredients:

7 lb (4.5 kg)	Belgian Pale Ale malt (MFB)	Mash
3 lb (1.4 kg)	German Munich (Best)	Mash
2 lb (907 g)	Dark Munich (Weyermann)	Mash
1.5 lb (680 g)	Belgian Aromatic (Dingemans)	Mash
4 oz (113 g)	Belgian CaraPils (Dingemans)	Mash
8 oz (340 g)	CaraMunich 60 (MFB)	*Vorlauf*
6 oz (170 g)	Special B malt (Dingemans)	*Vorlauf*
1 oz (28 g)	Chocolate wheat (Weyermann)	*Vorlauf*
1 lb (454 g)	Belgian candi sugar, dark	Boil

1.5 oz (43 g)	Styrian Goldings 4.5% pellets	@ 60
0.5 oz (14 g)	Czech Saaz 3% whole	@ 15
0.5 oz (14 g)	Czech Saaz 3% whole	@ 2
	Wyeast 3787 Trappist High Gravity yeast	

Water treatment: RO water treated with ¼ tsp 10% phosphoric acid per 5 gallons
1 tsp $CaCl_2$ in mash

Mash technique: Step mash, mashout, dark grains added at *vorlauf*

Mash rests: 142°F (61°C) 30 minutes
156°F (69°C) 30 minutes
168°F (76°C) 15 minutes

Kettle volume: 8.5 gallons (30 L)

Boil length: 90 minutes

Final volume: 6.5 gallons (25 L)

Fermentation temp: 64°F (18°C), allowing to rise freely

Sensory description: Chewy, rich malt base with deep bready, and toasty flavors. Balanced bitterness but retains a malty finish. Notes of dark and dried fruit, including plums and raisins. Spicy aroma complements the malt. The finish is dry and lightly warming, but the malt remains in control.

Formulation notes: Each ingredient has a purpose, but the key is including some dark Munich malt, and using Wyeast 3787 yeast. I could make a flavorful beer without dark Munich, but it never had the right malt *punch* to it. I enjoyed many of the other yeast varieties (I remember a good example using Wyeast 3522 Ardennes fermented warm that had some of the best esters of any batch), but 3787 is the Westmalle strain and it shows. The Special B malt gives the raisin notes, the CaraMunich brings the plum and some caramel. The chocolate wheat is for color adjustment only. It's important that the beer be malty but not sweet, so a lot of crystal type malts won't help. I don't like to get the alcohol above 7%; it's a good beer, but at higher ABVs it starts moving away from *dubbel* and into the dark strong territory. When using 3787 yeast, be aware that it is a vigorous fermenter and often needs a blowoff tube. It likes a rising temperature during fermentation, and will often stop and flocculate if you try to cool it during fermentation. I like to start it cool and keep the ambient temperature cool, but let the fermenting beer rise as warm as it wants. If it seems like it's slowing down but not done, I'll warm it up. Give it some extra time on the yeast after fermentation to help clean up by-products.

Variations: I've tried so many different variations of this beer that they're hard to count. I've done split batch yeast experiments, changed sugars, varied base malts, changed percentages of specialty grains, used different mash schedules (including decoction), played with alcohol level and IBUs, evaluated different maltsters, and explored spicing. All the beers were recognizable as *dubbels,* and all were enjoyable, so the style does have broad range. I do have some personal preferences based on all that experimentation, and those showed up in this recipe. But just when I thought I had it right, out came the commercial Belgian syrups and I had to start over. Still, that's the fun part of brewing: there's always something new to learn. If I were to make this as a single infusion beer, I'd shoot for converting at 151°F (66°C). I've mashed higher but the extra dextrins don't help with the dry finish. I'd rather mash lower and use a little CaraPils to ensure I get the right body. The yeast can handle a wide range of fermentation temperatures, so you can try this fermented cool and compare it against one fermented warm (72°F, 22°C). Westmalle and Westvleteren both use the same yeast, but Westmalle ferments cooler while Westvleteren goes warmer.

MODERN HOMEBREW DUBBEL

On trips to Belgium, I am often surprised to find that Belgian brewers tend to use simpler recipes than American homebrewers to produce classic darker beers. I was wondering how they managed to get such richness of flavor. As Stan Hieronymus' Brew like a Monk reveals, their secret weapon is their sugar. Much like some classic English recipes rely on flavorful specialty brewing sugars, the Belgians have long had access to syrups that supply the rich flavors and color the styles require. American homebrewers are fortunate to now have multiple sources of such brewing sugars, as well as instructions on how to make their own. This recipe is a modern adaptation of my classic recipe, showing how sugars can replace specialty malts to achieve the same goals.

Style: Belgian Dubbel (Classic BJCP Style)

Description: Malty, rich, moderately strong Trappist ale with fruity and spicy flavors.

Batch Size: 6.5 gallons (25 L)	**OG:** 1.064	**FG:** 1.012
Efficiency: 70% **ABV:** 6.9%	**IBU:** 22	**SRM:** 17

Ingredients:

10 lb (4.5 kg)	Belgian Pilsner malt (Dingemans)	Mash
1 lb (454 g)	German Munich (Best)	Mash
2 lb (907 g)	Dark Munich (Weyermann)	Mash
4 oz (113 g)	Belgian CaraPils (Dingemans)	Mash
1 lb (454 g)	D syrup (darkcandi.com)	Boil
1 lb (454 g)	D-90 syrup (candisyrup.com)	Boil
1.5 oz (43 g)	Styrian Goldings 4.5% pellets	@ 60
0.5 oz (14 g)	Czech Saaz 3% whole	@ 15
0.5 oz (14 g)	Czech Saaz 3% whole	@ 2
	Wyeast 3787 Trappist High Gravity yeast	

Water treatment:	RO water treated with ¼ tsp 10% phosphoric acid per 5 gallons
	1 tsp CaCl$_2$ in mash
Mash technique:	Infusion, mashout
Mash rests:	149°F (65°C) 60 minutes
	168°F (76°C) 10 minutes
Kettle volume:	8.5 gallons (30 L)
Boil length:	90 minutes
Final volume:	6.5 gallons (25 L)
Fermentation temp:	64°F (18°C), allowing to rise freely

Sensory description: Amazingly similar to the original recipe. Chewy, rich malt with fresh, dark fruit and caramel flavors. Balanced bitterness with a malty but dry finish. The yeast gives it a spicy profile with some balanced fruit.

Formulation notes: Similar to the Traditional Homebrew Dubbel recipe, but with Pilsner malt instead of Pale Ale malt as the base. Most breweries

I visited in Belgium were using Dingemans Pilsner malt as their base for all styles, so it's quite authentic. I chose to keep the richer base malts that bring the malty punch; that's a personal taste preference of mine. The dark Munich malt is not something that you'd typically see used in Belgium. The syrups fill in for the specialty malts and rock sugars. Hops and yeast are the same.

Variations: I first tried the candi syrups as a direct substitute for the dark candi sugar rocks, but that produced a very malty, fruity, and rich beer that seemed too dark and too intense for the style. A few sips tasted good, but it was hard to get through a glass. The syrups were duplicating many of the flavors from the base malts. I'm using two different types of syrups for added complexity, but you can choose one or the other as well. It would be a fun experiment to try this recipe against the same one made with all D syrup and another with all D-90 syrup. You can also try it as an exercise in minimalism—start with just the Pils malt and the syrup and see what minimum number of additional ingredients are needed to fit the target flavor profile. That's probably closest to how Belgians brew it, although formulations for this style do vary quite a bit between breweries. I sometimes use this as a base for a fruit beer, where you can add in any fruit that amplifies some fruity flavor present in the profile. Probably the easiest to do is the infamous cherry *dubbel*.

FLANDERS RED

I don't make a lot of sour beers, but have dabbled in brewing the various styles. I do like Flanders red ale, though. I think Rodenbach Grand Cru is the exemplar of the style, so I often turn to that beer for guidance. I think the sourness should be pleasant, not puckering. When I visited the brewery, I saw how after the beer came out of the barrel it was much more sour than their finished product. They must do some blending to hit a target sourness level, most likely like gueuze. A little bit of new to temper the old.

Style: Flanders Red Ale (Classic BJCP Style)

Description: Tart and fruity with a toasty, caramel malt base and dry finish.

Batch Size: 6.5 gallons (25 L) **OG:** 1.049 **FG:** 1.005
Efficiency: 70% **ABV:** 5.9% **IBU:** 19 **SRM:** 17

Ingredients:

8 lb (3.6 kg)	German Vienna malt (Best)	Mash
1 lb (454 g)	Dark Munich malt (Weyermann)	Mash
2 lb (907 g)	Flaked Maize	Mash
1 lb (340 g)	CaraMunich III (Weyermann)	*Vorlauf*
8 oz (227 g)	Special B malt (Dingemans)	*Vorlauf*
2 oz (57 g)	Chocolate wheat malt (Weyermann)	*Vorlauf*
1 oz (28 g)	Styrian Goldings 4.5% pellets	FWH
1 oz (28 g)	Czech Saaz 3% whole	@ 30
	Wyeast 3763 Roeselare Ale Blend yeast	

Water treatment: RO water treated with ¼ tsp 10% phosphoric acid per 5 gallons
1 tsp CaCl$_2$ in mash

Mash technique: Step mash, mashout, crystal malts and dark grains added at *vorlauf*

Mash rests: 144°F (62°C) 60 minutes
158°F (70°C) 15 minutes
168°F (76°C) 15 minutes

Kettle volume: 8.5 gallons (32 L)
Boil length: 90 minutes
Final volume: 6.5 gallons (25 L)
Fermentation temp: 72°F (22°C)

Sensory description: Reddish color, clear, with a wine-like acidity and a toasty, fruity, cherry profile. The beer starts bready, toasty, and malty with supportive bitterness and complementary esters, but then dries out and shows more acidity. The finish is tart and crisp with the fruity notes blending with the acidity.

Formulation notes: The 3763 blend is intended to mimic the Rodenbach fermentation profile (the Rodenbach brewery is in the town of Roeselare). Give the yeast blend plenty of time to work and to develop the sourness (at least a year), since it contains a blend of an ale yeast, a sherry yeast, two

Brett yeasts, and both *lactobacillus* and *pediococcus* bacteria. It's meant to be a complete *lambic*-like fermentation experience in one vial. I like it because it will not only provide the necessary attenuation and sourness, but will also develop a nice cherry flavor that is often characteristic of the style. The chocolate wheat malt is primarily for color adjustment; using a little bit of something dark will give a reddish hue. The rest of the grist is focused on toasty, rich malt flavors, the corn adds a rounded sweetness, and the crystal malts add to the dark fruit character.

Variations: Rodenbach used to make a version called Alexander that had cherries in it. An obvious pairing would be tart cherries (or even dried cherries). You can even blend it with tart cherry juice (or syrup, if you want the beer to be sweeter). Rodenbach is matured in wooden casks, so if you want a bit of wood character to the beer, use medium-toast French oak chips. You don't want a huge wood character, so taste frequently and don't let the wood get too prominent. The tannin from the wood is one of the factors that makes people think this beer is similar to red wine.

ALISON

Remember how I said I sometimes name beers after people who do something memorable when drinking the beer? At a work party at my wife's office, Alison took a liking to this beer but didn't fully grasp how strong it was. Among the more amusing things she did later was arm-wrestle the (male) host of the party and win. I like to think the beer had something to do with it, although her impressive biceps may have also been a factor.

Style: Belgian Tripel (Classic BJCP Style)

Description: A classic *tripel* in the style of Westmalle Tripel. Dry, bitter, and strong with a spicy and hoppy nose. Highly carbonated, and dangerously drinkable. Could lead to demonstrations of feats of strength. Should probably be saved for Festivus.

Batch Size: 6.5 gallons (25 L)	**OG:** 1.080	**FG:** 1.010
Efficiency: 60% **ABV:** 9.4%	**IBU:** 36	**SRM:** 4

Ingredients:

15 lb (6.8 kg)	Belgian Pils malt (Dingemans)	Mash
4 lb (1.8 kg)	White beet sugar	Boil
1.5 oz (42 g)	US Sterling 7% pellets	@ 60
1 oz (28 g)	US Sterling 7% pellets	@ 15
1 oz (28 g)	Styrian Goldings 4.5% pellets	@ 2
	Wyeast 3787 Trappist Ale yeast	

Water treatment:	RO water treated with ¼ tsp 10% phosphoric acid per 5 gallons
	0.5 tsp $CaCl_2$ and 0.5 tsp $CaSO_4$ in mash
Mash technique:	Step infusion, mashout, no sparge
Mash rests:	131°F (55°C) 10 minutes
	140°F (60°C) 10 minutes
	145°F (63°C) 40 minutes
	158°F (70°C) 20 minutes
	168°F (76°C) 10 minutes
Kettle volume:	8 gallons (30 L)
Boil length:	75 minutes
Final volume:	6.5 gallons (25 L)
Fermentation temp:	68°F (20°C)

Sensory description: Delicious Pils malt flavor with a dry finish and high carbonation. The hops also add fruity, spicy, and floral notes, and complement the yeast nicely. The yeast strain produces a peppery, spicy, and fruity quality.

Formulation notes: I used Sterling hops instead of the more traditional Saaz, since they often seem fresher at my local homebrew shop and their AA% is higher which means adding less vegetal content to the boil. If you can get fresh Czech Saaz, they are wonderful in this beer. Step mash and add sugar for attenuation. The best *tripels* start low and finish low so they have the right dryness. The same attenuation won't taste the same if the FG is too high. You can drop the OG (and the FG) even lower if you think this finishes too big (it's a little higher than a Westmalle) by cutting out a pound or two of the Pilsner malt while keeping the sugar the same. Using the *round-trip* mash program in *Tom Fitzpatrick's Last Saison* recipe in Chapter 10 could also give you a lower FG.

Variations: I provided a more modern *tripel* recipe in *Brewing Better Beer*, in the style of *La Rulles Tripel*. This same beer will taste different with other yeast strains, or fermented at different temperatures. My second favorite is White Labs WLP510 Bastogne. If you want to be a hipster, you can add an ounce or two of debittered black malt in the mashout and create a Black Tripel (that's a joke…). You can also dry hop the beer more to be more like an IPA. The style also lends itself to being fermented with *Brett Brux Trois* (White Labs WLP644) as the primary yeast strain, which produces a very dry and fruity beer. Finishing the original beer with *Brett Bruxellensis* (like White Labs WLP650) will give it more of an Orval feeling (if you want to go that route, swap the primary yeast for White Labs WLP510 Bastogne yeast).

9 | SPICED BEER RECIPES

"He who controls the spice, controls the universe!"

—Baron Harkonnen in Frank Herbert's Dune

I like creating spiced beers because I enjoy cooking and creating flavor combinations. When creating a spiced beer recipe, I start by envisioning the final beer, and how each spice provides a distinct contribution to the flavor. That line of thinking is very similar to recipe formulation in general, but spices add another dimension of variety and complexity. Most of the beers in this section are cold weather beers, suitable for the fall and winter holidays (in the northern hemisphere at least).

My only warning when brewing spiced beers is to avoid adding raw spices to finished beer. Lightly toasting the spices helps to extract important essential oils, and really makes the flavors bloom. Avoiding an extended cold steep reduces the potential for harsh tannins and other undesirable flavors. I normally steep the spices at the end of the boil in a mesh hop bag, or make a tea from the spices and blend it in after fermentation is complete. Sometimes I use both methods: a post-boil steep to get most of the flavor and then some spiced-tea additions to tweak the taste of the final beer.

This collection of recipes includes some of my favorite seasonal beers, including several Belgian Christmas ales inspired by classic commercial examples. Many Belgian seasonal specialties are simply stronger (2% ABV higher, on average), darker, more full-bodied versions of flagship beers. Some will have additional spicing, although Belgians don't typically smash you over the head with spices. The best spices are subtle and noticeable, although not necessarily individually recognizable or identifiable. When making Belgian-influenced beers, think about a well-blended final product, not making sure everyone knows what spice you used.

Personal preferences with spicing can influence your recipe design as well. Try to make a blend that you find personally pleasing, and that complements the underlying beer. Stronger, darker, and sweeter beers can take more spice before it gets overwhelming. Sometimes, in larger beers, I will increase the spicing since I know I will be aging the beer, and also know that spices can lose potency over time as bitterness and alcohol intensity subsides.

- **Christmas Beer** – It is fun to have a Christmas beer to take to holiday parties. Darker, stronger versions work well with spices, and have the flavors of holiday desserts and the aromatics of the season.

- **Pumpkin Ale** – My goal with this beer is to brew pumpkin pie in a glass. The problem with many pumpkin beers is that all you taste is spice. This one has pumpkin flavor, and also adds the flavors of the pie crust and optionally, some vanilla ice cream.

- **Llamarada Stout** – Inspired by a Chilean espresso drink with honey and smoked chile pepper, this recipe pairs a foreign stout with those flavors. The name means *bursts of flame*.

- **Kokonut Stout** –This foreign stout is best made through blending and tasting. The flavor of the coconut pairs beautifully with the dark flavors of the base beer.

- **Spiced Belgian Strong Ale** – The first of my selection of Belgian winter ales, this recipe pairs warming spices with a rich Belgian dark strong ale.

- **Christmas Saison** – A strong, dark *saison* with spices. This beer balances flavorful malt with the fruit contributions from spices, hops, and yeast.

- **Belgian Christmas Beer** – A fruity and strong Belgian ale spiced with bitter orange and thyme. This beer is malty with layers of dark fruit complexity.
- **Silent Night** – A Belgian barleywine-style strong ale that uses a significant amount of honey. As warming as your favorite blanket on a cold winter night.
- **Winter in Antwerp** – A darker, spiced version of a Belgian pale ale. Pairs vanilla and cinnamon with biscuity, fruity, and caramel malt flavors.
- **Spiced Bière de Garde** – The dark malts of a *bière de garde* paired with hops and spices. Warm-fermented as a lager to produce a fruity but smooth flavor profile.

CHRISTMAS BEER

This has been a favorite style of mine since I won my first best-of-show with a Christmas beer at the Ohio State Fair. The recipe for the fifth batch I ever brewed is in Brewing Better Beer. This version is one I have been making more recently, and has a richer, more complex malt profile, increased strength, and a slightly stronger spice balance than the original recipe.

Style: Winter Seasonal Beer (New BJCP Style, Experimental)

Description: A moderately strong, chewy, malty Christmas ale with seasonal spices.

Batch Size: 6 gallons (23 L)	**OG:** 1.067	**FG:** 1.018
Efficiency: 70% **ABV:** 6.6%	**IBU:** 24	**SRM:** 22

Ingredients:

7 lb (3.2 kg)	UK Golden Promise (Simpsons)	Mash
2 lb (907 g)	Dark Munich malt (Weyermann)	Mash
2 lb (907 g)	Belgian Aromatic malt (Dingemans)	Mash
1 lb (454 g)	Flaked Barley	Mash
4 oz (113 g)	UK Chocolate (Fawcett)	*Vorlauf*
1 lb (454 g)	UK Crystal 80 (Crisp)	*Vorlauf*
1 lb (454 g)	Cara 45 (Dingemans)	*Vorlauf*

2 lb (907 g)	Orange blossom honey	@ 0
2 Tbsp (30 ml)	Black treacle	@ 0
1 oz (28 g)	UK Challenger 8.3% pellets	@ 60
1 oz (28 g)	Styrian Goldings 3.8% pellets	@ 5
	Wyeast 1318 London Ale III yeast	

Steeping spices:	(put in mesh bag, add at end of boil, steep 10 minutes, remove)
	The zest of 2 oranges
	2 vanilla beans, split, scraped
	6 cinnamon sticks, broken up
	12 coriander seeds, crushed
	1 whole nutmeg, chopped
	8 whole allspice, crushed
Water treatment:	RO water treated with ¼ tsp 10% phosphoric acid per 5 gallons
	1 tsp CaCl$_2$ in mash
Mash technique:	Infusion, mashout, crystal malts and dark grains added at *vorlauf*
Mash rests:	154°F (68°C) 60 minutes
	170°F (76°C) 15 minutes
Kettle volume:	9 gallons (34 L)
Boil length:	120 minutes
Final volume:	6 gallons (23 L)
Fermentation temp:	68°F (20°C)

Sensory description: Rich malty base with toasty, bready flavors and deep caramel. Flavor and aroma of spices are prominent, but blend in with the richness. Warming and chewy, with a malty finish.

Formulation notes: A collection of flavorful malty ingredients sets the base for the spices. The spices are to taste, so feel free to omit any that you don't like. I would always avoid clove, since it reminds people think of an off-flavor. If the treacle flavor is too strong for you, try light molasses instead.

Variations: I've tried this beer with fresh ginger and didn't like it (candied ginger might be fine, though). It's fun to play around with different blends, sometimes showcasing Indian or Chinese spices, but if you're brewing a beer for Christmas itself, stick with traditional spices; those seem to be in the flavor memory for most people that celebrate Christmas.

PUMPKIN ALE

I've been making pumpkin beers for years. I often take them to Halloween parties and the kegs go dry pretty quickly. If handling the pumpkin wasn't such a pain, I'd make a double batch.

Style: Autumn Seasonal Beer (New BJCP Style, Experimental)

Description: Pumpkin and pumpkin pie spices combine with a malty-sweet, bready, toasty amber base beer that suggests pumpkin pie filling, crust, and even a dollop of whipped cream or vanilla ice cream.

Batch Size: 6.5 gallons (25 L)	**OG:** 1.058	**FG:** 1.015
Efficiency: 70% **ABV:** 5.7%	**IBU:** 12	**SRM:** 14

Ingredients:

5 lb (2.3 kg)	UK Golden Promise (Simpsons)	Mash
3 lb (1.4 kg)	German Vienna (Durst)	Mash
2 lb (907 g)	Dark Munich (Weyermann)	Mash
8 oz (227 g)	UK Brown malt (Crisp)	Mash
1 lb (454 g)	Rolled oats	Mash
1 lb (454 g)	Flaked wheat	Mash
1 lb (454 g)	CaraVienne (Dingemans)	*Vorlauf*
4 oz (113 g)	UK Pale chocolate (Crisp)	*Vorlauf*
9 lb (4.1 kg)	Pumpkin puree (See note)	Boil
3 oz (89 ml)	Light molasses (Grandmas)	Boil
8 oz (227 g)	Milled golden cane sugar (Billingtons)	Boil
0.7 oz (20 g)	UK Goldings 6.6% whole	@ 60

Steeping spices: (add at knockout in mesh bag, steep 10 minutes then remove)

	6 cinnamon sticks, broken up
	1.5 Tbsp crystallized ginger, chopped
	1 whole nutmeg, roughly chopped
	10 whole allspice, crushed
	4 green cardamom pods, crushed, husks discarded
	Wyeast 1968 London ESB yeast
Water treatment:	RO water treated with ¼ tsp 10% phosphoric acid per 5 gallons
	1 tsp CaCl$_2$ in mash
Mash technique:	Step mash, mashout, dark grains added at *vorlauf*
Mash rests:	131°F (55°C) 20 minutes
	146°F (63°C) 20 minutes
	151°F (66°C) 20 minutes
	158°F (70°C) 30 minutes
	168°F (76°C) 15 minutes
Kettle volume:	8.5 gallons (32 L)
Boil length:	90 minutes
Final volume:	6.5 gallons (25 L)
Fermentation temp:	68°F (20°C)

Using Pumpkin: The pumpkin used in this recipe is canned, unspiced puree (Libby's or equivalent store brand). Put the puree into a large baking pan, and roast in a 400°F (204°C) oven for 1:00 to 1:15, turning every 15 minutes until fairly dry and caramelized but not burned. Put the roasted pumpkin into a large mesh bag at the end of mash, recirculate on top of it, sparge through it, and then move to the kettle during heating. Remove the bag when the wort starts to boil, but allow the drippings to collect in the kettle.

Sensory description: Beautiful reddish amber-orange color. Big spice nose. Seems sweet but it's actually just low in bitterness. Pumpkin is noticeable in the flavor, and recognizable with pumpkin pie spices. Creamy mouthfeel. Medium-full body but dry in the finish.

Formulation notes: I don't like to use too many hops in spiced beers, and this one is no exception. The bittering hops are kept low, so as to preserve the malty-sweet impression. Late hops are not used so the spicing can shine through, unimpeded. Use pumpkin puree instead of wasting time with fresh pumpkins. If you must start with pumpkins, be sure to use pie (sugar) pumpkins, not field pumpkins (the kind you carve for Halloween). Split in half, remove seeds, roast for 1 hour on a baking sheet in a 350°F (177°C) oven. Let cool until you can handle it, then scoop flesh from skins. Puree in a food processor and save for use in recipe. Measure amount by finished pumpkin extracted, not starting weight of pumpkins.

Variations: If you vary the spices, I recommend leaving out cloves. I know they are a common ingredient in pumpkin pie spice, but experienced beer drinkers will almost always associate it with a flawed beer even if they know it is part of the spicing. I guess the judge training really does sink in. The vanilla is optional. The base beer can be used to experiment with other spices as well. This beer can also be made as into a larger beer (go ahead, make the obvious "Great Pumpkin" joke), but be careful about the alcohol being too bold. I don't normally drink alcohol along with my pumpkin pie, so try not to associate those flavors too strongly.

LLAMARADA STOUT

While on a trip to Chile in 2013, Kris England and I created this as a collaboration recipe with local brewers. Kris had tasted an espresso drink seasoned with honey and the smoked merkén seasoning and thought this would be a great flavor pairing for a beer. I later brewed it using some of the spice I bought at a market in Santiago. When I had Kris try it a few months later, he said, "You made this?" A Chilean woman at the same event tried it, and got a big smile on her face. "This reminds me of home," she said as she proceeded to slam down a pint in a few minutes. This recipe is a scaled up version of the original recipe Kris created, but he deserves credit for the concept and original recipe.

Style: Specialty Beer (Classic BJCP Style, Experimental)

Description: A foreign-style stout spiced with Merkén, honey, and coffee. *Merkén* is a spice blend using mostly a dried, smoked chili pepper from Chile with a little crushed coriander seed. The spice is made by the indigenous *Mapuche* people of Chile, but can be purchased from online retailers like Amazon.com. It's an interesting general purpose spice that I've begun using more frequently.

Batch Size: 7 gallons (27 L)   **OG:** 1.083   **FG:** 1.024
Efficiency: 75%   **ABV:** 7.7%   **IBU:** 24   **SRM:** 64

Ingredients:

9 lb (4.1 kg)	Euro Pils malt (Dingemans)	Mash
1.5 lb (680 g)	Flaked Oats	Mash
1.1 lb (510 g)	UK Brown malt (Crisp)	Mash
1 lb (454 g)	Wheat malt (Durst)	Mash
1.5 lb (680 g)	Carafa III Special (Weyermann)	*Vorlauf*
1.1 lb (510 g)	UK Chocolate malt (Crisp)	*Vorlauf*
12 oz (340 g)	Extra Dark Crystal (Baird)	*Vorlauf*
0.5 oz (14 g)	US Willamette 6.6% whole	FWH
2.5 lb (1.1 kg)	Honey (Tupelo)	@ 10
10.6 g	Merkén	@ 5 (add loose to boil)
2.4 oz (68 g)	Ground coffee (Sumatra) @ 0, steep 10 then remove	
	Wyeast 1098 British Ale yeast	

Water treatment: RO water treated with ¼ tsp 10% phosphoric acid per 5 gallons
1 tsp $CaCl_2$ in mash
Mash technique: Infusion, mashout, dark grains added at *vorlauf*
Mash rests: 156°F (69°C) 60 minutes
168°F (76°C) 15 minutes
Kettle volume: 9 gallons (34 L)
Boil length: 90 minutes
Final volume: 7 gallons (27 L)
Fermentation temp: 66°F (19°C)

Sensory description: Dark brownish-black color. Roasted, coffee, and chili aroma. Non-bitter , with a big coffee flavor. Spice is low, just a touch in the finish. Low notes of dark caramel. Moderately sweet finish with moderate fruit. Medium-full body. Medium bitterness.

Formulation notes: It's hard to substitute for the merkén; it's not as strong as chipotle. When used as a table seasoning, the blend is about 80% merkén, 10% kosher salt, and 10% crushed coriander seed, but the premium merkén doesn't include salt. A blend of some chipotle and sweet Hungarian paprika might taste approximately like the spice. The type of honey and coffee can be varied. I've listed what I used, and they both tasted great in this recipe. I would avoid using heavily roasted grains in this beer; this version works because of the smoothness of the roast. I would also be careful about using coffee that has a high acidity, as it could cause clashing flavors.

Variations: This beer already has a lot going on, so I'm not sure how much else you could add before it turns into a trainwreck. The intensity of the spice can vary with age and handling, as well as personal preference. I like it a little more prominent, so I sometimes add a pinch of fresh merkén to the glass at serving time. When I made the recipe, I used the blend with salt and coriander. The premium merkén without salt is a little smokier. When Kris made his commercial version (El Guerrero, or The Warrior), he used 100% indigenous South American ingredients; I think that would have a more rustic but authentic character.

KOKONUT STOUT

This recipe for a foreign export stout with coconut comes to me from longtime friend Keith Kost (who sometimes goes by the nickname Koko). I've judged his beer in competition, including when it won Best of Show at the 2014 Brewfest in Mount Hope. Once I found out it was his beer, I immediately requested the recipe. I think the key is that the coconut is recognizable but not so prominent that the beer reminds you of suntan lotion.

Style: Spiced Beer (New BJCP Style)

Description: Foreign Extra Stout with Coconut

Batch Size: 11 gallons (42 L)	**OG:** 1.073	**FG:** 1.018
Efficiency: 75% **ABV:** 7.3%	**IBU:** 37	**SRM:** 53

Ingredients:

15 lb (6.8 kg)	US 2-row (Rahr)	Mash
8 lb (3.6 kg)	UK Maris Otter (Fawcett)	Mash
3 lb (1.4 kg)	Flaked Barley	Mash
8 oz (227 g)	Extra Dark Crystal (Simpsons)	*Vorlauf*
2.25 lb (1 kg)	UK Roasted Barley (Bairds)	*Vorlauf*
1 lb (454 g)	UK Chocolate (Bairds)	*Vorlauf*
1.5 oz (42 g)	German Magnum 15.5% whole	@ 90
	Wyeast 1318 London Ale III yeast	
0.8 oz(24 ml)	Bakto Flavors Natural Coconut Flavor extract	

Water treatment:	RO water treated with ¼ tsp 10% phosphoric acid per 5 gallons
	1 tsp $CaCl_2$ in mash
Mash technique:	Infusion, mashout, dark grains added at *vorlauf*
Mash rests:	152°F (67°C) 70 minutes
	168°F (76°C) 15 minutes
Kettle volume:	14.5 gallons (55 L)
Boil length:	90 minutes
Final volume:	11 gallons (42 L)
Fermentation temp:	68°F (20°C) 3 days
	72°F (22°C) 10 days

Sensory description: Rich roasty stout with significant chocolate and coffee (mocha-like). Supportive, but not aggressive, bitterness. Coconut is apparent, but not over the top. The coconut enhances the chocolate and coffee flavors, much like coconut goes with chocolate in a Mounds candy bar.

Formulation notes: Keith says the key to making this beer is to brew a double batch, and only add the coconut extract to one keg. The two kegs are blended together for serving (or for competition). That way, the balance can be adjusted before serving since the flavors and balance can change over time. You are aiming for a final beer where you can just taste the coconut; anything more is too much (unless you're a coconut fanatic). Blend the beers at a 1:1 ratio to start; adjust as suits your taste. The beer tastes best between two months and six months old.

Variations: You can leave the coconut out entirely for a killer stout. Anything nutty would taste good in this beer. Once in Australia, I had a beer flavored with toasted macadamia nuts; those would blend well in this beer. As it goes when brewing with any nuts, the challenge is getting the nutty flavors without head-killing fat. In this case, a natural coconut flavoring works best. Keith bought as many different kinds of coconut and extract that he could, and tasted them all in the stout. He then picked what tasted the best and was easiest to use. I've done similar experiments and very much support this method of trial-and-error.

SPICED BELGIAN STRONG ALE

This recipe is a worst-to-first story. I love Belgian Dark Strong ales, and tend to make them every year. One year, I decided to try spicing my normal recipe. The spices were quite strong, but I liked the general balance. In the first competition I entered it in (when it was way too young), I got a very low score and the judges didn't care for the way the spices and the alcohol clashed. Being patient and aging it a proper amount of time for a 9% ABV beer lets the spices mellow and blend better. It really started peaking between one and two years of age. It eventually took Best of Show at the Mountain Brewer Open in West Virginia, which is pretty excellent for a beer I had considered dumping.

Style: Spiced Beer (Experimental)

Description: Malty, strong, dark Belgian ale with spices.

Batch Size: 5.5 gallons (21 L)	**OG:** 1.095	**FG:** 1.026
Efficiency: 65%	**ABV:** 9.3%	**IBU:** 23	**SRM:** 22

Ingredients:

9 lb (4.1 kg)	Belgian Pils malt (Dingemans)	Mash
2 lb (907 g)	Dark Munich malt (Weyermann)	Mash
2 lb (907 g)	Munich malt (Weyermann)	Mash
2 lb (907 g)	Wheat malt (Weyermann)	Mash
1 lb (454 g)	Belgian Aromatic (Dingemans)	Mash
1 lb (454 g)	Flaked barley	Mash

1 lb (454 g)	CaraMunich III (Weyermann)	*Vorlauf*
8 oz (227 g)	Belgian Special B (Dingemans)	*Vorlauf*
4 oz (113 g)	UK Chocolate (Baird)	*Vorlauf*
1 lb (454 g)	Dark candi sugar (rocks)	Boil
1 lb (454 g)	Amber candi sugar (rocks)	Boil
2 oz (57 g)	Styrian Goldings 4% whole	@ 60
0.5 oz (14 g)	Czech Saaz 3% whole	@ 12
0.5 oz (14 g)	Czech Saaz 3% whole	@ 3

Put spices in mesh bag, add to kettle at knockout, steep 10 minutes, and then remove from kettle:

4 g	Coriander seed, crushed
4 g	Bitter orange rind
4 g	Cardamom seeds, crushed
4 g	Cumin seeds, crushed
4 g	Fresh ginger, chopped
	Wyeast 1762 Abbey Ale II yeast

Water treatment: RO water treated with ¼ tsp 10% phosphoric acid per 5 gallons
1 tsp $CaCl_2$ in mash

Mash technique: Step mash, mashout, dark grains added at *vorlauf*, no sparge

Mash rests: 145°F (63°C) 15 minutes
151°F (66°C) 60 minutes
160°F (71°C) 15 minutes
170°F (77°C) 15 minutes

Kettle volume: 8 gallons (30 L)
Boil length: 60 minutes
Final volume: 6.5 gallons (25 L)
Fermentation temp: 75°F (24°C)

Sensory description: Strong, malty, rich, subdued bitterness, with a strong spice component when young, which balances as it ages. Spicy, fruity yeast character complements the malt and supports the spices.

Formulation notes: The spices can be fairly strong at the start, so let this beer age. The added benefit of aging is that the beer will mature and the alcohol will smooth out. It became very good at two years old. If you want to enjoy the beer sooner, cut the spicing level in half and omit the ginger. If the spices seem too low, make a tea with the same proportion of hops, then blend the tea with the beer after it cools.

Variations: This can make a solid Belgian Dark Strong if you omit the spices altogether. Using only the coriander makes it more like a traditional Belgian beer. Using coriander and orange peel gives it more of a *witbier*-like finish. Star anise and orange peel give it a deep, pungent character. Going a different route with more Christmas-like spices is an option, playing up the cinnamon and nutmeg. Or, to make it more exotic, pick some spice combinations from your favorite ethnic foods, especially ones that hail from Asia (Indian, Chinese, Thai, etc.).

CHRISTMAS SAISON

I came up with this recipe after I made several enjoyable saisons, *but still wanted something different and special for cold weather. While the combinations are new, the basic components are tried and true.*

Style: Winter Seasonal Beer (New BJCP Style, Experimental)

Description: A strong, dark *saison* for the winter season, spiced with orange peel, coriander, and thyme.

Batch Size: 6.5 gallons (25 L)	OG: 1.074	FG: 1.006
Efficiency: 70% ABV: 9.1%	IBU: 30	SRM: 18

Ingredients:

7 lb (3.2 kg)	Belgian Pilsner malt (Dingemans)	Mash
3 lb (1.4 kg)	Belgian Pale malt (Dingemans)	Mash
1 lb (454 g)	Dark Munich malt (Weyermann)	Mash
1 lb (454 g)	Belgian Aromatic malt (Dingemans)	Mash
1 lb (454 g)	German Wheat malt (Durst)	Mash
1 lb (454 g)	German Rye malt (Weyermann)	Mash
12 oz (340 g)	CaraMunich III (Weyermann)	*Vorlauf*

4 oz (113 g)	Carafa III Special (Weyermann)	*Vorlauf*
2 lb (907 g)	Turbinado sugar	Boil
0.25 oz (7 g)	Styrian Goldings 3.8% pellets	FWH
0.25 oz (7 g)	Pacific Jade 14.2%	pellets FWH
0.25 oz (7 g)	Czech Saaz 3%	pellets FWH
0.5 oz (14 g)	German Magnum 11% pellets	@ 60
0.25 oz (7 g)	Styrian Goldings 3.8% pellets	@ 0
0.25 oz (7 g)	Pacific Jade 14.2% pellets	@ 0
0.25 oz (7 g)	Czech Saaz 3% pellets	@ 0
1 oz (28 g)	Bitter orange peel (Curaçao), fresh	@ 0
0.25 oz (7 g)	Coriander seeds, crushed	@ 0
2 sprigs	Fresh thyme	@ 0
	Wyeast 3711 French Saison yeast	

Water treatment: RO water treated with ¼ tsp 10% phosphoric acid per 5 gallons
1 tsp $CaCl_2$ in mash

Mash technique: Step mash, mashout, dark grains added at *vorlauf*

Mash rests: 131°F (55°C) 15 minutes
144°F (62°C) 30 minutes
158°F (70°C) 20 minutes
168°F (76°C) 15 minutes

Kettle volume: 8.5 gallons (32 L)

Boil length: 90 minutes

Final volume: 6.5 gallons (25 L)

Fermentation temp: 72°F (22°C)

Sensory description: Rich malt up front with dryness, bitterness, and spiciness following. Significant aromatics from the spices, yeast, and hops, favoring fruity and peppery spice qualities. Orange, lemon, black pepper, thyme notes.

Formulation notes: The challenge for this recipe is balancing the contributions from the specialty malts, hops, spices, and yeast while still making the beer recognizable as a *saison*. The specialty malts give some dark fruit and light roast notes without astringency. The hop selections favor fruit and spice similar to the spice additions (orange, lemon, pepper). The bittering hop choice is clean and neutral. The yeast favors peppery flavors. I used fresh Curaçao orange peel, not dried. It can be harder to find, but I like the character better and it has less astringency and oxidation. If using dried, use maybe one-third the listed amount.

Variations: The hops and spices can be changed for personal preference. I think it would be a fun experiment to take the spicing in a completely different direction by adding exotic Thai flavors like lemongrass, lime, chili, and mint, or even perhaps fruit, such as mango. It could also be a fun experiment to go with a tropical fruit theme and use New World hops such as Galaxy.

BELGIAN CHRISTMAS BEER

A N'ice Chouffe inspired spiced Belgian winter ale with a fruity, spicy yeast. The Achouffe brewery is in the Ardennes mountains in Belgium, out in the woods. It's a beautiful location, and I think this beer epitomizes the feeling of fallen cold, snow-covered forest.

Style: Winter Seasonal Beer (New BJCP Style, Experimental)

Description: A dark Belgian winter ale with caramel, dark fruit flavors and fruity-spicy yeast, spiced with bitter orange peel and fresh thyme.

Batch Size: 6.5 gallons (25 L)	**OG:** 1.083	**FG:** 1.010
Efficiency: 70% **ABV:** 9.7%	**IBU:** 31	**SRM:** 26

Ingredients:

16 lb (7.3 kg)	Belgian Pilsner malt (Dingemans)	Mash
2 lb (907 g)	Belgian Aromatic malt (Dingemans)	Mash
8 oz (227 g)	Belgian Cara 45 (Dingemans)	*Vorlauf*
8 oz (227 g)	CaraMunich III (Weyermann)	*Vorlauf*
3 oz (85 g)	Special B malt (Dingemans)	*Vorlauf*
1 lb (454 g)	Dark candi sugar	Boil
2 oz (57 g)	Styrian Goldings 4.5% pellets	@ 60
1 oz (28 g)	Styrian Goldings 4.5% pellets	@ 15
1 oz (28 g)	Czech Saaz 3% whole	@ 5

1 oz (28 g)	Bitter orange peel (Curaçao), fresh	@ 0
2 sprigs	Fresh thyme	@ 0
	Wyeast 3522 Belgian Ardennes yeast	

Water treatment: RO water treated with ¼ tsp 10% phosphoric acid per 5 gallons
1 tsp $CaCl_2$ in mash

Mash technique: Step mash, mashout, dark grains added at *vorlauf*

Mash rests: 131°F (55°C) 15 minutes
144°F (62°C) 30 minutes
158°F (70°C) 20 minutes
168°F (76°C)15 minutes

Kettle volume: 8.5 gallons (32 L)

Boil length: 90 minutes

Final volume: 6.5 gallons (25 L)

Fermentation temp: 75°F (24°C)

Sensory description: Strong, with a malty base and balanced bitterness. The spicing is subtle and complements the yeast-derived esters and phenols. There is some caramel and dried fruit flavors backing up the malt, and supporting the alcohol. Needs some age to come into its own.

Formulation notes: Basically an artisanal Belgian amber ale, made dark with candi sugar and spiced with orange peel and thyme. The hop choices should complement and reinforce those spices, and in general, the spicing is not meant to clash with the malt flavors. This strain of yeast can be fruity and spicy, so watch out for interaction between the fruit and spices. Keeping them balanced is tricky, but remember that this beer ages well, so give it some time to let the flavors meld.

Variations: Spicing can be adjusted to your taste using some of the suggestions from previous recipes in this chapter.

SILENT NIGHT

Another Belgian Christmas beer, this time inspired by De Dolle Stille Nacht, which literally translates to "Silent Night" (even though the phrase, contextually, means Christmas Eve). This is a strong barleywine-style Belgian ale with honey. My birthday is a few days before Christmas, and this is the beer I normally drink to celebrate.

Style: Alternative Sugar Beer (New BJCP Style, Experimental)

Description: Like a Belgian braggot, beer-mead hybrid, or barleywine-strength beer that ages very well.

Batch Size: 6.5 gallons (25 L)	**OG:** 1.114	**FG:** 1.026
Efficiency: 70%	**ABV:** 12%	**IBU:** 30	**SRM:** 18

Ingredients:

10 lb (4.5 kg)	Belgian Pale Ale malt (MFB)	Mash
10 lb (4.5 kg)	Belgian Pilsner malt (Dingemans)	Mash
2 lb (907 g)	Belgian Aromatic (Dingemans)	Mash
1 lb (454 g)	Honey malt (Gambrinus)	Mash
1 lb (454 g)	Belgian Cara 45 (Dingemans)	*Vorlauf*
1 lb (454 g)	Dark candi sugar	@ 10
2.5 lb (1.1 kg)	Tupelo honey	@ 10
1.75 oz (50 g)	UK Target 8.1% pellets	@ 60
1 oz (28 g)	Czech Saaz 3% pellets	dry hop
1 oz (28 g)	Styrian Goldings 4.5% pellets	dry hop
	Wyeast 3942 Belgian wheat yeast	

Water treatment:	RO water treated with ¼ tsp 10% phosphoric acid per 5 gallons 1 tsp CaCl₂ in mash
Mash technique:	Step mash, mashout, crystal malt added at *vorlauf*
Mash rests:	142°F (61°C) 30 minutes 154°F (68°C) 30 minutes 168°F (76°C) 15 minutes

Kettle volume:	8.5 gallons (30 L)
Boil length:	90 minutes
Final volume:	6.5 gallons (25 L)
Fermentation temp:	68°F (20°C)

Sensory description: Bready-rich malt base with a noticeable honey flavor, and a smooth, full mouthfeel. The beer is soft but dry in the finish, with the alcohol and malt lingering in the aftertaste. The yeast provides some fruity and spicy notes, which combine with the fruity and caramelly malt flavors.

Formulation notes: Wyeast 3942 is reputed to be the De Dolle strain; this beer is at the upper end of its alcohol tolerance, so be prepared to repitch with a more tolerant strain if it stalls late (the Wyeast 1056 strain can handle these levels of alcohol, and the neutral character won't matter since the Belgian yeast will already have made its flavor mark). The honey malt reinforces the honey flavor, but the luscious quality comes from the honey itself. This isn't meant to be a honey beer, but a beer with a hint of honey flavor.

Variations: Light spicing may enhance this beer, particularly if it accentuated the character of the tupelo honey (like vanilla or nutmeg). Meadowfoam honey might also be a compelling choice in this beer since it has a vanilla-like flavor. Mesquite or desert blossom honey could also add robust earthy, woody, caramelly flavors without clashing with the beer. The proportion of honey can be increased to taste.

WINTER IN ANTWERP

Still working from my Belgian winter beer theme, this recipe is based on Winter Koninck, a stronger and darker beer from Antwerp that is spiced to my own taste with vanilla and cinnamon.

Style: Winter Seasonal Beer (New BJCP Style, Experimental)

Description: A darker, stronger Belgian pale ale spiced with vanilla and cinnamon.

Batch Size: 6.5 gallons (25 L) **OG:** 1.066 **FG:** 1.014
Efficiency: 70% **ABV:** 7.0% **IBU:** 29 **SRM:** 22

Ingredients:

8 lb (3.6 kg)	Belgian Pale Ale malt (MFB)	Mash
4 lb (1.8 kg)	German Vienna malt (Durst)	Mash
1 lb (454 g)	Dark Munich malt (Weyermann)	Mash
1 lb (454 g)	Belgian Aromatic malt (Dingemans)	Mash
6 oz (170 g)	Belgian Biscuit malt (Dingemans)	Mash
1 lb (454 g)	Belgian Cara 45 (Dingemans)	*Vorlauf*
1 lb (454 g)	CaraMunich III (Weyermann)	*Vorlauf*
4 oz (113 g)	Special B malt (Dingemans)	*Vorlauf*
4 oz (113 g)	Belgian chocolate malt (MFB)	*Vorlauf*
2 oz (57 g)	Styrian Goldings 4.5% whole	@ 60
1 oz (28 g)	Czech Saaz 3% whole	@ 10
1 oz (28 g)	Styrian Goldings 4.5% whole	@ 5
2	Cinnamon sticks, crushed	@ 0
1	Vanilla bean pod, split, scraped	@ 0
	White Labs WLP515 Antwerp Ale yeast	

Water treatment: RO water treated with ¼ tsp 10% phosphoric acid per 5 gallons
1 tsp CaCl$_2$ in mash

Mash technique: Infusion, mashout, dark grains added at *vorlauf*

Mash rests: 156°F (69°C) 60 minutes
168°F (76°C) 15 minutes

Kettle volume: 8.5 gallons (32 L)

Boil length: 90 minutes

Final volume: 6.5 gallons (25 L)

Fermentation temp: 70°F (21°C)

Sensory description: Toast, caramel, and biscuit malt flavors with a firm bitterness. Caramel and dark fruit with some nutty roast. Spicy and estery hops combine with the vanilla and cinnamon flavors to give a fruity, spicy, and sweet impression. Stronger than a typical pale ale, but not a huge beer.

Formulation notes: A Belgian pale ale recipe scaled up in size, with the addition of malty components, an increase in the amount of crystal malts, and some additional malts (dark Munich, Special B, chocolate malt) for darker flavors. The general balance is kept the same, but the beer is larger and finishes at a higher gravity. The spices are meant to complement the malt and evoke the spirit of the season.

Variations: Nutmeg would be another compatible addition, either in combination with the vanilla and cinnamon (or replacing the cinnamon). Using cinnamon oil instead of cinnamon can give it a red-hot candy kind of flavor. The beer could also be made at a higher strength, scaled up to the 8–10% range, but I'm not sure I'd spice that version. I'd first want to see what alcohol-related flavors were present, and then maybe think about adding some spices post-fermentation.

SPICED BIÈRE DE GARDE

A dark, spiced bière de garde, *inspired by Jenlain Noël. It's a stronger dark beer with bitter orange peel and allspice, which give impart a special character when combined with the French hops.*

Style: Winter Seasonal Beer (New BJCP Style, Experimental)

Description: A stronger dark *bière de garde* spiced with bitter orange peel and allspice.

Batch Size: 6.5 gallons (25 L) **OG:** 1.066 **FG:** 1.014
Efficiency: 70% **ABV:** 6.8% **IBU:** 22 **SRM:** 22

Ingredients:

5 lb (2.3 kg)	German Vienna malt (Durst)	Mash
3 lb (1.4 kg)	Belgian Pale Ale malt (Dingemans)	Mash
3 lb (1.4 kg)	UK Golden Promise (Simpsons)	Mash
1.5 lb (680 g)	Belgian Aromatic malt (Dingemans)	Mash
1.5 lb (680 g)	CaraMunich III (Weyermann)	*Vorlauf*
1 lb (454 g)	Belgian Cara 45 (Dingemans)	*Vorlauf*

8 oz (227 g)	Belgian CaraVienne (Dingemans)	*Vorlauf*
1 lb (454 g)	Dark Candi Syrup 'D'	Boil
1 oz (28 g)	German Spalt 5% pellets	@ 60
1 oz (28 g)	German Hallertauer 3.5% whole	@ 20
1 oz (28 g)	French Strisselspalt 3.5% whole	@ 10
1 oz (28 g)	Bitter orange peel (Curaçao), fresh	@ 0
6	Allspice berries, crushed	@ 0
	Wyeast 2206 Bavarian Lager yeast	

Water treatment:	RO water treated with ¼ tsp 10% phosphoric acid per 5 gallons
	1 tsp CaCl$_2$ in mash
Mash technique:	Infusion, mashout, crystal malts added at *vorlauf*
Mash rests:	156°F (69°C) 60 minutes
	168°F (76°C) 15 minutes
Kettle volume:	8.5 gallons (32 L)
Boil length:	90 minutes
Final volume:	6.5 gallons (25 L)
Fermentation temp:	64°F (18°C) primary
	34°F (1°C) lager

Sensory description: Toast and caramel malt richness with restrained bitterness and a dry finish make this a malty but easy to drink beer. The flavor is enhanced with deep fruity accents and a smooth but somewhat chewy palate. The spices are noticeable since the yeast is not producing any competing flavors. There is a pleasant but light herbal-floral hop aroma and flavor in support.

Formulation notes: A richer and darker *bière de garde* that emphasizes the malt and fruit components. The bitterness is set at a level to keep the beer from seeming sweet or cloying, but still decidedly malty. The spice complements this type of malt richness. The use of lager yeast keeps it smooth and adds to the fruitiness with the warmer fermentation.

Variations: Can be made as a bigger beer. The spices can be changed or omitted. I like the idea of star anise, fennel seed, or other licorice-like spices with this beer. Could also go a completely different direction and play up the chocolate component, which would still pair well with orange flavors. Or swap out the orange peel for dried cherries or other dark fruit that could mimic some of the malt flavors. Trying to develop Port-like flavors would be a fun exercise, too.

10 | EXPERIMENTAL BEER RECIPES

"You can't make experimental work by copying past work."

—*Trey Parker, South Park co-creator*

Even though I'm known for being the principal author of the BJCP Style Guidelines, I actually like to brew beers that don't fit into defined styles: variations on a style, historical recreations, or beers made using non-traditional brewing methods. I could have fit these beers into other sections of this book, but I decided to give them their own space since they are related by their unusual or unexpected twists. I'm not saying *all* of these beers would be entered in an Experimental category in a BJCP competition, but they are fairly different than other recipes for these styles.

- **Summer Rye** – A recipe that uses nothing but post-boil hops to demonstrate that hops added after the boil can still impart bitterness.
- **American Dubbel Brown** – An experiment in creating a hybrid beer using the malt flavors from a Belgian *dubbel* in an American brown ale.
- **Classic American Porter** – An attempt at recreating a historical beer: the smooth and lagered porter (it's something along the lines of what Yuengling produces today).

- **Tom Fitzpatrick's Last Saison** – A tribute to a dear friend who passed away much too young, this recipe uses a creative mash technique that produces a highly attenuative wort.
- **Vienna Hefeweizen** – A darker, maltier version of a German *weissbier* without being as dark as a *dunkles weissbier.*
- **Robust Cream Ale** – Who says flavor is bad in a light beer? This one pushes the boundary on style by adding a little toasty malt flavor and a late hop character, but I wanted something a little more interesting.
- **Gordian Strong Ale** – A scaled-up version of my Belgian Pale Ale from *Brewing Better Beer* (and a collaboration brew I did with Andy Tveekrem of Market Garden Brewery in Cleveland).
- **Dark Saison** – A non-traditional *saison* that uses the flavors of Belgian dark strong ale.
- **Light Mild** – A very sessionable beer; quite hard to find, even in England. I drank this all afternoon one day while watching the football playoffs with a friend, and barely felt it at the end of the day. This is a style not included in the 2015 BJCP Style Guidelines, so that would cause it to be categorized as an experimental or historical beer.
- **Sterling Bitter** – Non-traditional grain bill and hop varieties create a delicious English golden ale.
- **Australian Pale Ale** – The sparkling beer from Australia finally gets respect in the 2015 BJCP Style Guidelines. Now can you Aussies please stop harassing me? This recipe uses a combination of Australian hops and yeast along with some creative malt blending to simulate the profile of Australian malt.
- **Grodziskie** – *Grätzer* by any other name, this smoked wheat beer from Poland is becoming quite popular as a specialty beer in the summer.

SUMMER RYE

I brewed this beer as an experiment to demonstrate that post-boil hop addi-tions can contribute significant IBUs. Compare this to the hopping used in some of the American Blonde Ales earlier in the book. This beer uses nothing but post-boil hops, but tastes like it has around 25 IBUs. Combined with an unusual hop variety, this made for a fascinating beer.

Style: Alternative Grain Beer (New BJCP Style, Experimental)

Description: Fruity, spicy, and grainy, with a full body and clean fer-mentation profile. Uses an unusual hopping technique along with New Zealand hops.

Batch Size: 6.5 gallons (25 L)	**OG:** 1.049	**FG:** 1.006
Efficiency: 75%	**ABV:** 5.7%	**IBU:** 25 (?)	**SRM:** 4

Ingredients:

4 lb (4.5 kg)	US two-row (Briess)	Mash
3 lb (1.4 kg)	UK Golden Promise (Simpsons)	Mash
3 lb (1.4 kg)	Wheat malt (Durst)	Mash
1.5 lb (680 g)	Rye malt (Weyermann)	Mash
2 oz (57 g)	NZ Motueka 7.5% pellets	@ 0
	White Labs WLP001 California Ale yeast	

Water treatment: RO water treated with ¼ tsp 10% phosphoric acid per 5 gallons
1 tsp CaCl₂ in mash

Mash technique: Step mash
Mash rests: 131°F (55°C) 15 minutes
151°F (66°C) 60 minutes
Kettle volume: 8.5 gallons (30 L)
Boil length: 90 minutes
Final volume: 6.5 gallons (25 L)
Fermentation temp: 66°F (19°C)

Sensory description: Clear, with a deep gold color. Fruity nose, with a big fruity-spicy and grainy flavor on the palate. Intriguing combination of hops and esters. Medium bitterness. Dry finish.

Formulation notes: I like using rye malt rather than flaked rye; it's less gummy in the mash, and doesn't seem so heavy and thick on the palate. The hops steep for 20 minutes after the end of the boil. Most recipe software says this results in zero bitterness, but to my palate it was equivalent to hops added with 15 minutes left in the boil (about 25 IBUs). I picked the hop variety because it was unusual, and because it was reported to have a clean bitterness with a spicy, floral, citrus quality.

Variations: You might prefer to use fruitier yeast, like Wyeast 1272 or Wyeast 1335. Substitute any other hops, but try to use the same quantity as this recipe. You don't have to go the spicy route; you can try fruity or citrusy. I'd avoid hops with abundant resin smell and taste, as that character clashes with the graininess of the rye.

AMERICAN DUBBEL BROWN

I once wrote an article about fusion beers, or beers that tried to combine two styles to create something new. With this recipe, I decided to put my own suggestions into practice, and transplanted a Belgian dubbel grain bill into an American brown ale recipe.

Style: Hybrid Style (New BJCP Style, Experimental)

Description: The malt flavors of a Belgian *dubbel* with a New World hop combo.

Batch Size: 6.5 gallons (25 L)	**OG:** 1.055	**FG:** 1.014
Efficiency: 70% **ABV:** 5.6%	**IBU:** 31	**SRM:** 20

Ingredients:

8 lb (3.6 kg)	Belgian pale ale (MFB)	Mash
3 lb (1.4 kg)	Munich malt (Best)	Mash
1 lb (454 g)	Dark Munich malt (Weyermann)	Mash

1 lb (454 g)	CaraMunich 45 (Dingemans)	*Vorlauf*
8 oz (227 g)	CaraVienne (Dingemans)	*Vorlauf*
4 oz (113 g)	Special B malt (Dingemans)	*Vorlauf*
4 oz (113 g)	UK Chocolate malt (Fawcett)	*Vorlauf*
0.25 oz (7 g)	Australian Galaxy 13% pellets	FWH
0.5 oz (14 g)	US Cascade 8.7% whole	FWH
0.5 oz (14 g)	US Cascade 8.7% whole	@ 10
0.5 oz (14 g)	Australian Galaxy 13% pellets	@ 5
1 oz (28 g)	US Cascade 8.7% whole	@ 0
0.25 oz (7 g)	Australian Galaxy 13% pellets	@ 0
	Wyeast 1332 Northwest Ale yeast	

Water treatment:	RO water treated with ¼ tsp 10% phosphoric acid per 5 gallons
	1 tsp CaCl$_2$ in mash
Mash technique:	Infusion, mashout, dark grains added at *vorlauf*
Mash rests:	149°F (65°C) 60 minutes
	168°F (76°C) 15 minutes
Kettle volume:	8.5 gallons (30 L)
Boil length:	90 minutes
Final volume:	6.5 gallons (25 L)
Fermentation temp:	68°F (20°C)

Sensory description: Rich malty base with caramel, dark fruit, and light nutty, chocolate. Fruity and citrusy hop aroma and flavor. The bitterness is moderate and tempered by the malty depth.

Formulation notes: The grist is similar to a Belgian *dubbel,* except it includes extra chocolate malt to make sure it's a brown ale. The hops are a modern combination of citrus and tropical fruit.

Variations: If the citrusy notes aren't to your liking, try substituting Amarillo for the Cascade. If you want to try something even more unusual, try to use hops with spicy or peppery characteristics to compensate for using American instead of Belgian yeast. Try to have the hops fill in the spicy and fruity notes normally derived from Belgian yeast. If you want to dry out the finish more to make it seem more Belgian, add a pound (454 g) of white sugar.

CLASSIC AMERICAN PORTER

My wife enjoys Yuengling Porter, so I tried to come up with a recipe in the same style. Yuengling still brews this beer, but it represents a much older style of Porter that existed before the craft beer revolution. This style is sometimes called Pennsylvania Porter or Northeast Porter.

Style: Historical Beer (New BJCP Style)

Description: A dark, lagered porter in the style of historical Pennsylvania porters.

Batch Size: 6.5 gallons (25 L)	**OG:** 1.050	**FG:** 1.014
Efficiency: 75% **ABV:** 4.8%	**IBU:** 21	**SRM:** 30

Ingredients:

7 lb (3.2 kg)	US two-row (Briess)	Mash
2 lb (907 g)	UK Mild Ale malt (Fawcett)	Mash
1 lb (454 g)	Flaked Maize	Mash
1 lb (454 g)	US Crystal 60	*Vorlauf*
1 lb (454 g)	Carafa II Special (Weyermann)	*Vorlauf*
0.8 oz (28 g)	US Cluster 7.5% whole	@ 60
0.25 oz (14 g)	US Cascade 6% whole	@ 10
	Wyeast 2206 Bavarian Lager yeast	

Water treatment:	RO water treated with ¼ tsp 10% phosphoric acid per 5 gallons
	1 tsp CaCl$_2$ in mash
Mash technique:	Infusion, mashout, dark grains added at *vorlauf*
Mash rests:	152°F (67°C) 60 minutes
	168°F (76°C) 15 minutes
Kettle volume:	8 gallons (30 L)
Boil length:	60 minutes
Final volume:	6.5 gallons (25 L)
Fermentation temp:	50°F (10°C) 2 weeks
	32°F (0°C) 8 weeks

Sensory description: Smooth, balanced bitterness with a roasted and slightly sweet flavor. Moderate body with some residual sweetness to offset the roast.

Formulation notes: Tried for a basic grist but with some dextrinous grain for more mouthfeel. The corn gives a rounded sweetness more than a straight corn flavor, while the debittered dark malt provides that roasted flavor without the burnt aspects. It tends to be a sweeter beer, so the IBUs are restrained and crystal malt is used. Use a relatively neutral lager yeast and lager the finished beer.

Variations: Add some blackstrap molasses (1 tablespoon, at most) or brewer's licorice (maybe a half stick). If a more burnt flavor is desired, try a few ounces of black malt. For amore rustic and grainy beer, use US six-row instead of two-row base malt.

TOM FITZPATRICK'S LAST SAISON

Tom Fitzpatrick was a homebrewer, a beer judge, and a friend. He passed away unexpectedly on Easter Sunday 2013, and I wrote a tribute to him in Zymurgy. He had been working hard to perfect the saison *style, and most agree that he had nailed it. With the help of some friends in his Urban Knaves of Grain homebrew club, I was able to get his notes and brewing records for the beer. I published that version in Zymurgy. This is my reinterpretation of his recipe using some unusual techniques. I'm sure Tom would have approved (as long as the beer tasted good).*

Style: Saison (standard, pale) (Classic BJCP Style, Experimental)

Description: A dry, spicy *saison* with great balance; uses an unusual mash technique and unconventional hops. Finished at 1.002 without using additional sugar.

Batch Size: 6 gallons (23 L)	**OG:** 1.055	**FG:** 1.007
Efficiency: 70% **ABV:** 6.4%	**IBU:** 26	**SRM:** 4

Ingredients:

10.5 lb (4.8 kg)	Belgian Pils malt (Dingemans)	Mash
8 oz (227 g)	UK Golden Promise (Simpsons)	Mash
6 oz (170 g)	Rye malt (Weyermann)	Mash
1 lb (454 g)	Wheat malt (Durst)	Mash
4 oz (113 g)	Munich malt (Weyermann)	Mash
0.5 oz (14 g)	US Apollo 16.5% pellets	@ 60
	Wyeast 3711 French Saison yeast	

Water treatment: Plain RO water in the mash
0.5 tsp $CaCl_2$ and 0.25 tsp $CaSO_4$ in mash
Sparge water is RO water treated with ¼ tsp 10% phosphoric acid per 5 gallons

Mash technique: Round-trip continuously variable mash

Mash rests: Start mash at 153°F (67°C), begin recirculating while allowing to cool naturally to 140°F (60°C). Once mash hit 140°F (60°C), begin slowly heating while recirculating. Stop at 170°F (77°C). 168°F (76°C) 5 minutes

Kettle volume: 8 gallons (30 L)

Boil length: 75 minutes

Final volume: 6 gallons (23 L)

Fermentation temp: 73°F (23°C)

Sensory description: Bitter, bready, spicy along with lemony citrus note. Pale amber-gold color, clear, with an initial Pils malt flavor. The dryness accentuates the bitterness but it still has some body and comes across as balanced. It has what most people would call a 'Belgian' taste to it.

Formulation notes: I changed the original hops from Perle and Willamette, choosing to go with Apollo instead (described as having a grapefruit, orange, citrus quality, spicy, and clean bittering. I also made some grain substitutions, and changed the recipe to match my normal processes. The biggest change was using what I call a *round-trip* mash schedule: starting with a high temperature, letting it cool while it recirculates, then ramping it back up high. My target FG was 1.007 but what I actually hit was 1.002. I knew there would be doubters, so I took a picture of the hydrometer.

Fig 10.1: Tom Fitzpatrick's Final Saison finished at a very dry 1.002.

Variations: See my original recipe in *Zymurgy®* (September/October 2013, page 7) for another version. If I were to play with this recipe at all, I might explore whether any additional spices bring anything new to the beer. The yeast, rye, and hops already add quite a bit of spice, so I'm afraid pushing this too far will make the flavors clash. Using some Apollo hops late or even as a first wort hop addition might also create some pleasant aromatics.

VIENNA HEFEWEIZEN

This beer was brewed for a retirement party at work. Someone requested a hefeweizen, *and I asked if it was OK if I made it maltier and darker, kind of like a Schneider Weisse. The beer was a hit, as any wheat beer would be on a hot August afternoon. This beer probably wouldn't do as well in a competition since judges would be expecting Pils malt, so save it for parties where you can drink it young and fresh as intended.*

Style: Weissbier (Classic BJCP Style, Experimental)

Description: A classic German wheat beer with Vienna malt as the base instead of Pils malt.

Batch Size: 6 gallons (23 L)	**OG:** 1.048	**FG:** 1.012
Efficiency: 75% **ABV:** 4.8%	**IBU:** 11	**SRM:** 4

Ingredients:

7 lb (3.2 kg)	German wheat malt (Durst)	Mash
3 lb (1.4 kg)	German Vienna malt (Best)	Mash
1 oz (28 g)	German Hallertauer 3.3% whole	@ 60
	Wyeast 3068 Weihenstephan Weizen yeast	

Water treatment:
Used RO water with varying treatments
Add 0.5 tsp $CaCl_2$ to the mash initially
Add 0.5 tsp $CaSO_4$ after first mash rest
Treat sparge water with ¼ tsp 10% phosphoric acid per 5 gallons

Mash technique: Hybrid step mash and single decoction, mashout

Mash rests:	113°F (45°C) 10 minutes
	131°F (55°C) 10 minutes
	Pull thick decoction, heat to 158°F (70°C) for 15 minutes, then boil for 10 minutes
	Meanwhile, ramp main mash to 146°F (63°C) and hold during decoction
	Remix decoction with main mash, hitting 158°F (70°C)
	158°F (70°C) 15 minutes
	170°F (77°C) 10 minutes
Kettle volume:	8 gallons (30 L)
Boil length:	90 minutes
Final volume:	6 gallons (23 L)
Fermentation temp:	62°F (17°C) 2 days
	64°F (18°C) 2 days
	66°F (19°C) until done

Sensory description: A bit richer than a typical hefeweizen but still pale. A decent alternative to my usual Pils malt based beer. The additional malt provides color, a very slight toast flavor, and a fuller mouthfeel.

Formulation notes: Nothing fancy here; just a straight swap of Vienna for Pilsner malt. Add 1 lb (454 g) rice hulls to the mash to aid in lautering. Aerate the wort gently, but don't use any oxygen. Be ready with a blowoff tube for this yeast.

Variations: Could add other character malts, pushing it more towards an amber color. Try to split the difference between a *weissbier* and a *dunkles weissbier.*

ROBUST CREAM ALE

I enjoy cream ale in the summer as much as the next guy (I have a lawn that needs mowing too). If I want to make a standard cream ale, I can't really do any better than Curt Stock's Craptastic Cream Ale.[1] Instead, I decided to add extra character to the beer without taking it too far out of bounds (although I'm pushing the upper style limits on this one). This is another brewing project that is probably better suited to personal enjoyment than competitions.

Style: Cream Ale (Classic BJCP Style, Experimental)

Description: A slightly stronger cream ale with a bit more malt character and late hop character than standard.

Batch Size: 6 gallons (23 L)		**OG:** 1.051	**FG:** 1.009
Efficiency: 70%	**ABV:** 5.6%	**IBU:** 13	**SRM:** 3

Ingredients:

4 lb (1.8 kg)	Euro Pilsner malt (Dingemans)	Mash
4 lb (1.8 kg)	US two-row (Briess)	Mash
2 lb (907 g)	Flaked Maize	Mash
4 oz (113 g)	Vienna malt (Best)	Mash
1 lb (454 g)	Corn sugar	Boil
0.3 oz (8.5 g)	US Vanguard 4.6% whole	FWH
0.5 oz (14 g)	US Vanguard 4.6% whole	@ 60
0.3 oz(8.5 g)	US Vanguard 4.6% whole	@ 5
	Wyeast 1056 American Ale yeast	

Water treatment:	RO water treated with ¼ tsp 10% phosphoric acid per 5 gallons
	1 tsp $CaCl_2$ in mash
Mash technique:	Infusion, mashout
Mash rests:	154°F (68°C) 90 minutes
	168°F (76°C) 15 minutes
Kettle volume:	8 gallons (30 L)

---

[1] http://www.sphbc.org/mwhboy/signature-recipes/curt-stock-s-craptastic-cream-ale

Boil length: 90 minutes
Final volume: 6 gallons (23 L)
Fermentation temp: 66°F (19°C) primary
35°F (2°C) lager

Sensory description: Very clear, medium yellow color. Tall, tight white head. Mild grain, light corn, hint of hops in the aroma. Slight sweetness and a touch of toast. Medium-low spicy hops. Smooth, low bitterness, medium body. The late hops are at the upper end for the style, and the malt has slightly more complexity than is typical. Still very recognizable as a cream ale, especially with the super-smooth body and excellent drinkability.

Formulation notes: I made this once with polenta when I was out of flaked maize. Pre-boil as if you were going to serve it as food, then add it to the mash. It was good, but the corn flavor was subtle (flaked maize is more noticeable). Use 1 lb (454 g) rice hulls in the mash to aid lautering. I used one break-brite tablet in the last 15 minutes of the boil. This needs to be a clear style so I take steps to improve clarity, including using a settling tank before moving to the fermenter.

Variations: As an homage to my good friend Curt Stock, you can turn this into a Miller Chill-inspired summer drink. Add the juice and zest of 3 or 4 limes about 30 hours before kegging, plus some kosher salt to taste.

GORDIAN STRONG ALE

In 2011, I was very much looking forward to the opening of Market Garden Brewery in Cleveland. Brewmaster Andy Tveekrem, who got started at Great Lakes Brewing Company before moving on to Frederick Brewing and then Dogfish Head, was returning home to Ohio. I was expecting to try his beers and maybe get to chat with him. I was floored when I got an email from Andy, asking if I'd like to work on a collaboration beer to help them open their new brewery (is there a more positive answer than "hell yeah!"?). Andy wanted to do a variation on a recipe from Brewing Better Beer, *so we chose the Belgian Pale Ale since he had the right yeast in-house. We scaled it up to a special size, and Andy picked the name as a double entendre.*

Style: Specialty Beer (Classic BJCP Style, Experimental)

Description: I guess you could call this an Imperial Belgian Pale Ale. In Belgium, it would be a special version of a regular beer, which usually just means that it's about 2% stronger and maybe a bit richer than the base beer.

Batch Size: 6.5 gallons (25 L)		**OG:** 1.067	**FG:** 1.015
Efficiency: 70%	**ABV:** 7.0%	**IBU:** 28	**SRM:** 13

Ingredients:

9.5 lb (4.3 kg)	Belgian Pilsner malt (Dingemans)	Mash
5 lb (2.3 kg)	German Vienna malt (Weyermann)	Mash
12 oz (340 g)	Belgian Aromatic (Castle)	Mash
1 lb (340 g)	CaraMunich III (Weyermann)	*Vorlauf*
8 oz (227 g)	Belgian Biscuit malt (Castle)	*Vorlauf*
1 oz (28 g)	Carafa III Special (Weyermann)	*Vorlauf*
2.2 oz (62 g)	Czech Saaz 3.4% pellets	@ 60
1 oz (28 g)	Czech Saaz 3.4% pellets	@ 15
1 oz (28 g)	Czech Saaz 3.4% pellets	@ 5
	White Labs WLP515 Antwerp Ale yeast	

Water treatment:	RO water treated with ¼ tsp 10% phosphoric acid per 5 gallons 1 tsp CaCl$_2$ in mash
Mash technique:	Step mash, mashout, dark grains added at *vorlauf*
Mash rests:	131°F (55°C) 15 minutes 145°F (63°C) 30 minutes 158°F (70°C) 10 minutes 170°F (77°C) 15 minutes
Kettle volume:	8.5 gallons (32 L)
Boil length:	90 minutes
Final volume:	6.5 gallons (25 L)
Fermentation temp:	66°F (19°C)

Sensory description: Biscuity, moderately bitter, with a plum-like fruity notes and spicy-floral hops. Toasty, bready malt base with a dry finish. The alcohol is somewhat deceptive. The biscuit flavor can be a bit high when young, but mellows with age. This beer cellars well, and tastes very good at one year old.

Formulation notes: Essentially a Belgian pale ale recipe scaled up from 5% to 7%. Some changes made along the way to accommodate different systems, but nothing major. The general balance of the beer was fairly similar.

Variations: This beer is already a variation on another style. If you scale it up again to 9%, it could be a Belgian barleywine. Although unusual for a Belgian beer, I imagine this beer could be dry-hopped (or at least whirl pooled). I'd stick with Saaz, but Styrian Goldings would also be a fun choice.

DARK SAISON

Saisons *are traditionally summer beers, but it has become trendy to produce one for each season. Perhaps the trend was started at Fantôme, but there's no denying that the richer, stronger beers are delicious in the winter.*

Style: Saison (super dark) (Classic BJCP Style)

Description: A strong, dark, unspiced winter seasonal *saison*.

Batch Size:	6.5 gallons (25 L)	**OG:** 1.072	**FG:** 1.010
Efficiency: 70%	**ABV:** 8.4%	**IBU:** 31	**SRM:** 21

Ingredients:

10 lb (4.5 kg)	Belgian Pilsner malt (Dingemans)	Mash
5.5 lb (2.5 kg)	German Vienna malt (Best)	Mash
1 lb (454 g)	Dark Munich (Weyermann)	Mash
1 lb (454 g)	CaraMunich III (Weyermann)	*Vorlauf*
8 oz (227 g)	Carafa II Special (Weyermann)	*Vorlauf*
1.5 oz (43 g)	Styrian Goldings 5.4%	pellets @ 60
1.5 oz (43 g)	Czech Saaz 4% whole	@ 15
	Wyeast 3711 French Saison yeast	

Water treatment:	RO water treated with ¼ tsp 10% phosphoric acid per 5 gallons
	1 tsp CaCl₂ in mash
Mash technique:	Step mash, mashout, dark grains added at *vorlauf*
Mash rests:	131°F (55°C) 15 minutes
	145°F (63°C) 60 minutes
	158°F (70°C) 10 minutes
	168°F (76°C) 15 minutes
Kettle volume:	8.5 gallons (32 L)
Boil length:	90 minutes
Final volume:	6.5 gallons (25 L)
Fermentation temp:	73°F (23°C)

Sensory description: Starts with rich and toasty malt flavors and notes of dark fruit and light chocolate. Finishes somewhat dry and bitter, with a spicy, peppery flavor.

Formulation notes: The hardest part of this recipe is getting the necessary attenuation when using the more highly kilned base malts. The next hardest is balancing the spicy flavors from the yeast and hops with the base malts without clashing.

Variations: This can be made as a spiced beer using dried orange peel, star anise, black pepper, or traditional Christmas spices.

LIGHT MILD

This style wasn't added to the 2015 BJCP Style Guidelines, but it can sometimes be found in remote corners of the UK. It's fairly pale, like British Golden Ale, but less bitter and with more complex malt and sugar flavors.

Style: Historical Beer (Experimental)

Description: A pale golden beer with medium-low to medium bitterness, and moderate fruit and toffee flavors.

Batch Size: 6.5 gallons (25 L)   **OG:** 1.033   **FG:** 1.005
Efficiency: 70%   **ABV:** 3.6%   **IBU:** 19   **SRM:** 7

Ingredients:

3.5 lb (1.6 kg)	Belgian pale ale malt (MFB)	Mash
3 lb (1.4 kg)	UK Golden Promise (Simpsons)	Mash
1 lb (454 g)	Flaked maize	Mash
1.3 oz (37 g)	UK chocolate malt (Crisp)	*Vorlauf*
6 fl oz (177 ml)	Lyle's Golden Syrup Boil	@ 15
1 oz (28 g)	UK WGV 5.3% pellets	@ 60
	Wyeast 1335 British Ale II yeast	

Water treatment:	RO water treated with ¼ tsp 10% phosphoric acid per 5 gallons
	1 tsp $CaCl_2$ and 0.5 tsp $CaSO_4$ in mash
Mash technique:	Infusion, mashout
Mash rests:	147°F (64°C) 60 minutes
	168°F (76°C) 15 minutes
Kettle volume:	8.5 gallons (32 L)
Boil length:	90 minutes
Final volume:	6.5 gallons (25 L)
Fermentation temp:	70°F (21°C)

Sensory description: Brilliantly clear, pale gold color. Medium-light body. Medium to medium-low bitterness. Moderate fruit and toffee. Light caramel-like flavor. Clean but attenuative fermentation profile that favors the malt.

Formulation notes: Since the hopping is intentionally subdued (at least in flavor and aroma), the malt and sugar flavors carry this beer. I love the flavor of Golden Promise, but I didn't want it to dominate the beer so I'm blended it with another pale malt. I had some Belgian malt on hand, but anything British would be fine too (although I'd probably avoid the biscuity Maris Otter). The maize gives it some roundness, while the Golden Syrup provides some of the caramelized sugar flavor. I'm used the chocolate malt for color adjustment only. A darker brewing syrup or sugar could be used instead.

Variations: I didn't use late hops in this beer, but they could be used. I wouldn't go overboard (as this isn't supposed to be a hop-driven style), but additional hops could add a new dimension if they complemented the malt. Using other sugars like soft brown sugars, or amber caramel-type syrups would change the flavor profile, but could work with the right balance.

STERLING BITTER

British Golden Bitter was developed recently, but is not widely understood. It's a fairly broad style, like American Blonde Ale, but tends to be more bitter. It might be called a Golden Ale, although I prefer to call it a kind of bitter since it has that characteristic balance. This recipe is based on an example my friend Thomas Eibner shared with me. He kind of shrugged and said it was not a traditional recipe, but that it tasted delicious. I chose to call it a golden ale since it is paler in color and doesn't have the stronger caramel and fruity flavors that many US judges expect in English bitters.

Style: British Golden Ale (New BJCP Style, Experimental)

Description: A beautifully clear, pale golden beer with a clean, prominent bitterness, toasty malt, with a light caramel note in the background. The finish is dry, and there is a moderate fruity component.

Batch Size:	6.5 gallons (25 L)		**OG:** 1.043	**FG:** 1.011
Efficiency: 70%	**ABV:** 4.3%	**IBU:** 32	**SRM:** 7	

Ingredients:

5 lb (2.3 kg)	UK Golden Promise (Simpsons)	Mash
2.5 lb (1.1)	German Munich (Weyermann)	Mash
8 oz (227 g)	Wheat malt (Durst)	Mash
4 oz (113 g)	UK Carapils	Mash
4 oz (113 g)	UK Crystal 45 (Crisp)	Mash
1 lb (454 g)	Flaked Maize	Mash
4 oz (113 g)	Carahell (Weyermann)	Mash
1 oz (28 g)	US Sterling 7% pellets	FWH

1 oz (28 g)	US Sterling 7% pellets	@ 5
1 oz (28 g)	US Sterling 7% pellets	@ 0
1 oz (28 g)	US Sterling 7% pellets	dry hop
	Wyeast 1335 British Ale II	

Water treatment:	RO water treated with ¼ tsp 10% phosphoric acid per 5 gallons
	1 tsp CaSO4$_2$ in mash
Mash technique:	Infusion
Mash rests:	155°F (68°C) 60 minutes
Kettle volume:	8 gallons (30 L)
Boil length:	75 minutes
Final volume:	6.5 gallons (25 L)
Fermentation temp:	66–68°F (19–20°C)

Sensory description: Sterling hops have a floral-spicy note that works well with the bready-rich malt base. The beer finishes dry but with a moderate mouthfeel, and medium bitterness.

Formulation notes: Sterling is an unusual hop for an English style since it is a US-grown Saaz substitute, but it works in this beer. I use it because it is often fresher than any Czech hops I can buy. It's not traditional to use these type of hops in this style, but a pleasant fresh hop nose is always welcome. The base malt is fairly complex but the caramel is very restrained. The corn helps give it a rounded finish. Most English golden ales don't use crystal malts, and the Munich is certainly non-traditional, but I tried to play up a pale maltiness without getting too caramelly. Serving the beer at cellar temperatures (55–58°F/12–14°C) allows the malt to come through, but the hops will be apparent regardless. Be sure to use kettle finings since clarity is quite important in this beer.

Variations: Thomas pushes his version closer to 40 IBUs, but uses different yeast and a slightly different hop schedule. If you want to crank up the hops, feel free, but try to keep that malt prominent. For something closer to commercial English golden ales, drop the crystal-type malts and swap an English base malt for the Munich (I'd avoid the more biscuity malts like Maris Otter).

AUSTRALIAN SPARKLING ALE

I was a guest speaker at the Australian National Homebrew Conference in 2010. After telling me all about their great new Galaxy hops, the next thing people wanted to do was bend my ear over this style of beer, and demand that it be added to the BJCP style guidelines. It is finally in the 2015 edition, and I'm glad I had firsthand experience tasting the style fresh. It is certainly a different beer by the time it gets shipped to the other side of the world; it loses much of the yeast character and bright flavors, and often develops caramel oxidation flavors.

Style: Australian Sparkling Ale (New BJCP Style)

Description: A dry, highly carbonated, pale Australian beer loosely patterned after imported pale ales. When fresh, it has a light fruity dimension (often with a hint of banana). The Pride of Ringwood hops are traditional, but herbal and coarse. Many Australians drink it with the yeast roused, but I prefer it clear.

Batch Size: 6.5 gallons (25 L)   **OG:** 1.047   **FG:** 1.005
Efficiency: 70%   **ABV:** 5.6%   **IBU:** 27   **SRM:** 6

Ingredients:

2 lb (907 g)	US six-row (Briess)	Mash
2 lb (907 g)	UK Golden Promise (Simpsons)	Mash
2 lb (907 g)	German Pilsner malt (Durst)	Mash
2 lb (907 g)	US two-row (Briess)	Mash
6 oz (170 g)	Belgian Caravienne (Dingemans)	*Vorlauf*
1 oz (28 g)	Carafa III Special (Weyermann)	*Vorlauf*
2 lb (907 g)	White table sugar or corn sugar	Boil
1 oz (28 g)	Pride of Ringwood 9% pellets	FWH
0.5 oz (14 g)	Pride of Ringwood 9% pellets	@ 0
	White Labs WLP009 Australian Ale yeast	

Water treatment: Untreated RO water for the mash with 1 tsp $CaSO_4$ and 0.5 tsp $CaCl_2$
Sparge water is RO water treated with ¼ tsp 10% phosphoric acid per 5 gallons

Mash technique:	Step mash, mashout, dark and crystal malts added at *vorlauf*
Mash rests:	144°F (62°C) 60 minutes
	158°F (70°C) 10 minutes
	168°F (76°C) 15 minutes
Kettle volume:	8.5 gallons (32 L)
Boil length:	90 minutes
Final volume:	6.5 gallons (25 L)
Fermentation temp:	Start at 68°F (20°C) and let rise to 72°F (22°C) after 4 days.

Sensory description: The beer is highly attenuated and yeast-driven. Most flavors are fairly moderate. The hops can have an iron-like quality to them, and the grain can be coarse or grainy. The high carbonation and attenuation makes this a thirst-quenching beer. It shouldn't have a caramel flavor (if it does, it's likely from oxidation).

Formulation notes: You pretty much need the Australian yeast for this; it's so attenuated that other yeasts won't really taste right. I use a blend of base malts to give it a bit of grainy coarseness while still having bready and doughy flavors. I can't easily get Australian malts, so I'm blending a variety of other base malts to get a similar flavor. Sugar helps with attenuation, and a hint of color malt makes it a nice deep gold color (not sure if it's traditional, but it's the way I choose to adjust the color without adding flavor). Be sure to carbonate it highly; it's an important part of the style.

Variations: If you don't like the Pride of Ringwood hops, you can use a mix of Galaxy and Cascade, two Australian favorites, or possibly come up with a combination of New Zealand hops. If you can get Australian base malt, that would be even better, but I try a blend of base malts to give additional complexity.

GRODZISKIE

Also known by its Germanized name, Grätzer, *this style is unusual in that it is a low-gravity wheat beer that uses special oak-smoked wheat malt. Until recently, if you wanted to make this style you had to smoke your own malt. However, Weyermann came out with special malt just for this style—* Weizenrauchmalz®. *I want to thank William Shawn Scott for helping me with the BJCP Style Guidelines for this style; he also provided some helpful recipe tips based on Polish brewing records.*

Style: Historical Beer (New BJCP Style, Grodziskie)

Description: A low-gravity, light-bodied, pale, clear, highly-carbonated wheat beer featuring high bitterness and oak-smoked malt. A traditional beer style from Poland that died out but is now enjoying renewed interest.

Batch Size: 6.5 gallons (25 L)	**OG:** 1.031	**FG:** 1.012
Efficiency: 70% **ABV:** 2.6%	**IBU:** 34	**SRM:** 3

Ingredients:

7.75 lb (3.5 kg)	Oak-smoked wheat malt (Weyermann)	Mash
1 lb (454 g)	Rice hulls	*Vorlauf*
2.25 oz (64 g)	Polish Lublin 3.5% pellets	@ 75
0.75 oz (21 g)	Polish Lublin 3.5% pellets	@ 30
	Wyeast 2565 German Ale/Kölsch yeast	

Water treatment: RO water treated with ¼ tsp 10% phosphoric acid per 5 gallons
1 tsp $CaSO_4$ in mash

Mash technique: Step mash, mashout, add rice hulls at mashout and allow to settle to aid lautering

Mash rests: 104°F (40°C) 35 minutes
125°F (52°C) 40 minutes
Ramp up slowly using direct heat and recirculation, taking at least 20 minutes
158°F (70°C) 30 minutes
170°F (77°C) 15 minutes

Kettle volume:	8.5 gallons (32 L)
Boil length:	90 minutes
Final volume:	6.5 gallons (25 L)
Fermentation temp:	62°F (17°C)

Sensory description: Kind of similar to a Berliner Weisse, except that instead of being sour, it's smoky and bitter. Both are highly carbonated, pale, clear, low-gravity beers. The oak smoke has a drier, leaner, more mellow character than the typical beechwood smoke. The beer itself is very clean, and should never, be sour.

Formulation notes: You absolutely cannot substitute the Weyermann *weizenrauchmalz.* Their normal beechwood-smoked barley malt does not have the same profile; it is sharper, more intensely smoky, and often has a ham-like quality. However, the hops make up for the lower smokiness in this beer. Use Polish hops if you can find them, otherwise good-quality Czech or German hops. Use Biofine clear or another fining agent to clarify the beer; it should be brilliantly clear like a *Kölsch.* Carbonation should be very high.

Variations: This already uses some substitutions, but if you can find the original *Grätzer* yeast, use it. It's interesting in that it has a soft, red apple ester that is very unusual. But *Kölsch* yeast is a good stand-in. You can adjust the bitterness level and gravity to your taste. You can also add some Pilsner malt to the grist if the smoke is too much for you. Later year versions of this style were stronger and not as bitter, but try it's worth trying the version that was popular in its heyday.

A | BASIC BEER MATH

Although I use recipe software for most of my brewing calculations, sometimes I run them by hand to make a quick adjustment or double-check a result that looks dodgy. Here are the ten most common calculations that I use:

1. **Estimating your target final boil volume** – Your final boil volume needs to be large enough to account for the various places in transfer and fermentation where some beer gets left behind. To properly estimate the final boil volume, measure how much waste you have on your system (hop mass, trub, kettle waste, etc.). Now measure the usable volume of beer you have and compare that against your actual final boil volume. The difference is the overall waste of the batch. Make sure to adjust your batch size based on the final boil volume, not the final volume in the fermenter. Also remember that the waste will vary depending on how many hops you use, or if you have excessive break.

   It can be useful to record the volumes of your wort or beer at several points in the process: pre-boil volume, post-boil volume, volume transferred to fermenter, and finished beer volume available for packaging. The post-boil volume is your batch size, and should be used as a basis in your calculations.

   On my system, I find that if I have between 6.25 gallons and 6.5 gallons at the end of the boil, then I'll have plenty of beer to fill a 5-gallon keg. I shoot for 6.5 gallons at the end of the boil, transfer about 5.5 gallons to the fermenter (I use 6.5 gallon fermenters), and then ultimately rack 5 to 5.25 gallons from the fermenter for packaging. If I have more than will fit in a keg, I store it in a 2 L plastic bottle so I can watch the progress of the conditioning and maturation tapping into the keg.

This seems like a lot of loss (1.25 gallons), but I always rack the clearest portions of wort and beer. I'm trading volume for quality without having to perform additional steps to recover more usable beer. That's a tradeoff some homebrewers can make, but you won't see it in commercial operations. Understanding your losses lets you scale your batches accordingly to hit your desired final volume for packaging.

2. **Calculating evaporation rate** – Take the difference between your starting volume (Boil Vol$_i$) and your ending volume (Boil Vol$_f$) and divide by the boil length (Duration$_{Boil}$):

$$\frac{\text{Boil Vol}_i - \text{Boil Vol}_f}{\text{Duration}_{Boil}} = \text{Loss}_{hour}$$

This will tell you how much volume evaporates per hour. If you want to calculate it as a percent, take the number of gallons lost per hour and divide it into your starting volume. This rate can vary based on environmental conditions (altitude, humidity, temperature, wind, etc.), but you should have a baseline for your system.

For an average boil on my system, I start with 8.5 gallons, boil 90 minutes, and wind up with 6.5 gallons. I lose 2 gallons (8.5 – 6.5 = 2) in 90 minutes (1.5 hours), or 1.3 gallons per hour. Expressed as a percent, that's 15.3% (1.3 / 8.5) lost per hour. I lose the same 2 gallons in 90 minutes whether I'm making a 5-gallon batch or a 10 gallon batch, since I have the same surface area exposed and I'm maintaining a similar strength boil.

If you have a constant loss rate for different batch sizes, adjust the evaporation rate in your brewing software. For example, in 90 minutes I boil 13.5 gallons down to 11.5 gallons, so I'm still losing = 2 gallons (13.5 – 11.5) in 1.5 hours, or 1.3 gallons per hour. Despite the same overall volume loss, my evaporation rate percent is now 9.6% (1.3/13.5).

My recommendation for homebrewers is to understand how much volume you lose for your various boil lengths, and then adjust your starting volume to hit your target volume based. This is not a figure that should be the same for every brewer; it will be dependent on your particular system.

3. **Estimating post-boil gravity** – First, understand that the total gravity points[1] in your kettle are a constant, regardless of the amount of water. Before the boil starts, measure your specific gravity (SG, converted into points per gallon – $PPG_{pre-boil}$) and wort volume Boil Vol_i) to get a total gravity measurement (Gravity Pts_{Total}):

$$PPG_{pre-boil} \bullet Boil\ Vol_i = Gravity\ Pts_{Total}$$

Even if water boils off, your wort will still have the same gravity points. To get post-boil gravity ($PPG_{post-boil}$), divide by the post-boil volume (*Boil Vol_f*):

$$\frac{Gravity\ Pts_{Total}}{Boil\ Vol_f} = PPG_{post-boil}$$

If you are trying to hit a certain gravity and volume target, you may need to adjust the length of boil, or add water or additional fermentables.

For example, if you fill your kettle with 8 gallons of 1.042 wort, you have 42 points per gallon (PPG) of extract, or a total gravity of 336 (42 • 8).

Those 336 points of extract will remain constant throughout the boil. If you subsequently boil down to a final volume of 6.5 gallons, you will have 51.7 (336/6.5) points per gallon of extract. This equates to a specific gravity of 1.052. The trick is to drop the leading 1 from a gravity reading and use the decimal fraction as the points per gallon number. If you were using a brewing calculator, you could enter the formula as:

$$PPG = (SG - 1) \bullet 1000$$

---

[1] The term *gravity point* is used to describe the total amount of extract in solution. Specific gravity measures the concentration of sugar in solution, and is expressed as a number such as 1.048. The '48' portion of the specific gravity number is the points per gallon of extract.

Algebraically, the reverse equation is:

$$SG = (PPG/1000) + 1.$$

4. **Calculating efficiency** – When homebrewers discuss efficiency, they are talking about *mash* efficiency, or how completely sugar is extracted from the grains in the mash. To calculate this efficiency, determine how many gravity points per pound your grain would give you if its starches were fully converted into sugars. Most base grain contains around 36–38 points per pound (37 is a good average), crystal and roasts are less (roughly 32–34 for crystal and 25–31 for dark malts; 33 and 27 are good averages, respectively). Starchy adjuncts (like flaked wheat and flaked barley) are similar to base malts. Malt extracts and sugars are discussed in calculation #5. You can look up these values in most brewing software.

   Start by calculating the theoretical limit of your extract by multiplying the amount of each fermentable ($Weight_{fermentable}$) by the potential extract of the same fermentable ($PE_{fermentable}$) in gravity points per pound:

$$Weight_{fermentable} \bullet PE_{fermentable} = Gravity\ Pts_{Theoretical}$$

This value is calculated for each fermentable in the mash, then summed to get the total potential extract. You can simplify the calculation by combining fermentables that have the same potential extract (add their weights together, then multiply by the potential extract).

Compare that against your actual extract (total gravity points you get in your kettle). Your actual extract is obtained from your pre-boil specific gravity reading and your pre-boil volume; this is the first equation used in calculation #3 (Estimating post-boil gravity):

$$PPG_{pre\text{-}boil} \bullet BoilVol_i = Gravity\ Pts_{Total}$$

The actual extract ($Gravity\ Pts_{Total}$) divided by the potential extract ($Gravity\ Pts_{Theoretical}$) is your mash efficiency ($Efficiency_{mash}$) in percent.

$$\frac{Gravity\ Pts_{Total}}{Gravity\ Pts_{Theoretical}} = Efficiency_{mash}$$

For example, one of my dark mild recipes uses 7 lb. of English pale ale malt, 12 oz (0.75 lb.) of English crystal malt, and 7 oz (0.4375 lb.) of English chocolate malt. Using the ingredient database in my brewing software, I see that English pale malt has 38 gravity points per pound, English chocolate malt has 31 gravity points per pound, and English crystal malt has 33 gravity points per pound. So my total theoretical gravity points are about 304 ([7 • 38] + [0.75 • 33] + [0.4375 • 31]).

I ran off 8 gallons of wort, and it measured at 1.028. I have 224 (28 • 8) gravity points in my kettle. As a result, my mash efficiency is 74% (224 / 304) for that batch.

When looking at different recipes, you'll sometimes see terms such as *mash efficiency, total efficiency, brewhouse efficiency*, and simply *efficiency*; these terms have different meanings. On the homebrew (and typically the craft beer) scale, we are always talking about mash efficiency even if incorrectly using different terms. On the large commercial scale, brewhouse efficiency[2] is often used but it's a different (and more complex) calculation and is often in the range of 90% or more.

5. **Calculating fermentable or water additions** – If you want to add additional fermentables, know that most liquid fermentables (liquid malt extract, honey, syrups, etc.) add about *36 gravity points per pound* and most dry fermentables (dry malt extract, sugar, etc.) add about *45 gravity points per pound*. Specialty sugars and syrups for brewing (such as Belgian Candi syrups) often have the gravity points listed on the label. The common syrups add *32 gravity points per pound*, while soft sugars add *37–38 points per pound*. If you need to add to your total gravity points, use these to calculate the weight of your additions. Water adds 0 gravity points per pound and can be added to dilute the gravity.

Armed with this information, we can use the same formulas from calculation #3 to adjust our gravity. Suppose you have a final boil volume of 6 gallons with a specific gravity reading of 1.052. If you wanted to have a gravity of 1.064, then you'd have to add fermentables. You have 312 (52 • 6) points in your kettle,

---

[2] If you are interested, see Stephen Holle's *A Handbook of Basic Brewing Calculations* for more detail.

but you want 384 points (64 • 6). Your deficiency is 72 points (384 – 312). Knowing the points per pound of your fermentables allows you to calculate the quantity needed. If you use liquid extract (36 points per pound), then you'll need 2 pounds (72 / 36) to hit your gravity target. If you used dry malt extract, then you'd need 1.6 pounds (72 / 45).

If your gravity reading is too high, you can add water to bring it down. To properly dilute with water, you'll need to calculate the volume. Suppose you have the same 6 gallons of 1.052 wort but you really wanted a gravity of 1.045. You have the same 312 points (52 • 6) in your kettle, but need to know what volume will give you 45 points per gallon. Take the total points and divide by the points per gallon target to reach the volume needed: 312 / 45 = 6.9 gallons. You need 6.9 gallons but only have 6 gallons, so you need to add 0.9 gallons (6.9 – 6.0) of water.

6. **Estimating original gravity** – In order to estimate the original gravity of your recipe, you need to know the pounds of grain used (by type), your mash efficiency, and your batch size. You start by calculating the gravity point contribution of each grain addition:

$$\text{Weight}_{fermentable} \bullet \text{PE}_{fermentable} \bullet \text{Efficiency}_{mash} = \text{Gravity Pts}_{fermentable}$$

For example, let's assume my mash efficiency is 75% (0.75), my batch size is 5 gallons, and that I'm the using 7 lb. pale ale malt, 0.75 lb. crystal malt, 0.4375 lb. chocolate malt with potential extracts of 38, 33, and 31 points per pound, as my grist. The gravity point contribution calculation would be:

7 • 38 • 0.75 = 199.5 (pale ale malt contribution)
0.75 • 33 • 0.75 = 18.6 (crystal malt contribution)
0.4375 • 31 • 0.75 = 10.2 (chocolate malt contribution)
199.5 + 18.6 + 10.2 = 228.3 (total gravity points in kettle)

To estimate the original gravity, use this equation from #3 (Estimating post-boil gravity):

$$\frac{\text{Gravity Pts}_{\text{Total}}}{\text{Boil Vol}_f} = \text{PPG}_{\text{post-boil}}$$

In our example, the estimated original gravity calculates to 46 (228.3 / 5). This translated to a specific gravity of 1.046.

7. **Calculating grist additions** – To calculate the weight of grain additions for a specific batch size of your recipe, you essentially use calculation #6 (Estimating original gravity) in reverse. Let's continue to use the same recipe as in the previous example, but change the batch size to 11 gallons and the target gravity to 1.040 (or 40 gravity points per gallon). Let's also assume our mash efficiency remains at 75%. This example will not only show you how to calculate grain additions, but also how to scale the grist to a different batch size and gravity.

   If you were using this approach on a new recipe, you would start with your grist in percentages and then calculate the weight of grain additions based on the target parameters.

   We begin by calculating the total gravity points needed in the kettle using the equation from calculation #3 (Estimating post-boil gravity):

$$\text{PPG}_{\text{pre-boil}} \bullet \text{Boil Vol}_i = \text{Gravity Pts}_{\text{Total}}$$

   In our example, this is 440 (40 • 11).

   We now need to calculate the gravity point contribution provided by each fermentable in the recipe. It's easiest to do this by first converting the original recipe to percentages:

   Total grist weight = 7 + 0.75 + 0.4375 = 8.1875 lb.
   7 lb. pale ale malt = 7 / 8.1875 = 85.5%
   0.75 lb. crystal malt = 0.75 / 8.1875 = 9.2%
   0.4375 lb. chocolate malt = 0.4375 / 8.1875 = 5.3%

   Next we apply those percentages to the total gravity points required (440) to see what each fermentable needs to contribute:

85.5% pale ale malt = 0.855 • 440 = 376.2 points
9.2% crystal malt = 0.092 • 440 = 40.3 points
5.3% chocolate malt = 0.053 • 440 = 23.5 points

Almost done. We use the equation from calculation #6 (Estimating original gravity) to these gravity points. to work backwards and find the amount of grain that will give us these gravity points. The rewritten equation is:

$$\text{Weight}_{\text{fermentable}} = \frac{\text{Gravity Pts}_{\text{fermentable}}}{\text{PE}_{\text{fermentable}} \bullet \text{Efficiency}_{\text{mash}}}$$

Recalling that pale, crystal, and chocolate malts have potential extracts of 38, 33, and 31 points per pound, and that our mash efficiency is 75%, we convert the gravity point contributions to weights:

Pale ale malt: 376.2 / (38 • 0.75) = 13.2 lb.
Crystal malt: 40.3 / (33 • 0.75) = 1.63 lb.
Chocolate malt: 23.5 / (31 • 0.75) = 1.01 lb.

I would typically round those numbers to make them easier to work with. If using adjuncts, remember that a brewing sugar or malt extract have a mash efficiency of 100%.

8. **Estimating Color** – The general formula for color (in SRM, or Standard Reference Method) from a single grain addition is:

$$1.4922 \bullet \text{MCU}^{0.6859} = \text{SRM}$$

where MCU (malt color units) for each grain addition are calculated using the weight of the grain ($\text{Weight}_{\text{fermentable}}$), the color of the grain in degrees Lovibond ($\text{Lovibond}_{\text{fermentable}}$), and the batch size in gallons (Boil Vol_f):

$$\text{MCU}_{\text{fermentable}} = \frac{\text{Weight}_{\text{fermentable}} \bullet \text{Lovibond}_{\text{fermentable}}}{\text{Boil Vol}_f}$$

For example, calculating the color of the beer from the previous example:

Pale ale malt: 13.2 lb. • 2 L = 226.4 L pts
Crystal malt: 1.63 lb. • 120 L = 195.6 L pts
Chocolate malt: 1.01 lb. • 350 L =353.5 L Pts

$$\frac{L\ pts_{pale} + L\ pts_{crystal} + L\ pts_{chocolate}}{5_{gal}} = MCU$$

$$\frac{226.4 + 195.6 + 353.5}{5_{gal}} = 155.1\ MCU$$

$$1.4922 \bullet (151.1^{0.6859}) = 1.4922 \bullet 31.24 = \sim46SRM$$

9. **Estimating IBUs** – The general formula for estimating IBUs from a single hop addition is:

$$\frac{(0.749 \bullet Weight_{hops} \bullet AA\% \bullet U\%)}{Boil\ Vol_f} = IBU$$

The variables needed are the weight of hops in ounces ($Weight_{hops}$), the alpha acid of hops as a percentage (AA%), the hop utilization factor as a percentage (U%), and the batch volume in gallons ($Boil\ Vol_f$). The hop utilization is the percentage of alpha acids (AA) added to the kettle (by weight) that get converted into iso-alpha acids in the beer.

For example, if we add 2 oz of 5.5% AA hops at 60 min in 5 gal final volume, how many IBU do we add?

$$\frac{(0.749 \bullet 2\ oz \bullet 5.5\% \bullet 20\%)}{5_{gal}} = 32$$

$$\frac{(Boil\ Vol_f \bullet IBU)}{0.749 \bullet AA\% \bullet U\%} = weight_{hops}$$

If we want 60 BU of 11% AA hops at 60 min in 5 gal batch, how many oz do we need?

$$\frac{(5 \bullet 60)}{0.749 \bullet 11\% \bullet 20\%} = \sim 1.8 \text{ oz}$$

What if you don't know the weight of iso-alpha acids in your beer? You'll have to estimate that factor instead!

The Tinseth method[3] is a set of formulas to estimate hop utilization (U%). Glenn Tinseth fit a curve to research data and produced a fairly accurate formula based on boil time and wort gravity. He calculated utilization as:

Hop utilization = (gravity factor) • (time factor), where
Gravity factor = 1.65 • 0.000125(wort gravity – 1) and
Time factor = [1 – e(-0.04 • time in minutes)] / 4.15

For example, if you have a 30 minute addition of hops in 1.060 wort, the utilization factor would be:

$0.162 \{1.65 \bullet 0.000125^{(1.060 - 1)}\} \bullet \{[1 - e^{(-0.04 \bullet 30)}] / 4.15\}$, or 16.2%.

If that addition was 1.5 ounces of 6.3% AA Cascade hops in a 5-gallon batch, then the IBU contribution of that addition would be:

22.9 IBUs ([0.749 • 1.5 • 6.3 • 16.2] / 5)

But this is not an actual calculation you typically perform. You normally look up utilization based on wort gravity and time factor from a table where the calculations were already performed. There is such a table in the previously mentioned link to the Tinseth method. Most homebrewers I know just use recipe software, which will have the calculations built in. The advantage to using recipe software is that it will perform an exact calculation based on wort gravity and time, while tables might not have the values you need. In that case, interpolation (picking a number in between nearest values) or approximation (rounding to nearest value) is what most would use.

---

[3] http://www.realbeer.com/hops/research.html

Even with these formulas, the measurements are only an approximation. There are other factors not included in the equation, such as wort pH, boil vigor, break material present, boil temperature as a function of altitude, etc. The alpha acid percentage of the hops is nominal, and is reported by the hop supplier; the alpha acids could have degraded during storage because of storage temperature, oxidation (packaging), time, and hop variety.

The calculations of IBUs does not take into account the overall solubility of alpha acids in wort, as there is an upper limit on how many IBUs can be present in beer before they start to precipitate out (some say around 100 IBUs). The formulas also don't describe hops added outside the boil, such as whirlpool hops. Recent research[4] suggests whirlpool utilization can range from 12 to 22% (15% seems to be an average) in commercial craft beer operations. To my own palate, I thought whirlpool additions on my homebrew system were about the same as a 15 minute boil addition, which equates to roughly 10 to 11% utilization (but obviously that last measure is both anecdotal and subjective).

10. **Calculating ABV and ABW** – These are easy calculations everyone should know. In these formulas, use the actual specific gravity not gravity points per gallon:

$$(OG - FG) \bullet 105 = ABW$$
$$ABV = 1.27 \bullet ABW$$

For example, suppose your original gravity (OG) is 1.050 and your final gravity (FG) is 1.012. Your alcohol by weight (ABW) would be 4.0% ([1.050 – 1.012] = 0.038; 0.038 • 105). The alcohol by volume (ABV) is 5.1% (4.0% • 1.27). If I'm doing a quick approximation, I often multiply by 1.25 instead of 1.27 since that's easier to do in my head.

---

[4] *For the Love of Hops*, Stan Hieronymus, p. 201.

B | WORKING WITH RECIPE SOFTWARE

Many of the standard brewing calculations have been automated by recipe software. There is certainly not a one-size-fits-all type of solution available, so I recommend that brewers approach recipe software much in the same way they approach equipment selection. Find something that works for how you and your process, and try not to fight with it. If you force it to do something it wasn't designed for, you are unlikely to be happy with the results.

I'd like to explore how and when to use recipe software, and what common problems can arise. I'll discuss my use of recipe software as an example, and talk about some considerations for how you might select your own. In my experience, the best software supports the processes your existing processes, and does not force you to brew a certain way.

Keep in mind that any computer program that estimates or predicts an outcome based on inputs is a model, and models may or may not be accurate. The model may be based on assumptions that are different from the processes you actually use, so it's critical to validate the model by repeatedly comparing the predicted outcomes with your actual results. A single data point cannot validate a model, so be wary until you build confidence with your tools.

Types of recipe software – There are two basic types of recipe software: the recipe formulation or brew session management application, and single function calculator-type tools. Full recipe software tends to be more comprehensive, and can often perform many different functions, such as inventory control, formatted printing, batch cost estimation, and advanced process control. These full systems tend to be more expensive, and include features that range from necessary and helpful to the completely unnecessary to many brewers (such as label printing and cost calculations). The calculator-type tools can be single function or groups of tools in a single application (full recipe systems often include these tools as part of the overall software package). The standalone tools tend to be inexpensive or free, but typically lack the comprehensive recipe formulation and brew session management features.

Advantages – Recipe software is great for automating repetitive calculations, looking up reference information, and maintaining brewing records. When formulating recipes, it's great to be able to instantly see the effects of ingredient substitutions or varying percentages of grist components. Nobody likes to do IBU calculations manually, and thankfully, brewing software has completely automated the task. If you change your recipes or like to modify other people's recipes, brewing software lets you scale recipes, change efficiency, use different ingredients, convert between all-grain and extract, and generally adjust the recipe to your needs. Recording brewing records (including comparisons of the differences between standard recipes and as-brewed batches) can prove very useful when researching future recipes and deciding why one batch is better than another.

Disadvantages – Computer programs include models, which can be a problem if the basic way the brewing software works doesn't accurately reflect how you brew. Some software wants you to make brewing lifestyle changes, or develop different methods so that it can predict your outcomes more effectively.

For instance, some software assumes hop additions at the end of the boil contribute zero IBUs of bitterness. That's true if you chill your wort immediately, but what if you let it stand to help clarify or what if you add additional hops afterwards? If the software doesn't model hop stands correctly, your IBU estimates will be too low. Software often overestimates water calculations, resulting in beer that looks great but tastes like minerals. Software might not take into account that you aren't putting all your grains in the mash at the same time, or that you have loss between steps.

Despite how helpful it can be, software tends to make you dependent on it. You may be so focused on hitting a certain number that you lose sight of what those numbers represent. An IBU level is just a number that doesn't really take into account the quality of bitterness, the perceived bitterness, how IBU perception changes based on the final gravity, sweetness, alcohol level, carbonation, and pH of the beer. So yes, you might hit your target, but software won't help you understand whether you were aiming at the right target or not. Software is your assistant; don't delegate too much responsibility to it.

Selecting software – I think the two most important questions you can ask when it comes to selecting recipe software are, "How will I use it?" and "Where will I use it?"

When researching full recipe management systems, consider how many of its features you will use, how long it takes to enter a recipe, how cluttered the interface is, and how well the data entry matches your workflow. I also like to see how much it can be customized, and whether it can accurately represent my brewing system and process. Ask yourself if it can record all the information you need, and present it in a way that makes sense to you. Think about the learning curve, and whether it's something that you can see integrating into your overall process of recipe design, brewing, and review.

Some key features of recipe software include:

- Integrated ingredient database that allows you to quickly select the grain, adjuncts, hops, yeast, and other ingredients in your beer. The grain database should have the name, potential extract (how many gravity points could be extracted from the malt with 100% efficiency) and the color, as well as other helpful information like country of origin and maltster. The hop database should have the name, country of origin, and alpha acid content. The yeast database should include the product ID, name, and producer. The database should be searchable and sortable so you can find what you need quickly, and either regularly updated by the vendor or extensible so you can edit it yourself. I like to reset the default alpha acid levels to the hops I have in stock, for instance.
- Batch size scaling so that you can easily change the recipe to match any potential size.
- Mash efficiency scaling so that you can adjust a recipe to match your system.
- Goal-seeking that allows you to change the desired style parameters of the batch. For instance, if I enter my ingredients and the calculated original gravity is too high, I'd like to be able to set the desired target gravity and have the software scale the ingredients accordingly.
- Beer style reference so that you can compare the calculated parameters of your recipe against BJCP (or other) style guidelines.

When evaluating calculator-type applications, you should check whether the calculations you regularly perform are included, and what kind of interface is provided. You use calculators because they are fast, so check to see how long it takes to access each formula, enter the necessary information, and get a result. Does it let you specify variables in the units you want to use, and do the calculations seem accurate when checked against other methods?

It's also important to consider where you'll be using the software: on a traditional computer (desktop or laptop) or on a mobile device (phone or tablet)? Does the software run on the type of hardware platform and operating system you use? If the software is available on multiple platforms, can it access shared data or easily transfer data? Think about where you will actually need to use the software at each step in your brewing process, and if the platform matches what devices you are likely to be using in each step.

While not as important as how and where you'll use the software, you should still consider maintenance and support. Ask yourself some questions before committing to any one piece of software: How frequently is the software updated, and is it actively supported? If you have a question, can you get it answered through the vendor or a support forum? How responsive are they? Will they take product suggestions and fix reported problems? If the product uses databases, is the content regularly updated, or do you at least have a way to change it? The maintenance issue can become a problem if new versions aren't released when there are operating system updates, as they may not run properly on newer systems if not updated.

What do I use? Since I'm not always brewing the same way and I'm not really interested in automating inventory management, I find that comprehensive brewing management software is overkill. I also tend to need my recipes written in a style that can appear in a book, magazine, or email response, so I prefer to keep a text copy as well.

I turn to recipe software more frequently when I am able to make notes and actively use the software while I am brewing. My primary tool is *Beer Alchemy* on the iPhone. I use it to work on new recipes, and it is the tool I used to validate the recipes in this book. For straight brewing calculations, I use *BrewBot* (also on the iPhone). It has calculators, ingredient databases, and references, so it supports just about any process (especially calculating recipes using percentages). I also like that I can use it for a single calculation and move on without disrupting my brewing.

I use *Timer+* on the iPhone all the time. It lets me set simple timers so I remember to perform mash steps or hop additions at the correct intervals. When I was verifying recipes for magazines, I tended to use *Brew Pal* on the iPhone, mostly because I wanted to keep those recipes separate from my personal ones.

I tend to create recipes on paper, writing down ideas and adding notes, particularly if I'm doing online research. When I draft a concept, I'll put it into *Beer Alchemy* to validate the numbers and check the ingredient percentages. I also have an old copy of *ProMash*, and a newer copy of *BeerSmith 2*. I don't use these often since I do most of my recipe work away from my main computer.

Even though my recipe is electronic, I also write it out by hand to have a paper copy of my brew log. I do this primarily because I don't have to worry as much about my phone or computer getting wet, dirty, or damaged, and I can quickly take notes if something happens during brewing. I also tend to check off when ingredients are added, so the paper method helps to keep my recipes clean. When the brew session is done, I write up the recipe in a text file in my preferred format so I have it available when I need it. I store these on Dropbox so I can have my recipes handy at all times. When I have tasting notes or other feedback on the beer, I amend the text files to have a record. Using a cloud-based service means that I can edit those files from pretty much any location or device.

And that's how I use software. It's kind of a cobbled-together approach, but I find it flexible for my requirements. I'll be the first to admit that I'm not likely the average brewer, so I don't want to imply that this is an approach everyone should use. It's meant to illustrate how you can look at the full range of your requirements and pick the products that best meet your needs.

Products mentioned:

ProMash	www. promash.com
BeerSmith	beersmith.com
Beer Alchemy	www.beeralchemyapp.com
BrewBot	https://itunes.apple.com/us/app/brewbot/id542237024
Timer+	https://itunes.apple.com/us/app/timer+/id391564049

Brew Pal	https://itunes.apple.com/us/app/brew-pal/ id304022014
Dropbox	www.dropbox.com

C | WORKING WITH EXTRACT RECIPES

RECIPE CONVERSION

The ability to convert between all-grain and extract recipes is a skill every brewer should master. You shouldn't have to pass on a great-sounding recipe just because it's all-grain and you only brew extract beers. Likewise, you might sometimes find wonderful extract recipes in basic brewing books, and want to brew them on your all-grain system.

In the United States, more than half of all brewers are extract brewers, but the percentage of all-grain brewers keeps growing. Homebrewers in South America are all-grain brewers because malt extract is not available. Don't make the assumption that brewing using a particular method equates to skill level or experience. Brewers of all skill levels might need to convert recipes to suit their needs.

My recipes are all-grain because that's how I brew. I'm not comfortable giving extract versions if I haven't actually brewed them. I am, however, more than happy to describe the conversion process so that you can adapt them yourself.

CONVERTING ALL-GRAIN RECIPES TO EXTRACT

I'll first give you my method for converting recipes, and then walk through an example and discuss the various points where there might be alternatives. The basic method involves substituting malt sources; more advanced approaches look at other aspects of the beer (I'll cover those separately). Note that this method uses the US customary measurement system (sometimes colloquially known as English units), but the quantities can be converted to metric afterwards, if needed.

1. **Address malt first** – In the recipe, separate the mashed grains from the steeped grains. Steeped grains are crystal malts, dark/roasted malts and grains, and anything that does not contain convertible starches. If it's already a form of sugar, leave it alone, it doesn't need to be converted. Mashed grains are generally base malts (two-row, pale ale, Pilsner, Vienna, Munich, and similar) that make up the bulk of the grist.

2. **Get recipe parameters** – You'll need to have the batch size and the system efficiency in the recipe. If this information isn't present, you'll need to calculate it (recipe software can help). I'm assuming you'll be brewing a batch of the same size as the original recipe (if you're not, see the Advanced Topics). Keeping the volumes equal allows you to use the original recipe's OG and IBU, saving you considerable time and effort.

3. **Calculate total gravity points contributed by base malts** – Add up the total pounds of base malts. Multiply this number by the system efficiency. Then multiply the product by the theoretical extract from the base malt. This can vary by type of malt, but is generally 36 to 38 points per pound (if you are unsure, use 37). The result represents the total number of gravity points in the wort that must be replaced by extract.

4. **Replace gravity points with an equivalent amount of pale extract** – If you want to substitute liquid malt extract (LME) for the base malts, divide the total gravity points contributed by the base malts by 36 to get the pounds of LME (or liquid sugars) required. If substituting with dry malt extract (DME), divide the total gravity points contributed by the base malts by 45 to get the pounds of DME (or dry sugars) required. If you want to use both LME and DME, keep in mind that the total gravity points contributed by malt extract should match what was contributed by the base malts in the original recipe.

5. **Steep steeped grains, then boil with extract** – The most common extract brewing process involves putting crushed specialty grains in a mesh bag and holding it in the strike water at 150–170°F (66–77°C) for between 15 and 30 minutes. After the grains have been removed, the malt extract is added, and the kettle is brought to boil. From this point on, the converted

recipe should be the same as the original (hop additions, chilling, fermentation, and packaging).

As an example, consider this partial recipe for a dark mild (for the full recipe, see *Simplicity Mild*):

6.5 gallons	@ 1.036 (75% efficiency)	
7 lb.	Maris Otter	
12 oz	Crystal 65	
7 oz	Chocolate malt	
0.5 oz	Target hops	@ 60 (15 IBUs)
	Wyeast 1968 yeast	

Using my process step by step, we can convert this to extract:

1. Base malt: 7 lb.; steeping malts: 19 oz (12 oz + 7 oz)
2. Batch size: 6.5 gallons; Efficiency: 75%
3. 7 lb. • 0.75 • 37 points per pound = 194.25 points
4. 194.25 / 36 = 5.4 lb. LME (or 194.25 / 45 = 4.3 lb. DME)

The converted extract recipe would be:

5.4 lb.	pale liquid malt extract	
12 oz	crystal 65	
7 oz	chocolate malt	
0.5 oz	Target hops	@ 60
	Wyeast 1968	

Steep crystal and chocolate malt in mesh bag in 8 gallons 158°F water for 15 minutes. Remove bag from water, add liquid malt extract, bring to a boil, and boil 60 minutes. Ferment at 66°F.

Be sure to check your calculations:

5.4 lb. • 36 points per pound = 194.4 points.
19 oz = 1.2 pounds. 1.2 lb. • 30 points per pound = 36 points.
194.4 + 36 = 230.4 points.
230.4 points / 6.5 gallons = 35.4 points per gallon
35.4 is close to 36, or 1.036 starting gravity; recipe validated.

With rounding and approximation, the number won't usually be exact, but should be close. Note that I also averaged the gravity contributions from specialty malts, using 30 points per pound for combined crystal-type and dark malts. For a more accurate calculation, calculate the contributions independently.

With me so far? Let's try a bit more complicated example. Consider this Belgian *dubbel* (for the full recipe, see Traditional Homebrew Dubbel)

6.5 gallons	@ 1.064 (70% efficiency)	
7 lb.	Pale ale malt	
3 lb.	Munich malt	
2 lb.	Dark Munich malt	
1.5 lb.	Aromatic malt	
4 oz	CaraPils	
8 oz	CaraMunich 60	
6 oz	Special B	
1 oz	Chocolate wheat malt	
1 lb	Dark candi sugar	
1.5 oz	Styrian Goldings	@ 60
0.5 oz	Saaz	@ 15
0.5 oz	Saaz	@ 2
	Wyeast 3787	
	22 IBUs	

OK, maybe *a lot* more complicated. A version of this recipe was my first all-grain batch, since I knew I couldn't get the same malt flavors from extract. But let's see how close we can get when following my process:

1. Base malt: 13.5 lb. (pale, Munich, dark Munich, Aromatic); steeping malt: 19 oz (caraPils, caraMunich, special B, chocolate wheat); sugar 1 lb.
2. Batch size: 6.5 gallons; Efficiency: 70%
3. 13.5 lb. • 0.7 • 37 points per pound = 350 points
4. 350 / 36 = 9.7 lb. LME (or 350 / 45 = 7.8 lb. DME)

The converted extract recipe would be:

5 lb.	pale liquid malt extract
4.7 lb.	liquid Munich malt extract
4 oz	caraPils

8 oz	CaraMunich 60	
6 oz	Special B	
1 oz	Chocolate wheat malt	
1 lb.	Dark candi sugar	
1.5 oz	Styrian Goldings hops	@ 60
0.5 oz	Saaz hops	@ 15
0.5 oz	Saaz hops	@ 2
	Wyeast 3787	

Steep specialty malts in mesh bag in 8 gallons 158°F water for 15 minutes. Remove bag from water, add liquid malt extracts and candi sugar, bring to a boil, and boil 60 minutes. Ferment at 64°F.

Be sure to check your calculations:

5 lb. • 36 points per pound = 180 points

4.7 lb. • 36 points per pound = 169 points

19 oz = 1.2 pounds. 1.2 lb. • 30 points per pound = 36 points

1 lb candi sugar = 45 points

180 + 169 + 36 + 45 = 430 points

430 points / 6.5 gallons = 66 points per gallon

66 is close to 64, or 1.064 starting gravity; recipe validated

Did you see the extra trick I slipped in (it's something I cover in the advanced tips)? I noticed that some of the base malts included Munich-type malts (Munich, dark Munich, Aromatic) so I separated those from the pale ale malt, converted them into Munich malt extract, and used the more common pale malt extract for the pale ale malt.

This method will result in beer similar to the all-grain version, but it is unlikely to taste exactly the same due to the differences in ingredients and methods. If you're a perfectionist and want your extract brew to be an even closer match, there are still a few more advanced methods you can try.

ADVANCED TOPICS IN EXTRACT RECIPE CONVERSION

Not all recipes are easily converted. Sometimes there are ingredients that can't be found in extract form, or sometimes the recipe needs to be adapted to the size or idiosyncrasies of your brewing system. Rather than overly complicate the basic recipe conversion procedure, I've separated out the special cases and optimizations. Use any or all of them if they apply, and you want to make your recipe more accurate. Many of these methods can be calculated using recipe software.

Concentrated boil – If doing a concentrated boil (boiling less than the full wort volume, adding water post-boil to reach the target volume; sometimes called a *partial boil*), your original bitterness calculations will likely be wrong. The extraction of bitterness from hops is gravity-dependent, with higher gravities resulting in lower hop utilization. A concentrated boil has the same amount of sugar in a smaller quantity of water, so the gravity will always be higher. You can correct for this difference by first calculating the bitterness obtained using the parameters of the actual boil (which is a higher-gravity, smaller-sized batch than the full recipe), then further reducing the bitterness due to dilution as the partial boil is topped up with water in the fermenter.

If you're confused by what that means, here's a quick example. First, let's handle the dilution factor. If you have 3 gallons of 1.060 wort, and you top it off to 5 gallons by adding water, the final gravity of that batch will be 1.036. To reach that number, take the gravity points of the concentrated boil (60) and multiply by the volume (3) to yield the number of gravity points in the wort (180). Adding 2 gallons of 1.000 water doesn't change the total gravity points, just the volume. So the final gravity is the number of points of sugar (180) divided by the batch size (5), which gives 36, or 1.036 specific gravity. You could also do this by percentage scaling, if that makes more sense to you. The concentrated boil (3) is 60% of the total volume (5), so you can multiply by 0.6 to get the same answer.

How do you calculate hop bitterness? If you're only boiling hops in the concentrated boil, you need to determine the bitterness based on a 1.060 gravity beer, not a 1.036 beer. Perform the standard bitterness calculations (see Appendix A, or use recipe software) using the higher gravity and actual boil volume, which will estimate the bitterness of the concentrated boil. You can scale IBUs the same way as the specific gravity because IBUs are a measure of isomerized alpha acids in solution (diluting the bitterness with additional water reduces the IBUs accordingly). Apply the same scaling factor based on batch size to get the estimated IBUs of the final beer.

The basic point to remember is that if you use a concentrated boil, you will have to add more bittering hops to reach the same level of perceived bitterness as the full boil recipe. There are other limiting factors;

remember that it's nearly impossible to get more than 100 IBUs in a beer, so if your concentrated boil is above that limit, you should cap it. You won't get an 80 IBU beer by diluting a 160 IBU beer with an equal portion of water since a 160 IBU beer can't exist.

Different volumes – For homebrew-size recipes, you can typically apply a batch scaling factor to the weight of the malt and hops to get an equivalent recipe. If you want to brew a double-sized batch, double all the ingredients. If you want to brew a half-sized batch, halve all the ingredients. If you're converting a 6.5 gallon recipe to 5 gallons, use 77% as the scaling factor (5.0 / 6.5 = .769). This isn't perfect math, but it's close enough for the batch sizes homebrewers use. Recipe software works wonders for this type of scaling.

Matching malt to extract – You can replace specific malts with 'varietal' flavors (if available), but that can be expensive. Some styles (such as *bocks*) depend more heavily on the flavors of Munich or Vienna malt, for instance. Some brewers writing 5-gallon recipes will add in a pound of Munich (maybe 10% of the grist) here or there just to increase the overall maltiness (guilty as charged). If the flavor of a specific malt is an important part of the style profile, try to use an extract version of that malt. If an ingredient is used only as an accent, it's not vital to the recipe and can be substituted.

Munich, wheat, and rye malt extracts exist, and can be used as substitutes. It's also possible to find Maris Otter extract, which is pretty important for many English beer styles. You may need to search some of the larger online homebrew retailers for these products if you don't see them in your local shop. Given their specific uses, they can sometimes be hard to find.

I tend to use pale or extra pale LME and DME as much as possible. If using amber or darker extracts, you often have no idea what malt produced the color; therefore, the flavor of the extract is a big unknown (for example, was dark extract made using chocolate malt, roasted barley, black malt, dark crystal malts, caramel coloring, or something else? They all have different flavor profiles). You also have no idea what mash program was used, so you won't know the wort composition or fermentability. In general, I assume that pale malt extract is made with pale ale malt, and extra pale malt extract is made with two-row or Pilsner malt. If the malt extract comes from a certain country, I might further assume that the flavor will have a character typical of base malt that originates from there.

If you can obtain information about the composition of the malt extract, you can do a better job matching the extract to the base malt. Modern extract often comes with more information, and some is produced from single varieties of malt. Read the information packaged with extract carefully, as you might not be getting what you expect. For instance, some wheat extracts are actually a blend of a pale malt and wheat malt in a ratio common for brewing German weisse beers. You don't want to assume that it is 100% wheat malt, because it may be 50–65%, and throw off your recipe. Instead of just using the blend, you'd want to substitute the wheat malt extract for both the pale and wheat malts from the original recipe in the same proportion.

The earlier section on *Ingredient Substitution* has other ideas that you might want to use to add flavors that might be present in the all-grain base malt but not in the extract. If there are character malts in the grist that are providing flavor and not gravity points, you can steep them or perform a mini-mash. Note that steeping starchy grains will add unconverted starch to your wort, which could lead to clarity problems.

Some of the starch will likely go away as part of the break. Anything darker than light Munich malt that isn't a crystal or roasted malt falls into this category. I would generally treat these as minor grist additions, unless it has a signature flavor (dark Munich, brown malt, etc.). I'd generally use a mini-mash for these, or in a pinch, steep them since I care more about their flavor contributions than potential problems with clarity.

Eliminating small grist additions – Sometimes all-grain brewers have personal preferences for including a little bit of certain malts as a 'house character' ingredient, or add in certain grains only for their side effects (adding body, assisting with head retention, adjusting color). These grains can often be eliminated since the issues they are trying to address are generally not present in extract beers. For instance, if you see a brewer including less than 5% wheat malt in a recipe, chances are they included it to improve head retention. Small additions of CaraPils, flaked oats, flaked barley, dextrin malt, and the like are typically used to increase body. Less than 1% of a dark grain or malt is likely just to add a darker hue to the appearance, or to add a touch of dryness. As I mentioned previously, up to 10% of Munich or Vienna malt is likely being used to increase the general maltiness of the beer, and can be converted to pale malt extract (unless you want to perform a mini-mash).

Converting First Wort Hop additions – First wort hopping (FWH) is difficult to perform on extract batches since you never lauter the beer. You could mix together the full volume of extract and water, raise it to mash temperature, then slowly syphon it into another pot, and bring it to a boil when done. But it's probably easier to convert it to traditional additions. You could try using the FWH addition as a 20 minute boil addition instead, as equal levels of perceived bitterness and some hop flavor should persist. Or you can calculate the IBU contributions of the FWH addition, and add those IBUs through a flavor addition and a bitterness addition. Use the same quantity of FWH hops as a flavor addition at 10 minutes, calculate the bitterness of that 10 minute addition, and calculate how many hops need to be added at 60 minutes to reach the same level of IBUs. Or you can ignore the flavor contributions of the FWH hops and use them as a straight bittering addition at 60 minutes. That's admittedly a little sloppy, but certainly easy.

Accounting for the mash schedule and fermentability – Several mash techniques bring flavor and body contributions to the beer. For example, a step mash increases fermentability and attenuation, a decoction mash increases the maltiness and color of the beer, as well as improves efficiency and attenuation, and higher-temperature rests build body. An all-grain brewer controls wort fermentability through selecting rest temperatures in the mash program; if the rest temperatures are too high, or the wort contains excessive dextrins, then the wort fermentability is likely to be too low.

If your beer lacks sufficient fermentable sugars (i.e., you wind up with a high final gravity), next time substitute sugars for some of the malts. Corn sugar and plain table sugar are both highly fermentable and add little, if any, flavor. If the body of your beer is too thin (due to an excessively fermentable wort), reduce the amount of plain sugars. If there are no sugars in the recipe, add some malt with dextrins such as CaraPils. Start with 2 or 3% of the total fermentables.

If your recipe uses a decoction mash, try adding Munich malt (which is also available as an extract). Dark Munich and aromatic malts can all provide the extra color and flavor commonly produced during decoction mashes. You can add these (depending on the style, but try to limit them to 5 to 10% of the total fermentables to start), but you may cause other problems (such as needing to perform a mini-mash).

Economical purchasing quantities – While it's easy to crunch the numbers to find the necessary amounts of extract you need to exchange for malts, you can't always buy exactly the right amounts due to how they are packaged. So you wind up buying more than you need, and not using it all during that brew session. Using full cans or jugs of LME can reduce the possibility that the remaining amount will oxidize and ruin future batches. DME is more stable, as long as you keep it dry. Measuring DME over a pot of boiling water is a bad idea since steam can enter the bag and cause the powder to solidify.

It may be advantageous to first determine the weight of the LME you can buy in an individual container, then use whole multiples of that weight in your recipe. Determine the number of gravity points each container contributes (weight of container • 36), and then divide that into the total number of gravity points needed. Take the whole number of containers (mathematically this is the quotient) and allocate that towards LME. Calculate the remaining gravity points; this value is what the DME needs to contribute. Divide those gravity points by 45 to determine the number of pounds needed (it's easier to weigh out fractional amounts of DME than LME).

CONVERTING ALL-GRAIN RECIPES TO MINI-MASH

Mini-mash is a good option when your grist includes some character grains for which there are no extract equivalents. You can also use it with base malt when the character of that malt is an important part of the recipe. Any time you have the opportunity to use grain instead of extract, you are likely to get more of the flavor you want into the beer.

A mini-mash is kind of like a small scale brew-in-a-bag. You put the gains to be mashed in a mesh bag, and then put it inside a vessel where you hold the water. Unlike steeping, you don't use the full volume of water for the recipe. Use enough so the mash is on the thin side, but easily stirred with a wooden spoon (roughly 2 to 3 quarts per pound). You leave the mash alone for about an hour, remove the bag, and strain out the liquid. You can also sparge with hot water during this step, if that is part of your process.

Selecting which grains to mash involves more than just identifying what doesn't have an extract equivalent. Since you are actually mashing, you need to make sure there are sufficient enzymes to convert all the starches in the mash. Most base malts contain enough enzymes to fully convert themselves (plus some extra). In general, the paler the malt, the more enzymes. Six-row malt contains significantly more enzymes than two-row, but has a coarser flavor. Munich malt (light) has just enough enzymes to self-convert, but you'll need supplemental enzymes for anything darker.

Mini-mashes allow you to use starchy adjuncts like flaked oats, corn, and rye. They don't have enzymes at all, and as a result, must be mashed with other grains. Without getting into calculating amounts of enzymes, it's safe to have at least an equivalent weight of two-row, Pilsner, or pale ale malt with whatever other ingredients you're using. I wouldn't expect Vienna and Munich to fully convert (even though they will with the right conditions), so to be certain, add some Pilsner malt too. If you aren't sure if a malt has enzymes or not, assume it doesn't just to be safe.

I find mini-mashes to be more work than full mashes since they are harder to control temperature wise (unless you have more specialized equipment). I wouldn't worry about precise temperature control for the mash in a mini-mash; aim for around 150°F (66°C) but don't stress about it as long as you are over 140°F (60°C). Mash the grains for an hour, stirring every 15 minutes. You should try to maintain a constant temperature in the mash, but it's not the end of the world if you don't. Putting the mash in a warm (but not turned on) oven may help you maintain the temperature better than leaving it out in the open.

The process for converting an all-grain recipe to mini-mash is similar to converting to extract. First, separate out the steeping grains; don't include those in the calculation. Then identify the specialty or character grains that don't have an extract equivalent; those go directly into the mini-mash. Assess those grains to see if there are enzymes present (typically, there won't be), take an equal weight of base malt to match the weight of the character grains, and add them to the mini-mash. If the base malt is only Vienna or Munich, add an equal portion of Pilsner malt. To finish your mini-mash, add the steeping grains that were separated out.

For whatever base malt remains, perform the calculation from the extract-only section to come up with the equivalent amount of extract to use. The calculation is exactly the same once you have moved all the other grain to the mini-mash. Calculate the amount of extract to replace the remaining grain, and add that to the kettle once the mini-mash has ended (and the grain has been removed). Top off with the rest of the volume of water, bring to a boil, and proceed to brew as directed in the original recipe.

CONVERTING EXTRACT RECIPES TO ALL-GRAIN

To convert an extract recipe to all-grain, perform the extract conversion procedure in reverse. Keep specialty or steeping malts the same, but replace malt extract with grain. You will still need to know your mash efficiency to perform the calculation.

Determine how many gravity points are contributed by extract (multiply the weight of liquid extract by 36, and the weight of dry extract by 45). Sum those calculations to determine the total gravity points from extract. Divide that number by 37 to determine how many gravity points from base malts are needed. Finally, divide that number by your mash efficiency to determine the total weight of base malt needed.

Your next task is to choose *which* base malts to use. If there is a specialty type of extract used (such as Munich), then use Munich malt for that fraction of the grist. The remainder of the grist can consist of two-row, Pilsner, or pale ale malt if the beer was using pale malt extract. Look to the style of the beer to give you clues as to the proper type of malt rather than relying on a certain brand.

Start with a mash temperature of 150°F (66°C). You can adjust that if you know the style requires it, such as increasing the mash temperature if your beer needs a more dextrinous body. If you are brewing a style that traditionally uses another type of mash technique, you can obviously use that instead.

Converting extract recipes to all-grain is generally easier than going the other way since you have more control in your ingredient choices. Primarily you are seeking to hit the same gravity numbers first, then adjusting the bitterness to get the same balance, then finally selecting the ingredients that give you the desired flavor profile while hitting the color target. If you get the style parameters right, any mistakes made on the flavor profile can be adjusted in subsequent batches through malt substitutions. But if you selected your ingredients with knowledge of the style, you have a very good chance of being close on your first try.

INDEX

Entries in **boldface** refer to photos and illustrations.